Praise for *The Endless Practice*

"Mark Nepo is a treasure. His words invariably bring me to a place of greater depth, peace of mind, and lightness of spirit. In *The Endless Practice* he has given us a great gift. This lovely book is a field guide to being human."

—Dani Shapiro, author of *Devotion* and *Still Writing*

"Mark Nepo has created and encoded a work of wisdom, love, truth, and beauty. Reading his words will open your heart, expand your mind, and nourish your soul. Just holding this book shifted me into a state of grace."

—Arielle Ford, author of *Wabi Sabi Love: The Ancient Art of Finding Perfect Love in Imperfect Relationships*

"This book held me in its warm embrace. Mark is a true poet of the soul, using fresh, vivid language to capture realities that are too often cast as mere clichés. What a blessing!"

—Tosha Silver, author of *Outrageous Openness: Letting the Divine Take the Lead*

ALSO BY MARK NEPO

Nonfiction

Seven Thousand Ways to Listen
Finding Inner Courage
Unlearning Back to God
The Exquisite Risk
The Book of Awakening

Fiction

As Far As the Heart Can See

Poetry

Reduced to Joy
Surviving Has Made Me Crazy
Suite for the Living
Inhabiting Wonder
Inside the Miracle
Fire Without Witness
God, the Maker of the Bed, and the Painter

Editor

Deepening the American Dream

Recordings

Reduced to Joy
Seven Thousand Ways to Listen
Staying Awake
Holding Nothing Back
As Far As the Heart Can See
The Book of Awakening
Finding Inner Courage
Finding Our Way in the World
Inside the Miracle

THE
ENDLESS
PRACTICE

▼ ▼ ▼

BECOMING WHO YOU WERE BORN TO BE

MARK NEPO

ATRIA BOOKS

New York   London   Toronto   Sydney   New Delhi

ATRIA BOOKS

A Division of Simon & Schuster, Inc.
1230 Avenue of the Americas
New York, NY 10020

First Atria Books hardcover edition August 2014

ATRIA BOOKS and colophon are trademarks of Simon & Schuster, Inc.

Permission information for excerpts from previously published material is on page 311.

For information about special discounts for bulk purchases,
please contact Simon & Schuster Special Sales at
1-866-506-1949 or business@simonandschuster.com.

The Simon & Schuster Speakers Bureau can bring authors to your
live event. For more information or to book an event contact the
Simon & Schuster Speakers Bureau at 1-866-248-3049 or visit
our website at www.simonspeakers.com.

Manufactured in the United States of America

10   9   8   7   6   5   4   3   2   1

Library of Congress Cataloging-in-Publication Data

Nepo, Mark.
  The endless practice : becoming who you were born to be / Mark Nepo.—First Edition.
      pages cm
  Includes bibliographical references.
  1. Self-actualization (Psychology) I. Title.
  BF637.S4N4596 2014
  158—dc23   2014022115

ISBN 978-1-4767-7464-0
ISBN 978-1-4767-7467-1 (ebook)

For my grandmother, Maijessca Nepo (1893–1987)
who told me my hands are the oldest things I own,
and her son, my father, Morris Nepo (1920–2013)
who taught me how to use them.

Wakefulness is not a destination
but a song the human heart keeps singing,
the way birds keep singing at the first sign of light.

CONTENTS

A Dream We're Close to Living

The Mark of Our Hands

The Exchange That Brings Us Alive

TO MY READER

THIS BOOK IS an inquiry into how the soul works in the world, and how by engaging our soul in the world, we are shaped by the endless practice of becoming the person we were born to be. From the moment we open our eyes, we are meaning-seeking creatures, looking for what matters though we carry what matters deep within us. And more than the hard-earned understandings we arrive at, more than the principles or beliefs we stitch together out of our experience, how we stay in relationship to the mysterious Whole of Life is what brings us alive and keeps us alive.

From *The Book of Awakening* on, I've tried to offer a whole picture of the human journey, speaking whatever I know of truth while believing in my heart that life, for all its difficulties, is uplifting. And I've been committed to keeping each other company on this timeless journey we're all on, admitting that I have no answers. I believe we all seek this kind of company and find strength in it.

I believe everyone knows first-hand that life is messy and painful, beautiful and unpredictable, that we can't make careers of good running from bad, or positive muffling negative, but that life is full of wonder and obstacle alike. I remain devoted to the truth of that wholeness. Even as I write this—as my wife, Susan, and I are grieving the death of our beloved dog Mira and I am still making sense of my father's death this past year—I find myself in the endless practice of keeping my heart open to the whole of it. And the journey of becoming who we were born to be never ends. It's limitless, eternal. We don't arrive—we grow.

Throughout the evolution of my books, I've worked to expand our felt understanding of the totality of the human experience, to affirm our innate knowing of this.

With the subtitle of *The Book of Awakening—Having the Life You Want by Being Present to the Life You Have*—I began to discover the beautiful secret that there is nowhere to go. All we need and dream of is right here before us, within us. With *The Exquisite Risk*, I offered the sense that risk is not "negative" but necessary, beautiful, and enlivening. With *Unlearning Back to God*, I explored the notion that by reclaiming and reawakening the gifts we're given, resilience and peace are possible. Through all my books, I've been a witness to the mysterious truth that living with an open heart and bringing our being and doing together to form care is endless: waking, risking, finding courage, finding our way back to an innate sense of God, and simply but deeply listening. And now, *The Endless Practice*, the unfolding that never stops, the ever-growing journey of becoming who we were born to be.

Deep, Timeless Questions

So what does it mean to be a soul in the world and to be our truest selves? These are deep, timeless questions that we need to live into more than answer. While there are many insights and stories that can help, the work begins as we find our way and keep each other from retreating from life.

To bring who we are out and to let the world in is a brave and endless practice that clarifies and solidifies the gifts we are born with. There is no arrival point or destination here, only the chance to be more alive as we move closer to the Mystery.

What we can do is learn more specifically how to be a gardener of the soul, so it and we can keep growing. In this book, we will explore the difficult and rewarding aspects of being human, which are often inter-related, including how to restore our trust in life, when suffering makes us lose our way; how to begin the work of saying yes to life, so it can enliven us; and how to make our inwardness a resource and not a refuge.

The ever-changing practice of being human involves learning how to strengthen our heart by exercising it in the world, and how to refine who we are through caring, building, holding, and repairing. To do this, we must discover how to put down our old protections and stop interfering with the life-force that wants to open us like a flower. In this very personal journey, we have the chance to find our faith between who we are and what we do.

Toward this end, we will discuss how to find the courage not to waste our gifts, how to name the reliable truths we can return to, and how to enter and honor the magic of peace. We'll learn how to be accurate about what we feel, so as not to drown in it, and how to meet the troubles of living, so we can sense the common cry of life that allows us to feel the kinship between us.

To be a soul in the world, we must keep participating in the wisdom of an open heart, so we can be empowered by the life of expression. All this helps us to discover our own wisdom and to use our own gifts. All this helps us to become the particular person we were born to be.

Coming Alive

Every day, the heart keeps beating and the lungs keep breathing. Likewise, the endless practice of bringing our soul into the world lets us keep unfolding. It's a limitless journey of coming alive, which entails the messy, joyous, unfathomable drama of being human.

Like it or not, life keeps engaging us, asking that we follow what is real, until the light of the soul is drawn out of us, and that we carry what is real, until the depth of the world grounds us. By *real*, I mean any moment met face-to-face and heart-to-heart, without pretense or illusion. When we can follow what moves us, we break open what is possible and the light of the soul spills out of us. When we're moved to care and love, who we are extends into the world and we strengthen our roots.

Often, it's our love of life that gives us the courage to follow what is real. And our love of others that gives us the courage to carry what is real. Of course, there's no way to escape the need to do both: to let out the light of the soul and to let in the depth of the world. The challenge is to inhabit both.

While we constantly struggle with achievement and failure, with our want for fame and our fear of anonymity, it's the heartful commitment to be completely who we are—no more, no less—that awakens us to the full beauty and truth of being alive. These chapters explore the way in which we experience the light of the soul and the depth of the world. This is a journey of questions and stories that illuminate how we can inhabit the specific life we're given. Ultimately, each of us is an invaluable, irreplaceable seed in the ground of existence, each of us a small miracle waiting to blossom in the large miracle.

The Soul's Place on Earth

I believe and give my heart to the notion that spirituality is listening for and living into the soul's place on Earth. A life of spirit, regardless of the path we choose, begins with a person's acceptance that they are part of something larger than themselves. The want to know who we really are and to know the truth of our existence and our connection to a living Universe is, to me, the fundamental life-giving question that the heart commits to once opened by love or suffering. How we are led and pushed to our true nature is what spirituality and personal growth are all about.

At the heart of each spiritual tradition are the questions: How to be in the world without losing what matters, and is living an awakened life of any use if we don't bring what matters to bear on the world? Though every path offers some form of refuge, the journey of every human being is to discover—*through their personhood*—their own *living relationship* between the soul and the world, between being and experience, and between love and service.

Like those before us, we're left to make sense of the kinship between the mysterious forces of life that remain unseeable and the things of this world with all their weight and gravity. It's the interplay and friction between the mysterious forces of life and the things of the world that hone our qualities as particular beings.

To be living, growing, changing beings in a living, growing, changing Universe opens a larger, more dynamic sense of relationship, to each other and the world, as we journey through the depth and surface of life. To find our way, alone and together, is the purpose of spiritual friendship. All we can do is hold each other up in the journey of becoming who we are, while sharing our experience of the mysterious Unity of Life.

Come to the Well

Since my cancer journey over two decades ago, I honor two commitments in my struggle to be the person I was born to be. The first is to find and create inner food. The other is to stay awake and in love with the common center of all paths. Over the years, I've come to understand my life as a writer and a teacher to be that of an inner explorer. My books are lean-tos and campsites from which to commune with the interior. The teaching circles I'm blessed to convene are tents in which we compare notes on what it means to be alive, while sharing food and mapping trails, as we tell stories of our wanderings.

This brings me back to the endless practice, which for me has unearthed a path of questions, friends, and wonder. During the last five years, I've been drawn into yet another depth, awakened at yet another level by wonder and loss. And more than making sense of it, I've somehow kept my heart open to it all, letting it shape me. This journey, like the others, has taken longer than I thought, and, like any author, I've returned with this thing called a book. But more than the relic I've carved and polished, I want you to enter the depth from which it was taken. That's all a poet ever wants.

So, welcome, which means *come to the well*. Come to the well we all stumble on, the one that refreshes us, when we least expect it. If blessed, we'll meet at the edge of the world, where we can help each other live.

TO GLOW IN ALL DIRECTIONS

*To learn how to ask for what we need,
only to practice accepting what we're
given. This is our journey on Earth.*

During my days of cancer, I felt such fear from all directions, including the well-intended but negative scenarios of all the doctors preparing for what to do when this would fall off or that would stop working. The only place I could retreat to was the moment at hand. No matter how painful, that moment, paradoxically, had the calm certainty of already existing. No one could puncture it or take it away. It simply glowed. And so, without any wisdom but out of desperation, I took refuge in each glowing moment, one leading to the next. To my humble surprise, each moment was a threshold to the sanctity that waits inside any circumstance. I discovered that each moment contains an ounce of eternal perspective that doesn't eliminate what we have to go through, but which opens us to the stream of life that is always ready to carry us. And so, when weak and close to death, I learned that what we retreat to may at first be a refuge, but what we face and see our way through becomes a resource. I learned that authentic living begins with our acceptance of what we're given. Then the light of the soul can meet the light in the world. In those hard-earned moments, we glow in all directions. I've been trying to understand the truth and glow of being human ever since.

THE DAILY MIGRATION

We have been stopped for so many years by not being able to follow small things.

—LARS-ANDERS HANSSON

I RECENTLY LEARNED about the daily migration of microscopic zooplankton in the world's water supply—trillions of them. Plankton are organisms—comparable to sea larvae and tiny jellyfish—that drift in oceans, seas, and bodies of fresh water. The word *zooplankton* comes from the Greek *zoion*, meaning animal, and *planktos*, meaning wanderer or drifter.

Their migration isn't like the journey of whales or butterflies or flamingoes over thousands of miles or like caribou who circle the same arctic edge every year. The daily migration of these unseeable creatures is a persistent drift from depth to surface and back to depth. Along the way, they eat and process phytoplankton and, through their daily rite of survival, they serve as a filtering agent and so play their role in the aquatic food web. Innately, they both survive and contribute to the survival of the waters they live in.

This daily odyssey can span a few feet in small ponds or as far as five hundred yards in the open sea. Environmentalist Alan Burdick tells us that this is equivalent to a human being rowing a small boat five hundred miles every day to breakfast and back!

This is microscopic evidence that we need to work very hard to arrive where we are. The journey is inevitable—essential to our own survival and the health of the Universe we are a small part of. In fact, it's fair to assume that every part of life has its own version of this daily migration by which it exercises its being into place.

This persistent drifting from depth to surface and back is particularly instructive for the life of the soul, and how we need to stay in the world and process our experience in order to feed and cleanse both our working spirit and the small part of the Universe we inhabit. For years, I thought I was inwardly fickle, struggling to surface when drowning in the deep, only to be battered at the surface and long for the stillness of the depth. And now these microscopic creatures present a fractal of the larger physics at work. Now I wonder about *the practice of persistent drift*—from depth to surface and back—and how the many aspects of being and becoming are all part of the constant cleansing action that keeps us and life healthy.

In spiritually practical ways, this book is an inquiry into the practice of persistent drift: into the cleansing action of introspection, creativity, love, friendship, and how we deal with pain; into our need to stay in the world and process our experience; into the very hard and inevitable work to arrive where we are; and into the soul's daily migration from depth to surface and back. Relentlessly, the sea of life keeps us vital and buoyant while we in our small way serve as tiny cleansing agents of the sea of life. Mysteriously, spirit is known by its movement through the depth of the world, the way wind is known by its movement through waves and trees and prayer flags strung along the mountain's ridge.

So still yourself briefly and picture an infinite wave of zooplankton pulsing their way up through the planet's water and down again, cleansing it as they go. Imagine the tiniest cells of being rising within you this very moment, cleansing your thoughts and feelings. Imagine how you and I pulse our way through the days eating and processing the food of relationship, meaning, and care. All of us processing each other, drifting toward the healthiest exchange, the way plants and humans exchange oxygen and carbon dioxide.

Despite our endless plans, we are animals of being drifting with an instinct to survive and process. Despite our endless struggles, our need to survive and process is cleansing. It's beautiful and humbling to realize that the spirit inherent in each thing on Earth, including worms and flowers, is migrating to where it is and that this pulsation of being is the self-cleansing agent of all life-force. After all this way, it's never been about getting to the surface or getting to the bottom, but the inborn call to inhabit the journey in between.

....

∾ *The daily migration is a persistent drift from depth to surface and back to depth. This is how we deal with pain and stay in the world while cleansing life itself—through introspection, creativity, love, and friendship.*

....

A Reflective Pause

○ *In your journal, describe one way that you move between depth and surface during your day. Where are you more comfortable, in the world or the interior? One is a native strength, the other, an aspect of your self you need to know better. Name one way you might explore whichever you are uncomfortable with, the world or the interior.*

○ *In conversation with a friend or loved one, describe your own practice of persistent drift. Choose one of the following— introspection, creativity, love, or friendship—and explore how this inner way of being helps you deal with pain and stay in the world.*

SIX PRACTICES

▼ ▼ ▼

There comes a moment in every life when the Universe pre-
sents you with an opportunity to rise to your potential. An
open door that only requires the heart to walk through, seize
it and hang on. The choice is never simple. It's never easy. It's
not supposed to be. But those who travel this path have always
looked back and realized that the test was always about the
heart. The rest is just practice.

—JAIME BUCKLEY

WHETHER WINDED OR elated, exhausted or fresh, whether
grieving or beginning again, when we get up to try again, it
all comes down to inhabiting a living practice. So before we talk about
practice in particular, let me offer a spiritual context for all forms of
practice, in an attempt to remind us, myself included, why we engage
in practice at all.

Every gift life has to offer is endless, though we are not. The tasks
are endless. The wonder is endless. The pain of living is endless. The
chances to love are endless. In actuality, living is an endless practice,
through which we become who we were born to be, step-by-step, face-
to-face, heart-to-heart.

And being opened quietly for moments every day creates a path by
which life reaches us, the way rain carves a little stream in the earth
by which the smallest flowers are watered. We each need avenues by

which we can be watered. Sometimes such avenues are carved in us by our experience. Other times we're taught by loved ones or strangers. Mostly, we have to discover them for ourselves. However we come to this, creating paths by which life can reach us is the only way that aliveness roots in our heart.

No matter how hard we work, the aim and purpose of practice is not to be done with it, but to immerse ourselves so completely in life by any means that we, for the moment, are life itself living. Excellence, if we achieve it, is a welcome by-product of complete immersion. But the reward for practice is a thoroughness of being.

Our Work as Brother Sisyphus

In Greek mythology, Sisyphus was the cruelest of men, the deceitful, vengeful king of Corinth who would murder travelers and guests for their money and to heighten everyone's fear of him. He even betrayed Zeus, who then sent Thanatos, the spirit face of death, to chain Sisyphus in the underworld dungeon for the wicked. But Sisyphus even outwitted his captor, chaining Thanatos there instead. As long as Thanatos was chained, no one could die. The old began to suffer interminably and no sacrifices could be made to the gods. At this, Zeus and the others made life so miserable for Sisyphus that he himself wanted to die and couldn't. He was forced to restore the natural order.

As punishment, Sisyphus was made to roll a large boulder up a hill for eternity. Each time he would near the top of the hill, the massive stone would roll back down, forcing him to begin again. Ever since, Sisyphus has been a symbol of how life without compassion or integrity can become a pointless endeavor. His story warns us that in the long run greed and cruelty will disrupt the natural order and that unbridled deceit will eventually make our life unbearable and pointless.

∽ *Excellence is a welcome by-product of complete immersion. The reward for practice is a thoroughness of being.*

The existential philosopher Albert Camus wrote his famous essay *The Myth of Sisyphus*, in 1942, during the height of World War II when France and Europe were on their way to ruin under Nazi occupation. In the last chapter, Camus cites the fate of King Sisyphus as evidence that life is meaningless and absurd. In an era filled with such unspeakable destruction and genocide, who can blame anyone for thinking life meaningless? Still, Camus found meaning in the struggle itself. The last lines of the book read, "The struggle itself . . . is enough to fill a man's heart. One must imagine Sisyphus happy."

But in another long-forgotten world, we can imagine an opposite unfolding for Sisyphus. We can imagine him as everything he was not, inhabiting his greatest possibility with his entire heart. We can imagine King Sisyphus welcoming strangers and travelers and giving them refuge and seeding their dreams. We can imagine him so beloved that even Thanatos, the spirit face of death, would come to him and ask, "How can I break these chains that make me die in life?" We can imagine the kind old king journeying with him to the underworld like a wizened bodhisattva, keeping Thanatos company in the breathless dark until the spirit face of death itself could break back into life, the way a diver out of air might burst through the waves. We can imagine Zeus and the others so moved by his kind company that they offer Sisyphus immortality. But Sisyphus bows in humility, admitting, "I can't imagine so many years if I'm not able to give." In the hollow of their immortal hearts, the once envious gods are softened.

The reward they bestow on Sisyphus for his life of giving is the simple task of rolling a ball of light up a magical hill, the rolling of which seeds kindness and generosity throughout the world. And to ensure that this tender task will never end, the ball of light rolls back down as the ageless Sisyphus must begin again to slowly disseminate light with each step he takes.

To believe in one version of the myth of Sisyphus only opens half of the human story. We don't need to counter or negate the plight of the cruel and deceitful Sisyphus, just complete it. For we live daily at the crossroads of becoming the cruel king or the kind servant. Each day we're asked to choose.

Our time on Earth is spent carrying what is heavy and following the light. When the light turns heavy, life feels oppressive. When the heaviness turns to light, life surprises us with its wonder. What makes the journey turn? What makes us turn from rock pushers to light followers? And how can we remember the one, when we're deflated or inflated by the other?

The press of life makes us quickly learn how to work the task and love the light. The deeper part of life's practice, however, is to learn how to love the task and work the light. This can change everything. When we can love the task, we stop crossing the hill and start seeding it. When we're a slave to the rock we're rolling with no end in sight, the journey seem pointless: up and down, there and back, always crossing the tedium of hours, lifting and carrying, checking off our many lists and creating new ones. When following the light, touching it as we go, then like a farmer fertilizing the land, we seed light and kindness in each furrow.

It seems that loving the task is what turns the heaviness into light. Even so, no one can do this all the time. So how can we not just endure but be transformed by the difficult transitions from heaviness to light, from soul to world, from pain to peace, and back? This is the skill that can never be mastered, though we can't abandon trying. The endless practice is enlivened by our constant struggle to turn heaviness into light, which no one can tell us how to do.

⌒ The deeper part of life's practice is to learn how to love the task and work the light. This can change everything.

Given the pulls to be cruel or kind, to be clever or sincere, to hoard or give away, we can explore six practices that, if personalized, can help us turn the task back into wonder; practices that if listened to can help us transform ourselves from rock pushers into light followers, one more time.

The Practice of Uncertainty

The practice of uncertainty is patience. That is, the only way to move through uncertainty, the only way to listen for what it has to say, is by being patient. The speech of uncertainty is slow. When we move too fast, the lessons are unintelligible. For sure, it's hard to be patient. Waiting was one of the great teachers that appeared during my cancer journey, the most difficult teacher and greatest ally. In the three-year heat of my medical journey, every step required a different decision which only waiting uncovered. During that waiting, I became more and more grounded in the free fall of uncertainty.

We are born both patient and impatient. While our being is born moving slow, the life that carries it flits like a hummingbird, rapidly twitting even when we hover. Yet when our body, mind, and heart are aligned—like tumblers in a mystical lock—something eternal opens. When our body, mind, and heart move at the same pace, which requires slowing down, we know that congruence of being as the pace of what is real. Moving at the pace of what is real can move us through uncertainty and open us to the shimmer of spirit and the energy of aliveness.

> ∾ *The gift of patience opens when our body, heart, and mind slow enough to move in unison.*

How then can we learn to be patient? By slowing down when we speed up. By following whatever part of us is moving slow. If your heart is racing, let the calm at the center of your mind slow the rest of you. If your mind is racing, let the tiredness of your body slow the rest of you. Difficult as it is, the practice of patience centers on trying to have our body, heart, and mind pause until they all can move in unison, at the pace of what is real. An ounce of music, silence, or truth can bring us closer.

The Practice of Opportunity

The practice of opportunity is trust, which means following our heart. Opportunity always presents itself as an opening that seems a bit smaller than we think we can fit through. Following our heart means trusting that we will fit through the opening we have to go through. It might be the narrow opening back to health, or leaving a life of quiet secrecy to swim into the sea of love, or putting all our weapons down, even the invisible ones, so we can humbly shimmy through the tunnel of now to an authentic life. Trust means dropping closer to the earth so we can inch our way through the one opportunity that is presenting itself. Oh, there will be others, but we must practice trust every chance we get. We must grow humble, follow our heart, and lean in to the next opening.

Though it seems daunting, we never know what we carry or what we can seed until we strip down to meet our opportunity. We never know what is full-born or waiting deep inside our pain until we trust what is under all our explanations and doubts. Opportunity doesn't promise a destination or relief from the press of not being who we are. Opportunity provides fresh water for the fish of our soul to swim in. And it's the swimming in fresh water that cleanses us of all that doesn't matter.

The Practice of Courage

The practice of courage is doing small things with love. This was Mother Teresa's anthem. We begin to dismantle what is overwhelming by beginning the journey of involvement one hand at a time, one kindness at a time, one utterance of truth at a time. From the outside, things that require courage seem impossible, but once we begin, we're no longer on the outside. This lets us see more. This lets us feel the current of the situation we have to cross. Any small act of love shows us the next step to be taken. So it's imperative to stop rehearsing the perfect starting point and just begin.

We can practice doing small things with love when we're not afraid, so it will be available to us when we are afraid. You can do this by mak-

ing dinner for your dog, or getting coffee for your loved one, or holding the door for an elder who's taking way too long to cross the parking lot in the rain. The world is our practice ground.

The word *authentic* comes from the Greek *authentes*, which means bearing the mark of the hands. Doing small things with love is how we care for each other, one hand at a time. Doing small things with love releases our courage. And each small act we're led to leads to more. Doing small things with love is the atom of bravery. I tell myself when afraid, "To be courageous, I don't need to become my best self, I just need to open who I already am and courage will fill me."

We must try to do small things with love when we're not afraid, so the love will be available to us when we are afraid.

The Practice of Connection

The practice of connection is holding and listening. When we feel disconnected, any act of holding or listening will return us to the larger world.

With regard to listening, the difference in being an introvert or an extrovert is mostly the direction of our attention; where we naturally face when we listen, toward the inner world or the outer world. Just as some of us are born left-handed and some right-handed, some of us are born to listen inwardly first or outwardly first. One is a strength and the other is an unused capacity. The practice of connection requires that we complete the one that doesn't come naturally.

Entire cultures naturally lean one way or the other, too. It's telling that Eastern statues of Buddha traditionally have their eyes closed, implying an attunement to the inner world, while Western statues from ancient Greece and Rome traditionally have their eyes open, implying an attunement to the outer world. But to live an awakened, compassionate life, we need both.

Our daily life is the practice ground for the integration of our inner and outer attention. While tasks need to be done, they don't always

help us stay connected. Our evolving practice is to call the doctor, fix the car, cut the grass *and* to make amends and repair our torn connections to life. Our challenge is to do the dishes and pay the bills while somehow stilling ourselves, though there are so many places to go. If we can't stay connected to the stream of life in the midst of the thousand tasks, our frustration and disconnection will begin to hurt others. Tending and being go hand in hand. When we can tend and be in a way that complements our soul, we discover time and again that holding leads to finally being held.

Like everyone, I still struggle with this. My only thoughts, when feeling disconnected, are to stay open to the teachers around me moment to moment. I believe that each is a ready guide. And when I can practice holding and listening, no matter how poorly I do it, I find I begin to feel the wisdom of connection as it moves through me.

Just the other day, I was drawn to hold some of my father's tools, now that he's gone. I have a chisel, a T-square, an awl. And when I can't really fathom the fact that he's died and is no longer here on Earth, I hold one of his tools. I hold something he held. Because we can listen to what we hold. When we touch something that's been touched, it speaks to us. Not in words, but in the felt language of being from which all words arise.

Planting the Oar

These four practices lead to a fifth that we can call *Exploration, Mastery, and Abandonment.* This is a practice we're drawn into over time. Throughout our lives, we begin and discover, grow and mature, and then we're asked to shed our gown of mastery in order to begin again.

Regardless of what we learn, we're never so in wonder as when we begin. The greatest position of aliveness is when we're full of wonder and curiosity, when we're exploring. Then comes the work of immersion, commitment, and devotion, through which we become accomplished at a skill, an understanding, a practice, or a relationship. This marks the deeper immersion of effort that transforms us and sustains us on our way to some form of mastery.

But if we stay there, sooner or later, we grow numb. There's certainly a value in doing things well, but the heart wants to keep living and learning. The heart is not satisfied by mastering anything. It needs to keep applying what it knows.

Eventually, we come upon the necessary yet difficult moment when, in order to stay fresh and vital, we need to abandon, not what we've learned, but our identity as a master of anything. We need to put down our identity as an experienced know-it-all, because encased in that we deaden ourselves to life. Think about the ways in which we're bored with all that we know, but reluctant to let go of our earned position, because we've worked so hard to learn these things. Yet if we refuse to return to a beginner's mind and heart, our self-regard as a master can turn hollow and suffocate the soul.

I'm not referring to emotional or relational abandonment, but rather the peeling away of a skin that helped us grow when it hardens into a bark or callus that prevents us from growing further.

A crucial example of this for me happened in my forties. I had worked for more than twenty years to become a true poet. Only to discover that being a poet had revealed the depth of spirit I was born to inhabit. My identity as a poet had become too small for the spirit I was led to. I discovered I was the soil and not the pot and like a plant that outgrows its container, my spirit needed to be repotted in something larger. I had to abandon being a poet in order to keep growing. This was very disorienting but ultimately liberating. I will always write and always be a poet with a small *p*. But being a poet is the means by which my Spirit with a capital *S* speaks and moves in the world. Paradoxically, only by being faithful to my own cycle of exploration, mastery, and abandonment was I able to become a better poet.

A mythic example of this is powerfully rendered by Helen Luke in her book *Old Age: Journey into Simplicity*. Helen conveys a little known part of the story of Odysseus. After twenty years at war and wandering home, the master seaman is finally living peacefully as an old man in Ithaca with his wife, Penelope.

After a time, the great and clever warrior finds himself restless and bored. He decides to go back to sea where he is skilled and respected.

He gathers his things and leaves a letter for his wife. With a small sack of belongings and an oar, he sets out for the harbor. On his way, he's stopped by the great, blind soothsayer, Tiresias, who hovers before Odysseus and says, "No. Your time as a master seaman is over. You will turn around and walk inland, as far as you can, until you meet someone who doesn't even know what an oar is. And then, you will plant the oar and start a garden."

To be clear, there is nothing wrong with returning to what we love and what we're good at. The reason Tiresias compels Odysseus to go inland is because he knows that Odysseus is heading back to his mastery for the wrong reasons—for comfort, respect, and familiarity. We gather what we know but shed our posture as the grand knower in order to stay a vital learner.

My dear friend Robert and I devoured Helen's book on old age together. A few years later, Susan and I moved to Michigan, beginning another phase of our lives. It was exciting but troubling to start over. After a few weeks in our new home, we received a long, narrow package in the mail with no return address and no note of any kind. I opened the box to find an oar! I knew immediately what it meant and who it was from! We laughed as we carried it up the hill in our new backyard and planted the oar.

That oar has weathered many seasons, most beautiful with dustings of snow on its paddle. And more than one stranger has asked about the oar and what it's doing so far from the sea. But every day, while pouring my coffee, I bow to the need to explore, master, and then to learn and build something new.

The Life of Expression

The sixth practice is to stay devoted to the life of expression. This is imperative because *the life of expression is the tuning fork by which we find our way to the sacred.* Only by allowing what we feel, think, and experience to move through us can we be animated enough to sense what matters, and so join with it.

Consider that the tuning fork was created in 1711 by John Shore, a legendary trumpeter for the royal court in England. Tuning forks are designed to evoke pure tones that allow us to hear a larger harmony. When struck, the handle of a tuning fork is usually pressed on a table or wood surface to amplify the tones.

In a similar way, what we feel, think, and experience is often inaudible until it's expressed. The life of expression that moves through us allows us to hear a larger harmony. When we ground what we feel by touching another, the interwoven nature of things is amplified and we're brought closer to what matters.

When we don't give voice to what moves through us, we become entangled with life, but not connected to life. When silent with our love and pain, we can't distribute what we feel and so our heartaches and pains are intensified as they only bounce around within us. The way a lightning rod standing in the open attracts and grounds the lightning, the life of expression grounds the intensity of what we feel on any given day.

To practice the life of expression enhances all the other practices, the way blood is needed for each organ to do its work.

> ⌁ *What we feel, think, and experience is often inaudible until it's expressed.*

Being a Teacher

I return to the fact that the aim and purpose of practice is to immerse ourselves so completely in life that we are life itself living. Given this, we are daily at the crossroads, trying to turn our heaviness into light. We are constantly challenged to love the task and work the light. Whether we are cruel or kind depends on the practices we enliven.

When faced with uncertainty, we're asked to practice patience. When faced with opportunity, we're asked to practice trust. When faced with a need for courage, we're asked to do small things with love. When faced with disconnection, we're asked to remember how to hold and listen. And when encased in the weight of our own knowledge, we're asked to abandon what contains us and begin again. Yet none of these practices can help us, if we don't let the life of expression move through us, so it can lead us back to what matters.

I was letting our dog out before bed, as I do every night, when I was stunned by the moon. It was full and thin clouds were drifting past it, which only made its reflection brighter. It led to this poem:

BEING A TEACHER

Like the moon standing full
reflecting as much of the Source
as it can so those unaccustomed
to the dark can find their way,
this is the path you have chosen,
that has chosen you.

To be a teacher means that we take our turn standing in our life as full as possible, so we might reflect what matters and be bright enough for those nearby to find their way. If practice can lead us here, we will not want for sanity or company.

A Reflective Pause

○ *In your journal, choose either patience, trust, holding, or listening, and describe the history of your agility and awkwardness with one of these inner skills. How might you deepen your practice here?*

○ *In conversation with a friend or loved one, tell the story of one form of practice that has captured your interest and passion at one time in your life. It might have been gardening or listening to jazz or birding or carving spoons. Share how the experience of deep practice has affected you.*

○ *In conversation with a friend or loved one, tell the story of one small thing you found yourself doing with love and how this changed you.*

THE NECESSARY RAIN

▼ ▼ ▼

I have always been high strung. Perhaps others are strung too low. Or missing a string entirely. I just know that without strings you can't make music.

—HOWARD NEPO

WITHIN EACH OF us is a spirit, which knows from birth how to say yes and not question that yes. In some ways, the path of our spirit is that of a hawk. It doesn't need to pay attention to roads or terrain. Our spirit simply flies directly to the heart of the matter. But the life we live is human and we can't escape the weight of feet and legs and arms. We can't fly like a hawk, so we need to break trail and follow paths. We need to stop and cut down limbs when they block the way. We need to accept when we make a wrong turn. It's a dead end and now we need to back up and start over.

In our humanness, we need to plod, one step at a time, and find our way, while our spirit is already there. In our own way, we each have to reach an agreement between our spirit and our humanness or there will be no peace for the life that carries them. The spirit in us can be very impatient with the person that carries it. It can say, "C'mon, why are you taking so long? I see where we need to go. Let's do it!" And the human in us can become very frustrated with its spirit, "I can't get there that quickly. Stop pushing me."

We have this tension between the part in us that needs to work through the days and the part in us that is instantaneously attuned to everything. Sometimes, being high-strung means that our spirit is tugging at us, ever more insistent that we come along. But it's of no use to bemoan this paradox. We need the skill and commitment to inhabit it.

Ultimately, the human in us must accept that it will never transcend this life into what its heart knows is eternal. We can feel and taste what is limitless but never stay there because being human by definition is to live here with limits. And the spirit in us that glides like a hawk, which we can also call our being, must accept that what carries it walks; must accept that while it lives in the sky, the life it is incarnated to help lives on the ground.

So, our being will always see more and move faster than our humanness, which must step over rocks and through mud. If we don't accept this imperfect marriage, we will never fully know our gifts. Instead, our being will break our body, insisting that it catch up, and our heart will drag us into impossible situations, insisting that the sun can fit in a thing as small as a dream. And trying to eat more of life than we can, we will burn the things we love along the way. Reaching this agreement between what is human and what is spiritual is the practice of meeting the world with vulnerability and acceptance until who we are releases what we know.

Clearly, we are both the flawed human being hacking through the brush and the hawk-like spirit gliding to what matters. We are the troubled apprentice, never sure what to do, nudged by our deep knowing spirit toward yes, even when we don't know what we're saying yes to.

Do you know these voices? Do you recognize the knowing one who says yes? Do you recognize the troubled apprentice who hesitates? Can you recall a moment in the last month, in the last year, when you've been the troubled apprentice slogging away, breaking trail, confused, not sure?

And can you recognize a moment when you said yes, even though you didn't know what you were saying yes to? These voices are aspects of life-force we're born with which we need to discover and relate to. To arrive at this necessary agreement is part of the pilgrimage of the heart.

Through the Briars of Fairness

If we can't arrive at an agreement between our being and our human-ness, the frustrations of living will eventually turn us into sour victims. There's no question that the journey we're given from birth is often difficult. We can say with legitimate frustration and despair, "I don't deserve any of this," whatever *this* is, and yet it still affects us. I don't know why we're given what we are. We have every right to every bless-ing there is *and* it's relentlessly true that life is mysterious, wondrous, and unfair. This is our long-standing argument with life. Under our sense of purpose, our history of being loved or not, under our elusive dance with all we want, this quarrel with life persists.

Regardless of what seems fair or not, we're each asked to settle this underlying argument, to arrive at some kind of acceptance of the para-dox that much of what happens to us is painful *and* it's the one life we have. I'm not suggesting that this means giving up on finding what will fulfill you. Rather, that working to make peace with life will give your heart new eyes that will enable you to make more wholehearted deci-sions about the things that live close to your soul.

Polishing the Heart

The Sufis speak of polishing the heart into a mirror, so that through our love we can reflect the heart of everything. This is one practice that in time can help us make the necessary agreement between our being and our humanness. By its very nature, living in the world creates a film over our heart, while our thoroughness of being and our gestures of love remove that film. There is no arrival in this process. The goal isn't to stay clean or get dirty, but to stay engaged in the unending transfor-mative cycle of life. And when we can't summon the effort or courage to clean the film from our heart, there is always the necessary rain by which life will clean and refresh itself. In this way, the work of being and the inevitable friction of becoming are inextricably knit together.

We all film the heart and we all polish the heart. We all move between these points of wakefulness and weariness. All the while, the resources of life wait like a great sea to cleanse us. This is why we polish the heart into a mirror—to open and touch the place within us where all life lives, where all hearts feel, where all things resound through the inlet of our soul. The endless practice here is to live out a constant commitment to aliveness, to stay engaged in the ongoing journey of being filmed over, only to be scoured into a clear vessel, again and again.

> ᔕ *Regardless of what seems fair or not, we're each asked to arrive at some kind of acceptance of the paradox that much of what happens to us is painful and it's the one life we have.*

Another Crucial Pairing

Our being and our humanness are part of a larger Whole. To better understand their relationship, it helps to better understand the nature of Life's Wholeness. To begin with, in the essential water of life, love and suffering are inseparable. We can only hope the love we imbibe renews us before we're enervated by the suffering. This overwhelming aspect of Wholeness is one way that God or the Mystery of the Universe (whichever name you prefer) ensures that we walk this journey together. Life is made just difficult enough that we need each other.

Only when we can take Life in as a Whole does Life bestow its resources of resilience. It's the dynamic Unity of Life that creates resilience. Broken down, the mystery is no longer carried and the potency of life dissipates. But the challenge in taking Life in as a Whole is that we never know whether we will receive more love or suffering in any one mouthful. And so, when we take in more suffering than love, we need each other to make it through. When we take in more love than suffering, we need one another to keep each other grounded.

As if by design, life is demanding enough that no one can make it alone. This ensures our interdependence. It seems a requirement of experience: to receive Life in its Wholeness, we need to hold each other up, and open.

....

⌒ꞔ The work of being and the friction of becoming are
inextricably knit together.

....

Being the Part, Feeling the Whole

Since we're each a living part in a living Whole, one challenging art in being human is to live out our particular life while comprehending the Whole. One aspect of the endless practice is to feel both the depth of our feelings and, at the same time, to stand on the ground of all being which exists independent of what happens to us. Often, we slip to one side of this: either denying the impact of our feelings in order to stay grounded or we're swept away by the strength of our feelings and lose the larger perspective. Being fully awake comes from staying close to both, when we can.

Let me share two personal examples. I was teaching in a beautiful remote setting. The folks attending had traveled quite a distance to be there. As we broke for lunch the first day, a rather distinguished-looking man approached me. He introduced himself as a marine biologist. I had used a metaphor that morning from the biology of fish and he went on to let me know with some vigor and edge that I was dead wrong. I felt the sting of this at once, not the sting of whether the metaphor I used was accurate or not, but the sting of being chastised.

For some reason, though, perhaps because I was holding the space as a teacher, I leaned in and looked into his eyes. I could sense he'd been drawn to attend this retreat, knowing that I speak in metaphor and that I bow to the mystery and the indecipherable logic of paradox. I could see in his eyes that he was testing the waters beyond his world of science and was floundering a bit. Rather than ask for help, he was lashing out.

I found him rude and couldn't deny the harshness of his comments, but I sensed more deeply that this argument was between the way his mind had always worked and the way he was feeling drawn to explore. So I went the other way and said, "Oh, you're a marine biologist! Please, tell me all you know about fish." This seemed to disarm him and he began to secure his footing in this new world by sharing what he knows.

When he finished, I thanked him and said, "You know, I think it's important to realize that, no matter how well or poorly I may have drawn the metaphor, the truth it brings into view is just as true. I would invite you to reflect on your discomfort with that truth."

By the time he left, it was clear that if I had challenged him, the argument he needed to have within himself would have been played out between us. I think the job of a teacher is to give the internal argument back to the person wrestling with their own growth. The entire exchange wasn't easy. And while I stepped aside from his impatience with metaphor and his anger at having to think in new ways, I was still stung inside.

During lunch, I called Susan who was thousands of miles away and blurted out, "You won't believe the asshole I just encountered!" Now, clearly, he's not an asshole. He took the risk to come quite a distance to participate in something that's at his growth edge. But the point here is that I needed to honor my own particular feelings while also honoring his learning struggle. Both are true and my learning in that moment was to feel my own feelings, while also feeling the Whole of Life moving us both along.

The second example is much more personal. During the last eight months of my father's life, he was in and out of hospitals and rehabilitation centers. I had flown in to see him again. When I arrived, he was sleeping and my brother said he was having a hard day. I sat by his side. When he woke, he didn't know who I was. This had never happened before.

I was stunned and it felt odd and evacuating to have my father stare with enormously wide eyes, as if I were a stranger. My heart began to sink. I thought, *So this is what it will feel like when he's gone.* I took his hand and tried to remind him, "Hi Dad, I'm Mark. I'm your son." He looked at me like an old miner trapped underground. He looked at me as if to say, *Am I still here? Are you here to help me?* My heart began to tumble in this canyon between us. But it was suddenly clear that in this moment, I had to be a kind stranger.

I gave up trying to have him recognize me and sat closer, introducing myself for the first time, "Hi, I'm Mark. I'm here to help you, to keep you company. How are you today?" His stare softened and he gripped my hand, thankful for the company. Then he looked beyond me, as if to say, *No one can get me out of this. No one.*

Later that night, he knew me again. But this was a humbling episode in which I was challenged to feel the unnerving moment that I was erased from the consciousness of the man who fathered me *and* to enter a reality that existed beyond my feelings, my story, or even my life. Without denying either. It was also a deeply personal moment of knowing that all things are true. This was my father, the man who held me as a boy, who cried but didn't show up when I had cancer, who was lost to me for fifteen years, who cried in my arms when he was ninety, who didn't know I was his son at ninety-three. All of it is true. And it's imperative not to choose between them, but to let the many faces of my father wash into the many sides of his son's aching heart.

What I've learned from these passages is that the heart not only has room for both, but that life demands that we embrace both what is particular to each of us and what exists in mysterious complexity beyond our singular life. I've learned that the bird must feel both its broken wing and the current of wind that lifts and twirls and carries it. This is what it means to be a bird. As a person, we must feel both the break in our heart and the current of life that lifts and twirls and carries us. This is what it means to be openhearted.

Another Set of Mysteries

So here we are in the midst of another set of life's mysteries: working the tension between our humanness that needs to plod through the days and our spirit that is attuned to everything; working to settle our underlying argument with life; working to polish our heart into a mirror, so our love can reflect the heart of everything; working to receive Life in its Wholeness; and working to feel what is ours to feel while never losing sight of the Whole.

Who knows how to do this, to inhabit this, to honor this? Each of us is a work in progress, not sure what progress looks like on the inside, only feeling closer to what it means to be alive. Yet we can try.

It helps to realize that the sun never stops shining, no matter the variety and constancy of the clouds that drift and enclose us. So much depends on our tender resolve to outwait the clouds and maintain our trust that the sun never stops emanating light and warmth, never stops being a resource, even when we can't see it, even when the blanket of clouds makes us cold.

Similarly, on the inner plane, the common source of Spirit never stops shining, no matter the variety and constancy of psychic clouds that drift and enclose us. So much depends on our tender resolve to outwait the psychic clouds that roll in. The challenge is to maintain our trust in the common source of Spirit that never stops emanating light and warmth; that never stops being a resource, even when we can't see it, even when the blanket of our worries and confusions makes us cold.

We are humbly and beautifully left in the middle. Perhaps one of the most important acts of faith is to never lose sight of the mystical fact that the sun never stops shining no matter the weather, and that the common source of Spirit never stops shining no matter what we suffer. Perhaps one of the most important acts of courage is to move with sincerity through our daily weather of circumstance and emotion till we can be renewed by the inner and outer light.

And when all our efforts just fall short, we need the necessary rain to clear the clouds wherever they linger.

A Reflective Pause

o *In this chapter, we spoke of the Sufi notion of polishing the heart into a mirror, so that through our love we can reflect the heart of everything. In your journal, describe what you do in your day that creates a film over your heart. Then describe what you do in your day that polishes the film from your heart. How do you experience this unending rhythm of being and becoming?*

THE SANCTITY OF EXPERIENCE

▼　▼　▼

Every [person's] condition is a solution in hieroglyphic to those inquiries [we] would put. [We] act it as life, before [we apprehend] it as truth.

—RALPH WALDO EMERSON

THE POINT OF experience is not to escape life but to live it. Each of us carries some wisdom waiting to be discovered at the center of our experience, and everything we meet, if faced and held, reveals a part of that wisdom. We have a language of truth growing in our heart that only living can decode. Truth is a seed hidden in the days until watered by our experience.

In Greek, *ginosko* (ghin-*oce'*-koe) means to come to know, the recognition of truth by experience. As impatient as we are, this recognition can only happen through time. Like it or not, time slowly exposes the story of our lives with its friction, wearing away the film that covers our eyes and the calluses that guard our heart, till we can apprehend the wonder waiting just under the skin of everything. Can we facilitate this process? I'm not sure, but we can ready ourselves.

In Japanese, *wa* means harmony and *doryoku* means effort. Together, they suggest that the job of experience is to bring us closer to harmony through effort. It helps to think of experience as a music we must live to hear. But how do we hear the music of our journey? Who and what do we listen to along the way? How do we make sense of our experience?

How do we listen to life and not what life does to us, when suffering and loss meet us at every turn?

This is a quandary no one has been able to answer since the beginning of time, and I won't either. But we can look at it together and feed the paradox of life like a fire that warms us, one kept going by the stories and questions we add to it. This story from the life of Buddha speaks to our struggle to be heartened or disheartened in our time on Earth.

Come to Your Senses

Patacara lost her family and her home to a flood. She became mad with grief. Ripping the clothes from her body, she moaned aimlessly through the countryside, grief-stricken and naked. Known as the "cloak walker," she wandered into a field where Buddha was teaching. At first, the attendant monks wouldn't let her in, fearing she was crazed, but Buddha beckoned her to him. At once, he saw her inconsolable suffering. It is said that Buddha took her by the shoulders and, with a firm compassion, spoke directly into her raw and broken heart, "Sister, come to your senses."

After a while, she calmed and stayed with Buddha, studying for years. Though her grief had quieted, she had not yet found her place. She had not yet awakened. But one day, while pouring bathwater into the ground, she could see that some streams were short, some were of medium length, and some trickled a long way after the pouring. It was then she realized that some lives are short, some of medium length, and some are blessed to trickle a long way from their birth. She dropped the bucket and finally cried a soft stream, apprehending at last how impermanent and precious life is and how suffering wears down our resistance to this fact. She knelt and cried softly and watched her tears join the three streams of bathwater soaking into the ground.

The questions we're left with are penetrating: When Buddha tells Patacara to come to her senses, what senses is he referring to? What resources does he imply are there? And what is it that finally allows Patacara to turn her suffering and grief into something heartening? These are not questions to be solved but entered. When Buddha calls Patacara to her senses, he seems to be invoking more than a quiet stoicism. More than the will to *contain* her feelings, he seems to be asking her to enter the holy ground of her experience, which can *absorb* her feelings. Patacara's revelation suggests that all of our experience wears us down to something essential that moves through everything. When we can recognize this essential being that moves through everything, accept it and love it, we can feel the place that no one can hold and know we are home.

ᴄᴡ The paradox of life is a fire that warms us; one kept going by the stories and questions we add to it.

Ever-Present Choices

When we can absorb our feelings rather than contain them, the way earth absorbs bathwater, our roots are fed. And feeding the roots of heart and soul with the water of our experience is a quiet irrigation we understandably lose track of while wrestling with our suffering. But no matter how often we fall, the gift of wakeful effort allows us to find our way back to what is heartening and affirming, without denying the suffering we encounter. Still, the things that dishearten and drain us are always near, as near as all that is affirming.

Our stories remain an ever-present medicine. They are mysterious cups of remedy that carry the choices each person has to face. Consider these two stories and the choices they present. The first speaks to our capacity to awaken or numb each other and ourselves. The second speaks to how resentment can drain us of our own possibility.

Aslan and the White Witch

We always have the choice to be one who affirms or one who drains. This choice is beautifully rendered in the C. S. Lewis classic The Chronicles of Narnia. There, Aslan, the life-affirming, mystical lion, appears from time to time to restore balance and empower others. His counterpart, the life-draining White Witch of Narnia, freezes the life out of others, turning them into statues. Theirs is a classic battle; it is our battle. Ultimately, it is Aslan's mystical breath that brings those drained of feeling back to life by thawing their numbness. Isn't this the gift of encouragement: to thaw our numbness by breathing life into each other and ourselves? Isn't this the blessing of the lion-hearted?

We could say that the mystical breath is the heartening influence we carry within us and that freezing the life out of things is the disheartening influence, the coldness we're capable of when we withdraw our attention and care. When we stop listening long enough, that inattention can be numbing.

It is imperative to remember that we are both the lion and the witch. As such, we carry tremendous powers within us to affirm life or to drain it. Each time we turn away from life and deny the living, we numb some part in the world. But each time we turn toward life and accept everything that lives, we thaw some part in the world. While we can't avoid turning away from life and at times denying the living, while we can't escape moments of numbness, working with what we're given is the first step to decoding the hieroglyphic of our time on Earth. Our resilience is the mystical breath that thaws us and brings us back to life.

Jupiter and the Bee

Another insidious condition that drains us of all that is heartening is the murkiness of harboring resentments until they boil into vengeance. Of course, vengeance and spite are not new. Consider this ancient myth. A bee from Mount Hymettus, the queen of the hive, ascends to Olympus to present Jupiter with some honey fresh from her combs. Jupiter, delighted with the offering, promises to give whatever she would ask. She is quick to implore, "Give me, I pray thee, a sting, that if any mortal shall approach to take my honey, I may kill them." Jupiter is sorely displeased, but can't refuse his promise. Carefully, he answers the bee, "You shall have your request, but at the peril of your life. For if you use your sting, it shall remain in the wound you make, and then you will die from the loss of it."

This small but potent tale offers many choices. At what point do we consider the honey we make ours and when do we accept it as a gift that comes through our labor of being? If we think the honey ours, then, like the queen of the hive, we can become obsessed with hoarding it and protecting it. If we accept the honey as a gift, then we're a carrier of a sweetness whose purpose is to be given. And what does this tale say of promises? Does Jupiter make his promise too soon? Is his trust in the queen of the hive misplaced? Though his deep cleverness reveals a truism about the cost of spite, which is more important: keeping his promise or keeping his response to the queen of the hive authentic? Different lives unfold from these choices. Not just among the gods, but in our ordinary lives.

Throughout history, the queen of the hive has taken many incarnations, both female and male. In truth, the bee from Hymettus possesses us each time we let the bottom of our hurt define the world. Then the law of spite will plague us. For whenever we let our sting remain in the wound, a part of us dies to life.

The Temptation of Fear

Nothing disheartens us more than fear. It is wildly paralytic and numbing. It keeps us from listening and what we do hear through fear is often distorted. So let's look at the dynamics of fear. As human beings, we're born with a fight-or-flight reflex in which we're physiologically wired to respond to life-threatening situations by either fighting off a threat or running from it.

However, this impulse is often exaggerated and triggered by situations that, though stressful and uncomfortable, are *not* life threatening. Yet we respond the same way, fighting or fleeing *as if* our life depends on it. Such overreactions can leave incredible damage in our path. As when we kill a bee that's made it to our kitchen because we fear its sting. Or when we swat at someone because we fear being stung by their neediness or pain. Or not letting a woman torn open with grief, like Patacara, into our church because we fear she is mad.

But what if this fight-or-flight reflex is evolving like everything else?

What if we are in the midst of an evolutionary process in which our basic understanding of what it means to fight or flee is being redefined by our experience? The evolving questions could save us. Can we grow the skill to determine what is truly life threatening from what is simply ego or identity threatening? And how might we respond more precisely to situations that *seem* life threatening though they are not?

The longer we can resist the temptation of fear, in order to discern what is truly threatening from what is stressful and uncomfortable, the less violent our reactions are. This requires a special kind of listening, awakened by our strength of being and our strength of compassion. This discernment is a reflective practice that deepens our integrity. I believe that over time the art of facing things openly and honestly can evolve our fight-or-flight reflex beyond its primitive response. Facing conflict and fear can keep us in relationship with our experience long enough to uncover what we have in common with every living thing.

> *All of our experience wears us down to something essential that moves through everything. When we can recognize this essential being that moves through everything, accept it and love it, we can feel the place that no one can hold and know we are home.*

Things That Hearten and Dishearten

There are many. And while all the thinking and talking can't keep us from the suffering and loss we will encounter for being human, neither will all the suffering and loss keep us from the sanctity of our experience, if we can help each other to it.

Here are some fears that dishearten us into life-draining positions:

o The fear of the unknown—*that I won't see it coming*—infects our distrust of the days.

○ The fear of being undone—*that the worst possible outcome will happen*—breeds cynicism.

○ The fear of breaking—*that things will shatter and fall apart*—makes an occupation of anticipating pain.

○ The fear of rejection—*that I will speak the truth and everyone will leave*—leads to the practice of hiding.

○ And the fear of death—*that the clock will keep beating louder*—enslaves us to panic and urgency.

All of these fears in passing are quite normal, but when allowed to take over our lives, they become life draining and disheartening.

Thankfully, there are also intentions that hearten us into life-affirming positions, intentions that can counter these fears. Let me name a few:

○ *To strengthen trust,* we can expand our ways of being to include surprise and deepen our ways of feeling to include wonder and curiosity.

○ *To strengthen what is possible,* we can imagine and spend equal time with what might go right as with what might go wrong.

○ *To strengthen our ability to integrate pain,* we can try to be like water and learn how to absorb what falls into us and how to flow instead of shatter.

○ *To shrink our habits of hiding,* we can listen to experience as a teacher and wait in the open for truth to show itself, the way trees grow toward the sun.

○ *And to shrink the press and urgency of time,* we can linger in the moment and try to accept our death.

Often, we struggle between what is heartening and disheartening, brought along when feeling affirmed and tossed about when feeling drained. But one thing is clear: when we cling to our situation, we can fall into the trap of viewing whatever happens from the vision of the part, from which things seldom make sense and fear takes over. When we can surrender our pain—that is, stop holding it tightly—we chance to view whatever happens from the vision of the Whole. From here, our experience can open us to a mystery that will carry us. There are few things in life that are as challenging or as rewarding as moving from what disheartens us to what heartens us.

Toward What Is Precious

No matter how lost in fear or distrust we may be, no matter how consumed or disoriented by hurt and anger, we can find our way back to all that is heartening by giving ourselves over completely to attention and appreciation. It doesn't even matter toward what.

The simplest and bravest way to counter the plight of disheartenment is *to move toward what is precious*. This is the original meaning of the word *appreciate*. Repeatedly, a life of appreciation uncovers the freeing truth that life itself is one miracle after another passing through us. Ultimately, moving toward what is precious returns us to what matters. It's through this deeper sense that we are able to discern what is heartening and what is disheartening. It's through a life of appreciation that we are refreshed.

In the fifth century BC, the Greek philosopher Heraclitus said, "You can't step in the same river twice." And in our own time, the Standing Rock Sioux elder Vine Deloria Jr. said, "We may *mis-understand*, but we do not *mis-experience*." Both elders speak to the inescapable fact that we and the life we wake in are constantly emerging and evolving. We and life are constantly dynamic. They speak with Emerson and Buddha to the mysterious vitality of *directly* engaging the life we are given as the most immediate way to discover the wisdom hidden in our days. After all our attempts to reframe, deny, project, or simply run from what's upon us, we have no real choice but to meet our own experience until, moving through us, it makes our song knowable.

The paradox at the center of the sanctity of experience is that while we can learn from each other, while I can quote these sages from across history and cultures as a way to affirm that we're not alone, we are left to live our lives. As the Italian novelist Umberto Eco said, "If [you were given] the truth immediately, you would not recognize it, because your heart would not have been purified by the long quest."

So, in a world where tragedy is broadcast every half hour; where situation comedies are rerun nightly; where confusions and betrayals replay themselves; where dark histories repeat themselves, help me put my stinger down and I'll help you take the deep chance to come to your senses. We can take the time to move toward whatever we sense is precious. Let your experience-worn lips feel the air and I'll dare to listen before fighting or fleeing. We can dare to offer something we haven't rehearsed. We can dare to effort our way into harmony, where each moment will birth us and each will gift us something as it dies.

A Reflective Pause

○ *In your journal, describe two or three things that are disheartening you right now and two or three things that are heartening. What do the things that dishearten you have in common? What do the things that hearten you have in common? How can you calm what disheartens you and lean into what heartens you?*

WHAT'S IN THE WAY
IS THE WAY

❯ ❯ ❯

W HILE TEACHING AT the Sounds True Wake Up Festival, a global
gathering in Estes Park, Colorado, I read William Stafford's
poem "The Way It Is":

> There's a thread you follow. It goes among
> things that change. But it doesn't change.
> People wonder about what you are pursuing.
> You have to explain about the thread.
> But it is hard for others to see.
> While you hold it you can't get lost.
> Tragedies happen; people get hurt
> or die; and you suffer and get old.
> Nothing you do can stop time's unfolding.
> You don't ever let go of the thread.

I've always been moved by this poem and invited our group to journal, asking each person to describe the thread they hold on to.

In exploring this, several people described being sidetracked from
what matters. One woman said she couldn't move from her head to her
heart long enough to find the thread. A young man said he was afraid
holding on to the thread would cause him to lose himself. Another person said she'd lost the thread since her husband died seven months ago.

A fourth person said she was afraid she'd given the thread away and couldn't get it back.

As more people shared, we discussed how being in conversation with what seems in the way is how the heart presents the next step in our journey. It suddenly became clear that what's in the way *is* the way. Facing the things that prevent us from making our way *is* the road of freedom we each must suffer in order to become authentic enough to follow the thread of what matters.

Frustrating as it is to keep retreating into our head, learning to stay in our heart is not a distraction but how we prepare the ground for living a full life. Afraid as we are that we will lose our self for getting involved, loosening the tightness of our identity is how we let our soul experience the Living Unity of Things. Thrown off course by the loss of a loved one, we discover that grief is the stripping away of all that doesn't matter. And even giving the thread away and feeling thoroughly lost allows us to practice the emptiness necessary to begin again. Despite all our plans, learning to stay in our heart, losing our tight hold on our self, being made humble and gentle through the erosion of loss, and feeling empty enough to begin again—these are steps to finding and refinding the thread of all that matters.

Often, we so furiously insist on what we want or where we think we're going that we ignore, resist, or deny what life brings as the next step. Often, we are so intent on the goal we have worked toward and so in love with the dream that has seized us that we miss the teachers trying to get our attention along the way. All the while, truth is a seed hidden in the days until watered by what life brings us.

Sooner or later, just by living, we're reduced to what matters; as many of the things we thought were important and irreplaceable are broken or snapped like small branches in a storm. And somehow, as we heal from the scratches and bruises, we stand taller, covered by less. It's then we begin to feel gratitude, even though it's hard to be grateful for what is difficult. In the earned nakedness that follows honest experience, we are very close to the thread that connects us to everything.

Five years ago, I was in the crucible of a difficult life change. I had lost my job at a time when I was sick. I kept retreating into my head, trying to douse the urgency I felt, trying to land my wife and me in a safe situation. I was shaken to my core, afraid I was losing my self. I was tumbling in my grief, having lost my position, my community, my health insurance, afraid we would lose our home. I felt dark and empty, unsure how to continue.

It was then I went to be by the sea, to clear my head, to open my heart, to imagine next steps. But I couldn't imagine anything. What I found was the beauty and resilience of life waiting under my trouble and under all trouble. I was forced by the weight of my situation to look beneath my pain and confusion. I was emptied of all plans till I could remember that though what happens can be dark and alarming and hurtful, the fact that we're alive is all that matters. In this very moment, a gull landed a few feet away, as if to look out into the sea of time with me.

Suddenly, this tender, unbreakable silence in the company of a gull showed me the thread I could hold on to. I can't name it, other than to say that under the particular things we want and don't want, there is a sacred is-ness that can't be destroyed. I felt an unexpected sense of peace, though I was raw and weak and beat-up.

When we least expect it, what's in the way *is* the way. The broken door lets in the light. The broken heart lets in the world. Like shattered fruit, our broken plans attract the angels who feast like songbirds on the sweetness we've hidden, now finally in the open. And so we grow.

Under the particular things we want and don't want, there is a sacred is-ness that can't be destroyed.

A Reflective Pause

○ *This is a meditation. Center yourself and breathe slowly. Meditate on your sense of what feels stable in your life under everything that changes. Without trying to name it or control it, just settle into the feeling of constancy that waits under all your changing thoughts. This is the thread that connects all things. Feel it connecting you to the web of life.*

○ *In your journal, describe how you first became aware of this thread.*

○ *In conversation with a friend or loved one, describe what's in the way for you right now. How might you hold this, if what's in the way is the next step in your path and not a distraction or an obstacle?*

OUR INCH OF LIGHT

❱ ❱ ❱

I T WAS PLATO who said we are born whole but we need each other to
become complete. This is a law of nature. Flowers have every inch
of their petal and color but need to be pollinated to become complete.
Every seed has its full form within it, but it needs the rain and the heat
of the sun to become corn or wheat or potato. And every poem or
painting or piece of music—indeed, every act of love—is carried within
us like a seed, but each needs the rain and heat of experience to become
its full expression in the world.

This paradox is especially true of the light we carry inside. Some
call this inner light spirit or soul. Others call it grace. But we can simply call it our *eternal aliveness*, which is constantly looking for a way to
express itself. Each being born to life is like a simple wooden match
with its phosphorus tip. We have the lighted fire within and carry it
everywhere we go. The nature of living as a spirit on Earth is that, like
a simple match, we enter the days needing to strike or be struck against
the things of the world, in order to ignite our aliveness. How we do this
determines the kind of life we live.

There is no getting around the fundamental fact that we need to
interact with everything in order to manifest the wholeness we are born
with. Sometimes we do the striking; sometimes we are struck. Sometimes the friction of life is painful, even devastating, and sometimes the
rub of life can be liberating. Often, out of fear, we avoid the touch of
life, as if this will somehow protect us from the wear and tear of existence. But touching nothing keeps our match from being lit.

41

The mysterious difference between a wooden match and the dormant spirit we carry within is that the light we carry can be lit more than once. In truth, the more we lean into life, the more we authentically interact with the world, the brighter our flame. No one knows how this works, just that it does. Every spiritual tradition affirms this. Our honest meeting of experience is key to finding our light.

The story of addiction can be seen as the human match falling in love with the strike, against ourselves or the world, and not the light that is awakened. Without facing what is ours to face, without owning our innate gifts and capacities, we can become addicted to whatever jarring surface we run into and mistake that shock or rush of adrenaline as our aliveness. That jarring strike could be alcohol or drugs or sex or danger or gambling or the various forms of high-risk adventure.

An even more insidious misunderstanding of how our soul meets the world is when we become addicted to the act of striking itself, when we are so far removed from our inner light that we go about seeking things to strike, as if this taste of violence is what brings us alive.

It seems like it should be easy to remember that we strike a match for the light it carries, and that we live in the world for the soul that experience releases. But being human has never been easy, though it's always been simple. It's interesting that there are two types of matches: *safety matches*, which can be struck only against a specially prepared surface, and *strike-anywhere matches*, which can be struck against any solid surface. Herein lies another dangerous truth about our way in the world.

Clearly, safety matches were designed to prevent accidental fires. But in the realm of our soul coming alive, which are we: *safety souls* or *strike-anywhere souls*? Often, we have preconditions for letting our soul out. It has to be the right person or the right movie or a particular piece of music. We only like certain foods and only keep certain company. But while quarantining our involvement in the world, we run the risk of letting our soul sleep for never meeting life. On the other hand, the vulnerability in being a strike-anywhere soul holds the innocence of children and saints. But there's a responsibility not to set reckless fires and not to open the hearts of people in ways we can't tend.

The first known match was used in China in 577. It was a small stick of pinewood infused with sulfur. The state of Northern Qi was surrounded by the soldiers of the Northern Zhou and Chen. Supplies were sparse. The ladies of the court were out of tinder and needed a way to start fires for cooking and heating. And the pinewood-sulfur match was created. About 950, some four hundred years later, Tao Gu mentions the incident in a book called the *Records of the Unworldly and the Strange*:

> If there occurs an emergency at night it may take some time to make a fire to light a lamp. But an ingenious man devised the system of impregnating little sticks of pinewood with sulfur and storing them ready for use. At the slightest touch, they burst into flame. One gets a little flame like an ear of corn. This marvelous thing was formerly called a "light-bringing slave," but afterwards when it became an article of commerce its name was changed to "fire inch-stick."

So, too, for us. When we find ourselves in an emergency at night, in a life-changing crisis or a passage that feels quite dark, we need to lean *into* life, not away, and strike ourselves against the situation in order to release our soul and see by our own light. How we hold this is crucial. Is our deepest resource of spirit a light-bringing slave, a one-time rescuer? Or has our inch of fire been waiting for the transformative chance to let our light out, into the world for good?

....

Every act of love is carried within us like a seed, but each needs the rain and heat of experience to become its full expression in the world.

....

A Reflective Pause

○ *In your journal, tell the story of a time when the rub and friction of an experience brought some of your true self to the surface. What made you show up at such a time?*

o *In conversation with a friend or loved one, give a personal example of the difference, as you experience it, between immersion and addiction. For you, when is the complete giving over of yourself life-giving and when is it depleting?*

PRAISE AND BLAME

▼ ▼ ▼

Praise and blame, gain and loss, pleasure and sorrow come and go like the wind. To be happy, rest like a giant tree in the midst of them all.

—BUDDHA

THE SWAY AND grip of being here happens to us all. Events wear us down and prop us up. Experience chips and cracks our masks. We want so badly to be seen and heard and loved that the reactions of others eat at us. All the while, our worth grows like a root, an inch at a time, as our limbs reach in every direction.

When lost in our wounds, we want everyone to bleed. When drunk on despair, we want everyone to bend or break. This is what envy and despair can do. It happens to us in the other direction as well. Afraid to take the risk that is only ours to take, we lionize others in order to take the light off of us. Inflating others beyond the truth of who they are is how we try to hitch a ride out of our own insecurity. It's all terribly human and inescapable. We're thoroughly here one moment, trying to leave town the next. Only honest company can lead us back to our own possibility.

My last encounter with envy surprised me. Someone I know went out of her way to speak to me about my work, only to be as cutting as Zorro. Afterward, I felt fatigued and diminished. I've learned that envy works like undertow, giving with one hand while taking out from under

with the other. More than sleight of hand, it's slight of heart. Once home, I felt a sense of being on guard, as if something were about to come at me from behind.

A week later, I found myself in the company of someone very sweet who adores me, a little too much. The contrast of these meetings has been very instructive. While envy has us blame another for becoming what we long to be, inflated praise has us put our possibility in another's hands. And while envy doesn't feel good and praise does, neither has anything to do with the journey of our soul or the work we're called to in our time on Earth.

This brings us to Buddha's sturdy tree, withstanding the winds of praise and blame, gain and loss, and pleasure and sorrow. Like it or not, each of us grows like this tree, in both directions. The soul spreads its roots steadily into the ground of being, no matter what happens in the weather above. All the while, our limbs and leaves grow every which way, branching further into the world of relationships. The practice of being human is staying alive to both: the ground of being that pulls our roots to lengthen and the weather of life that swirls our leaves.

⌒ *Only honest company can lead us back to our own possibility.*

Inevitably, our lives are affected by the tangle of reactions we encounter from others. Yet how we inflate and deflate each other has nothing to do with our fundamental being. Still, we're not exempt from being worn down or propped up by the turbulence that comes our way. This does not mean we can hide in our being. Appealing as it is, we can't complete ourselves by retreating into the dark stability of our roots alone. Each of us sways in the storm of the world, while the roots of eternity spread in us and grow. Our job is not to deny any of the journey.

It's thoroughly human to be stalled by the criticism of others and intoxicated by the fragrance of praise. However, the thing about listen-

ing too closely to blame is that we become a prisoner of the need to correct its wrong view. And the thing about exaggerated praise is that we become a prisoner of the need to maintain the sudden regard we are bathed in. Neither is life-giving and both are eventually draining. But like a giant tree, we gain in true beauty when we soak up the water from the storm, though it beats us to and fro.

Standing firmly in things-as-they-are is a way to outlast the distortions we heap upon each other. This brings to mind two recent teachings. While guiding a group, these insights came from those in the circle, as they often do.

Linda is committed to having more relationships in her life. She feels isolated and is determined to take emotional risks to find some sense of authentic community. Her cousin, Michael, a devout evangelical Christian, is a kind person with strong opinions about religion. He and Linda, a progressive seeker, have never really shared in any deep way. Recently, without warning, Michael asked Linda about her values. She was shocked. The next time they spoke, she heard herself saying, "I want to talk about our experiences, *not* our beliefs."

This is a profound instruction: sharing the evidence of our journey and not our conclusions removes distortion and brings us closer. Without the judgments in which we carry our beliefs and principles, we are free to compare notes of simply being alive. Without the mask of our conclusions, we can be touched by the very personal aspects of being human. This is authenticity.

Later the same weekend, I asked the group how everything we'd been exploring was sitting with them. Dan looked very pensive. I saw this and without a word leaned his way. He felt me giving him attention and soon he blurted out, "I really want to control all this."

I gave the depth of his feeling space to surface and land in the group. Then I invited him to take that sentence with him, to live with it for a while. I offered that the word *control* didn't seem precise enough, given his depth of feeling. I invited him to find some synonyms, to open *control* like a box and see what's stirring inside.

The conversation went on and about twenty minutes later, Dan burst back into the circle, saying, "I've got it! I really want to *trust* all this!" I was in awe at how, given space and encouragement, the wisdom that sleeps under our tongue can wake. Humbled by how such self-honesty benefits us all.

While control makes us strategize, trust lets us experience a larger set of resources. To move from controlling to trusting life is like exhausting ourselves by trying to put our arms around a river until we realize we have to enter the river and let the current take us. So when struggling to hold off what's happening, we can look for the opening of exhaustion by which we might slip into the river of life and see where it's taking us.

Beliefs tend to harden us by confirming our own view, while sharing what happens to us lets us discover the common center that lives within all personal experience. So when feeling envy, we can open our fear of never becoming who we were born to be by being honest with ourselves and vulnerable to the world. When putting someone on a pedestal, we can solve our insecurity by inquiring into the truth of what we admire.

....

∽ *Sharing the evidence of our journey and not our conclusions removes distortion and brings us closer.*

....

If we could ask the giant tree, it might confess that it both desires and fears the wind, the way we desire and fear praise and blame. If we could ask the salmon being carried in the rough current, it might confess that it both desires and fears the slap of white water, the way we desire and fear gain and loss. If we could ask the spirit of someone about to be born or about to die, it might confess that it both desires and fears the journey of living in a body on Earth, the way we desire and fear a life of pleasure and sorrow.

Like everyone before me, I endure the distortions of being human while trying not to turn them into intractable beliefs. I really want to trust all this, the way a tree trusts the Earth and Sky it grows between.

A Reflective Pause

○ *In your journal, describe the tension you feel between your want to control the life around you and your need to trust life.*

○ *In conversation with a friend or loved one, tell the story of a time when you experienced either praise or blame that seemed inaccurate and how that affected your sense of self.*

LOSING YOURSELF

▼ ▼ ▼

*The more uncertain I have felt about myself, the more there
has grown in me a feeling of kinship with all things.*

—CARL JUNG

I'M HAVING LUNCH with my dear friend Bob, who loves jazz. Earlier in
life, he was a DJ for an FM show. One of his heroes is John Coltrane.
A few times a year we have a jazz night, where he leads me through
some of the great improvisations and points out the legendary moves,
the way an Olympic judge will marvel at some clean pivot no one else
sees.

But this day we're having lunch and just before our salads arrive,
Bob starts talking about losing himself in certain pieces of music. Not
losing track of time or forgetting to meet me in half an hour, but that
who he is pools, for the moment, in a larger sea. He says it's scary,
because he's not sure he will come back as himself. Yet being drawn out
this way makes him feel alive.

This threshold moment—of being yourself and losing yourself—
is at the heart of being human, at the heart of waking the soul. In
our deepest moments, we're challenged to hold our center, to not be
washed away by the weight and press of the world. But toward what
end, if we never open ourselves to be touched and changed by life?

Because survival is so demanding, fending off burden and mistreat-
ment can easily become a habit or reflex by which we fend off everything

that comes along. Yet every spiritual tradition leads us through suffering to the mystical moment when we're asked to put down all protection and relax the boundaries of our identity, so we can be touched by the Unity of Life that waits under everything, and so grow and be changed.

Though we're always moving forward, the peak moments of living—those moments that change everything and sustain everything—permeate us because we go deep, not forward. To open this depth requires facing sacred moments, which are everywhere: in the music we fall into, in the sudden truth that stops us, in the realization that what we've been carrying is ready to be born. Entering such moments completely lets us feel and taste the Universal Being that brings all things alive. And facing sacred moments requires us to engage the paradox of being ourselves and losing ourselves.

As a shore is constantly eroded for receiving the sea, we are constantly asked to lose the edge of who we are in order to absorb the sea of life that rushes us every day. I return to the lines of the Sufi poet Ghalib, which I have worked with for years: "For the raindrop, joy is entering the river." In joining with all that is larger than itself, the raindrop doesn't lose its substance, but surrenders its shape and previous identity. It doesn't vanish, but relaxes its boundaries and joins something larger than itself. It both loses itself and maintains itself.

This losing and not losing who we are happens when we experience even the slightest amount of love or suffering. It happens every day. We fall in love with some sense of what matters, then move in the world accordingly. We set goals, make plans, effort our way here and there, even contribute. Then, along the way, we're distracted from our well-meaning list of tasks and appointments, and invited into new and deeper forms of experience. Now we suffer a tension, which we try to quiet, but which is a doorway itself. Do we stray from our good work and put down our plan? Or do we lose the next step of aliveness, resisting what we're being called into? There is never a right or wrong response. This constant reassessment is part of facing sacred moments, part of the soul's work in being here.

Moments that immerse us and renew us often stand like invisible doors we must open. Only honest gestures open such doors, gestures that minimize what stands between us and life. Letting things near us opens doors. Leaning into what comes our way opens doors. Putting things down, so we can meet life freely, opens doors. Letting things clear, like muddy water settling, opens doors. Dropping our conclusions lets us view life freshly. And the humility of wonder opens everything.

So the next time you're three tasks behind and something compelling quietly calls you—some rush of light busting through the trees, or a wash of music too moving to ignore, or you're in a conversation too truthful or loving to end on time—lean in for a while and feel your heart expand. Smile as you drink from the stream of aliveness, smile as you try to pick up where you left off, smile as you lose yourself and deepen yourself at the same time in the journey that is both personal and Universal. Smile as the raindrop of your being pulls you into the larger sea.

⤳ *In our deepest moments, we're challenged to hold our center, to not be washed away by the weight and press of the world. But toward what end, if we never open ourselves to be touched and changed by life?*

A Reflective Pause

○ *In your journal, describe a time when something new challenged your sense of who you are and how your identity evolved.*

○ *In your journal, discuss which you spend more time and effort at: moving forward or going deep. Describe the rewards and costs of each for you. Which needs more of your attention?*

○ *This is a meditation. Close your eyes, and breathe slowly. For the moment, put down your plans and concerns. Inhale fully and let everything that is not you greet you. Exhale fully and put down your conclusions, just for the moment. Be still and let the thousand thoughts and feelings slowly settle like water going clear. Breathe simply and let your heart slip into that water. Relax the boundaries of your identity and let who you are breathe its way into everything around you. Open your eyes and notice that you are still you and that everything is closer.*

EXHAUSTING THE STRUGGLE

IN MY SIXTIETH year I had a disturbing and liberating dream. I woke, went to my study, and watched the sun come up till it parted the trees with its fingers of light. Finally, a stream of light inched across my desk and I tried to capture the dream in this poem:

FOR A LONG TIME

I had this idea and imagining it and
building it brought me alive. I was never
as engaged as when it was half-built. I'd read
the blueprint in my heart and carve another
piece. Once finished, I lived in it. It was where
I'd go to look out on the world. For years it was
a peaceful place in which I grew. I thought it was
my nest. But slowly, I grew so big that I couldn't
get out of my idea. It became a cage. I panicked
and railed at what I'd made, afraid to give up
any of my growth. Trapped and exhausted, I
sat in the middle of all I'd built and began to
listen to the rhythm of things that never die.
In time, I grew smaller and smaller till I was
thin as the breath of life. Only then could
I slip through the bars of my idea. Like a
quiet breeze, I returned to the world.

This dream paints a journey that seems archetypal. We start with such an urge to build. We think it's to create something lasting, but early on, the building is how we tease who we are into the world. Though we may indeed create something worthwhile, may even contribute to the common good, the idea we devote ourselves to, whatever it might be, is chiefly a vehicle for the soul to show itself on Earth. And the soul showing itself on Earth is the greatest contribution we can make.

Personally, this dream comes as an instruction on inner freedom. For my idea has been a life's work as a poet and a teacher, and the creative maker in me has imagined book after book, which has kept me engaged and growing for decades. I still feel enlivened at the prospect of creating anything, but the self-expectation and press to complete all these books feels stifling. So the need to build and achieve has been dissipating. I am who I am. I am where I am. Life is now about uncovering the essence in each moment, each conversation, each experience, and less about building anything or journeying toward some imagined destination. At this stage of life, I'm being asked to exhaust the struggle and deepen my relationship to the mystery.

Though I'm healthy and hope to live to a hundred, I'm beginning to feel the limitations of a single life on Earth. In my twenties, I'd immerse myself in a book, feeling limitless. If the inquiry took years, I had a lifetime. Now, as I'm aging, I'm becoming more of a filament. There's more to dive into and less to surface with. I feel like an old whale who lives more in the depths though he must surface to breathe. I confess I used to feel such an urgency to bring as much as I could to the surface. But now it's enough to break surface, all wet with the deep, enough to *be* the deep breaking surface before heading back down. This has changed the way I write: more simply, with less explanation, more from the heart that lives below the heart. The words I write are simply the wetness of the deep splashed on the surface.

When fearful of my end, the press of time is everywhere and the life I'm living feels more like a cage in which I don't have room to do or say all the things I want to do or say. And the more I press, the more my single-mindedness makes the life I have too pointed and small. Though once in a while, I'm stopped in my race through the days, like driftwood near the bank of a river, caught for a second in the mud before being swept along. In those moments, I get a rare view of the nonstop world we are a part of. Then I remember that, like the sun, we're asked over a lifetime to glow in *all* directions.

And so, I'm in the process of exhausting the notion of getting anywhere, of building anything, in the process of putting down what is not essential. Until, like the breeze in my dream, I can slip through the bars of my own idea of life and join the actual pulse of life.

We spend so much of our early life wanting to be as forceful as the elements. As I get older, I only want to be as unseeable as the wind that lifts sad faces weighed down at the end of the day, as gentle as the breeze that lifts the colorful side of flowers so that children can find them. I simply want to receive the softness of those I encounter, to be a conduit of the nature that threads us all. I'm surprised to admit, I no longer want to rebuild the world, but to *enliven the world that has always been.*

....

The idea we devote ourselves to, whatever it might be, is chiefly a vehicle for the soul to show itself on Earth. And the soul showing itself on Earth is the greatest contribution we can make.

....

A Reflective Pause

o *In your journal, begin to tell the story of a recent struggle between keeping up with the race you find yourself in and your effort to widen an unexpected moment of stillness.*

o *In conversation with a friend or loved one, describe two things that make you feel alive. What place do they have in your life? How can you make them more central to your path? Tell the story of a sacred moment you are being asked to face. What does that doorway look like? Where do you think it's leading you? What are you being asked to do in order to open that door?*

SAYING YES

▼ ▼ ▼

Ubakharta bakhaim.

—Hebrew for "You shall choose life and the living."

L IFE IS DIFFICULT and beautiful, soft and hard. It's fragmented and whole. Within a single day, our cells are both dying and being born. Our tissue is disintegrating and rejoining, even while we sleep. Likewise, our consciousness and heartfulness is both fragmented and whole. Within each experience, our understanding of life is being torn apart so new perspectives and insights can rejoin. Like our cells, the very makeup of who we are is both dying and being born, through our moment-to-moment struggle in being human.

In the face of this gritty, mysterious, and ever-changing dynamic we call being alive, it's nothing short of heroic that we are asked to choose life and living, again and again. Not just to put a good face on things while we're here, but because saying yes to life is how the worm inches its way through earth. It's how salmon leap their way upstream. It's how flowers grow out of stone. The word for such flowers, *saxifrage*, from the Latin, means stone breaker. Saying yes is the way the flower of the soul breaks through the stone of the world.

But how do we do this? Some deep part of us knows and needs no instruction, while the part of us sore for meaning needs to uncover the practice of saying yes. In the next two chapters, I will offer several ways to look at what it means to say yes to life.

Yes and No

Ultimately, saying yes is synonymous with opening who we are and giving our attention to whatever is before us. Once open and attentive, discerning *how* to relate to what we meet is the ongoing challenge, especially when what we meet is painful.

What often keeps us from the resource of aliveness, what keeps us from strengthening our own resilience, is how we inflate a particular experience into a code to live by, as if that will protect us from experience. We're caught in a squall while swimming and almost drown. It's traumatic. What do we do? Do we learn how to better read the weather and how to better swim in disturbed water? Or do we conclude that water is untrustworthy and banish swimming as dangerous? We're wounded in love and almost drown in the heartache. What do we do? Do we learn how to better read the weather of the heart and how to make better choices about who to love and how to love? Or do we rely on a worldview that people are untrustworthy and that love is dangerous?

When we construct a philosophy out of our hurts rather than better understand the physics of how we were hurt, we cut ourselves off from any form of saying yes and shrink our world. To mitigate our want to do this, two recurring questions serve as the heart's compass: What are we saying yes to? And what do we rely on inwardly in saying yes?

The saying yes that joins us to life is our openness to lean into the very pulse of existence wherever it finds us. The presence of such lifeforce is always near. It can touch us and in-form us and re-form us, whenever we can stop what we're doing, what we're anticipating, or what we're regretting—even briefly.

This animated and dynamic presence waits inside every silence we ignore. We know this presence the moment we're born, before language, before our eyes even open. We know life directly by our innate sense of Oneness; our inborn sense that we and everything on Earth are already complete, if we just embrace being alive and let life embrace us. None of this will remove the difficulties we face or remove us from the endless disintegrating and rejoining that is being alive. But saying yes to the very pulse of life can hold us up, and make us buoyant and resilient.

Saying yes to the human tangle is another thing. When we say yes for approval, to avoid conflict, to barter for a sense of belonging, or to put off fear—that yes is really a no. Anytime we give up who we are or muffle our own authority of being, we are stalling our chance to be fully alive. We all do this, because we want so badly to be loved or because fear sometimes gets the best of us. I have done this many times over the years, and can find myself in a moment of giving myself away, even today. Of course, anyone, no matter how dear, that wants us to be other than who we are does not truly love us or doesn't know how to love.

Paradoxically, while a false yes to others is really a no to life, it takes an authentic no to others to free up our vulnerability. This, in turn, makes us available to say yes to all the majestic currents of life. Saying yes is the filament that connects us to everything.

Our Journey on Earth

I began the opening section of this book with this stanza from a poem of mine:

> To learn how to ask for what we need,
> only to practice accepting what we're
> given. This is our journey on Earth.

These are two eternal practices that bring us in alignment with the Unity of Life. At first look, they seem to contradict each other, but they are two sides of one paradox. Together, they lead us into the way of being called saying yes, through which we are returned to meeting life rather than hiding from it, to receiving truth rather than inventing it, and to joining with other life rather than pushing off of everything different from us.

While we don't always get what we need, the reward for asking for what we need is that this allows us to be who we are. And the reward for accepting what we're given is that we get to participate in the living Universe. Asking for what we need is a practice in being present and visible that lets us become intimate with our own nature. Accepting what we're given is a practice in being present to everything beyond us that lets us become intimate with the nature of life. As a way of being, saying yes is the ongoing dance of intimacy between our own nature and the nature of life. Through a life of asking for what we need and accepting what we're given, we feed the fire of our soul, which glows its brightest the moment our aliveness is ignited.

Inch by Inch

To know the fullness of being human, we are challenged repeatedly to look up from the mud and peer through the storm. This is never easy. For slogging through the mud and storm of life, we each encounter our own form of despair, which if endured reveals a resilience of being. If you are in despair as you read this, I know this doesn't seem possible; for that's the nature of despair, it makes everything seem impossible. But despair is often the nut in which the fruit of resilience ripens. When we can crack the hard nut of it, a small taste of despair softens us and readies us for the fruit of resilience. Though none of this seems viable when in the mud and storm.

My own experience is that we can grow our resilience in response to despair inch by inner inch, the way that immunization works; where we are fortified against something toxic by ingesting it or injecting a small dose of it into our bloodstream. Vaccines work by stimulating our immune system to build a set of healthy antibodies to the sample dose of the disease. In the same way, we need inner time to build a set of healthy responses to the taste of difficulty and despair we experience, if we can limit the dose we take in. This doesn't mean the mud and storm of life won't make us sick or fatigued, but the serum of our hard-earned resilience will keep the mud and storm from killing us. Saying yes to life means accepting a taste of despair, at some point, so our soul can inoculate us in some degree to the difficulties of living.

....

⁓ Asking for what we need is a practice in being present and visible that lets us become intimate with our own nature. Accepting what we're given is a practice in being present to everything beyond us that lets us become intimate with the nature of life.

....

Emerging, Again

Short of being killed, we always emerge from difficulty in a stronger if rearranged form. And waking as human beings, where the human is finite and the being is infinite, there's always more spirit in us than one life can carry. By our very nature, each of us is challenged to grow out of one self into another. I am not the same person I was ten years ago, nor was that self the same as the one I inhabited twenty years ago—though I am the same spirit. We blossom and outgrow selves the way butterflies emerge from cocoons. Except that, being human, we have the chance to emerge from many cocoons. Mysteriously, saying yes is one of the ways we begin to emerge. Saying yes is how the infinite spirit we're born with keeps moving through us into the world, redefining us each time it emerges.

Given this, we could say that one purpose of spiritual education is to renew and rename the meaning of life and that one purpose of spiritual friendship is to restore our trust in life and in life's journey. It seems our job as souls in bodies is to let our spirit rise from within to meet and inhabit the world, every chance we get.

Still, no one can truly know what another carries or goes through. But putting down our fears, long enough to meet life outside of our own stories, it becomes astonishingly clear that tripping through hardship into what matters is both timeless and ordinary. Each of us feeling alone in our pain, only to discover, when forced open, that we are part of the same fragile family on Earth. Each of us struggling with the weight of living other people's values, only to learn that direct, first-hand, first-heart experience is the only way to know eternity. Meeting the transformations that hardships hold is a deep form of saying yes that makes every soul on Earth blossom.

Still, like mountain climbers who throw ropes ahead of them, hoping to find a toehold in the future, we toss our dreams and plans ahead of us. But once climbing, once falling, once gathering ourselves to climb again, it's the moment our hand holds our weight that we become aware of the simple courage necessary to stand in a life. It takes inner fortitude to stand firmly in what we're given, no matter where it leads. That we can stand at all in the face of pain and fear is nothing short of anonymous magnificence. So never diminish or underestimate your worth or connection to the nature of things, because stress or pain blocks your sureness. An archer's bow is always stretched before it releases its arrow, as the arc of a soul is always stretched before releasing its wisdom.

⌒ *Each of us feels alone in our pain, only to discover, when forced open, that we are part of the same fragile family on Earth.*

A Reflective Pause

○ *In your journal, describe the deepest yes you have been asked to give in your life so far and the situation that prompted such a deep voice in you.*

○ *In conversation with a friend or loved one, tell the story of a time when you were compelled to ask for what you needed and what this calling forth did to you. Listen to each other. Then tell the story of a time when you were asked to accept what you were given and what this acceptance called forth in you.*

MEETING DIFFICULTY

❯ ❯ ❯

THERE IS NO escaping difficulty, because difficulty is part of being alive. It's how we hold the difficulty that lets us move through it. While obstacles on the surface require problem solving, the lessons in experience often wait below our efforts to analyze or decode them. Instead, we're asked to take very small steps to let our experience in, to let it work and shape us. Why? Because often the intimacy of experience is where the simplest teachers present themselves. There are infinite circumstances through which the majesty of life presents itself. Given this, we're constantly asked to enter the conversation that difficulty opens till it reveals the gift or tool it is carrying.

Being Vulnerable

At the deepest level, the reason to be vulnerable has nothing to do with whether we have company or not, and nothing to do with whether we belong or are seen or heard. A flower blooms not because it has an audience, but because that's how it becomes what it was born to be. A hawk flies not because birders are watching, but because that is what it was put here to do. For human beings, how we grow is inextricably linked with being vulnerable, because being vulnerable makes us malleable enough to transform, find our place in the larger Universe, and feel the Oneness of things.

Being vulnerable is how we begin to unfurl our petals, how we begin to spread our wings. If in doing this we're not seen or heard, becoming that blossom or that bird in flight will give us the strength to endure our loneliness. If we're seen and heard, we'll know true company and intimacy and the beauty of relationship, though we'll have to resist muffling who we are in order to belong. Of course, the practice of being human means we know both. We will be seen and heard for who we are and we will not. Feeling both is inescapable. Working with both is necessary. Ultimately, the reason to be vulnerable is to blossom into a full and complete life.

All That Is Not Us

The challenges in being fully here build on each other. We must meet difficulty in order to grow, which requires us to stay vulnerable. For only when vulnerable can we be touched and shaped by life. This is important because the things that matter can't be felt except through first-hand experience: through our mind, our heart, our skin, our touch. And being vulnerable always restores first-hand experience.

At the same time, the world is not just our experience. I know what I feel, but can't imagine what you feel. As I write this in southwest Michigan, the sun is starting to set. If you're in South Africa, Australia, or Nova Scotia, you're experiencing a landscape I know nothing about. Wherever we are, there is much to life that is beyond what we know. In order to lead a healthy life, we need to open our hearts, so we can be completed by everything that is *not us*.

How do we do this? Paradoxically, we have to open our hearts to ourselves first. Because the web of our own being, mind, and heart is the lens through which we receive the rest of life. And knowing ourselves thoroughly is how we clean our lens, which means feeling completely what is ours to feel, and leaning into our questions and doubts and confusions. When we clean the lens that is the self, we're ready to receive everything that is beyond us.

Since life manifests its mysterious unity through its endless diversity, the goal of all experience is to find and inhabit our common center, our common Wholeness. When I lean into things and experience you or some place I've never been, or a culture I know nothing about that opens me to an entirely different way of thinking and feeling, I can't help but enliven a dormant part of that common Wholeness that I've been carrying since birth.

As we honestly encounter each other, we move through our unique personalities and eventually experience that common center, which lets us know the Oneness of Life. Since the heart of everywhere is the same, the revelation of all experience is that we are all made of the same Spirit. Yet we have to move through our differences to get to what we share, the way pathfinders break trail from different directions to uncover the same interior that no one has seen, though everyone knows it as home.

....

Knowing ourselves thoroughly is how we clean our lens, and when we clean the lens that is the self, we're ready to receive everything that is beyond us.

....

Looking with Love

Our best chance to find the Oneness of Life is by looking with love into everything and everyone we meet. Looking with love is a form of saying yes. We give birth to everything we look at with love, including our own soul. This shining forth is the one gift we're born with that is always near, though we often lose sight of it or lose faith in it. I've watched those I love break through their entanglements many times like trees that keep growing closer to the light. And they've watched me break through trouble like a stubborn root. But looking with love is different than watching. Like sunlight, looking with love is a warm presence that helps everything looked upon find its strength. The presence of love is how questions grow under the moon in the open patch of yard; how in our pain we suddenly find a way to create peace; how being with each other, in the midst of great difficulty, creates a sense of home.

Knowing Our Core

We often think, *When I get through this difficulty, when I get through being weak, when I get through this illness or that heartache or my sadness, then I'll be strong. Then I'll find my core.* But life has taught me that it's actually the other way around. When we fall down, we're touching the foundation of things. Understandably, the pain of falling frightens us and we quickly want to get up. But no matter where we want to go in life, no matter where we stumble, we're always led to right where we are. And physically, metaphysically, spiritually, and emotionally, we always have the opportunity to feel the ground we're standing on. When we can stand still and feel the pulse of life run through us, we start to sense the foundation of things.

Knowing that ground means that, despite the life of questions, at some point, we have to trust a certain depth of feeling and stop questioning. When we stumble and touch the essence of life, we have to trust our deep, first-hand knowledge. Why? Because we feel it and know it. And we build from there. No one can tell you what this foundational moment is or what it feels like. Ultimately, it defies words. Paradoxically, all the questions that matter rise from this feeling and lead to this feeling.

It's often in the depths of love and suffering and wonder that we touch on this unnameable center. One of the wonders and rewards for saying yes to life is that we chance, through our authenticity, to experience the essence of all those who ever lived. When we love completely, we chance to feel everyone who ever loved. When we listen completely, we chance to feel the presence of everyone who ever listened. When we allow ourselves to feel this moment completely, however we come upon it, we often feel the moment of aliveness that all people have shared and that all people have suffered. In that moment, we're touching our core, which, felt deeply enough, brings us to the core of all life. To know this moment releases tremendous foundational strength. To know this moment is to glow and know the glow is to feel our place as a living atom of the mystery.

Returning to Center

We have moments of clarity and then we're confused. We're awake and then we're numb. We're buoyant and then we're sinking. Just as we inhale and exhale constantly, our wakefulness ebbs and flows.

The practice of being human is the practice of coming awake, staying awake and returning to wakefulness when we go to sleep. We go to sleep because we're mortal—not because there's anything wrong with us. This opening and closing is part of the human journey. Therefore the practice of being a spirit—in a body, in the world—is a practice of returning to our center where we can know the world fully. This return to center is a foundational form of saying yes to life.

Life has taught me two things about being centered. First, returning to our center, our solid place of inborn knowing, is only nourishing because it is through our core that we find our connection to the common Center of All Life. As thirst would drive you to a well, to drop your bucket and pull up water from the underground spring that feeds all wells, the individual soul is such a well that draws on the water of Spirit that feeds all souls. We need to know where our well is.

Secondly, the fact that we need to *return* to our center lets us know that we *will* drift away from what matters. This drifting is part of being human, and so, there is an ongoing need to find our way back to what matters.

Most of us are educated to think that if we work hard enough, are good enough, and disciplined enough, we'll crack the secret of life and live at the end of all trouble. While these traits are helpful tools, being human doesn't work that way. From the very start, we're asked to stay as close as we can to all that is alive. The tides of experience are endless: the wakefulness and sleepiness, the agitation and calm, the joy and suffering we encounter are continual. Our aim is not to eliminate these conditions but to navigate them from a living center, the way you'd steer a boat at sea while balanced in its stable bottom.

We each have to discover a very personal practice of how to return to what matters when we lose access to what we know. Losing our way is even more painful in a world of judgment and duality, a world of good and bad, up and down, and more and less—none of which is specific enough to be helpful or to let us decipher the wisdom in direct experience.

I use the word *wakefulness* as a term for enlightenment. I believe enlightenment isn't a place we arrive at but a process we stay in. Our time on Earth is constantly shifting and changing, and being human itself is a paradox—an endless formation of our being and becoming. We are wonderfully left to live out the gifts and tensions of both.

The first lesson of wakefulness is to keep opening our heart so we can meet what we're given, for it's meeting what we're given that reveals the heart's deeper logic and therefore the logic of Spirit. The first step to wakefulness, again and again, is putting down what we carry and saying yes to what life has to offer.

Though Sometimes We Fail

Chasing Paradise keeps us from living here in paradise.

Sometimes, we don't realize there is nothing to be done, until we've tried everything. I don't think this means we've failed, though sometimes we fail. I think it means we've been thorough in our humanness. And it's only through our humanness that we can meet difficulty, stay vulnerable, and be completed by all that is not us. Only by inhabiting our humanness fully can we know our core, and so know the core of all things. Only by meeting life completely, in all its entanglements, can we find our way back to the aliveness we all need in order to go on.

In the last two chapters, we've surfaced some insights about saying yes and meeting difficulty that we can return to. I invite you to personalize each by exploring how you feel the presence or press of each in your life. I invite you to pause with any of these and to discuss the space it opens with a friend:

○ Saying yes is how the infinite spirit we're born with keeps moving through us into the world. *How do you know the presence of your spirit?*

○ Saying yes is the way the flower of the soul breaks through the stone of the world. *How is your soul inching through the stone of the world?*

○ Two recurring questions serve as the heart's compass: What are we saying yes to? And what do we rely on inwardly in saying yes? *In your most alive moments, what are you saying yes to and what does saying yes feel like?*

○ To learn how to ask for what we need, only to practice accepting what we're given—this is our journey on Earth. *Describe what keeps you from asking for what you need, and what keeps you from accepting what you're being given.*

○ Meeting the transformations that our hardships hold is a deep form of saying yes that makes every soul on Earth blossom. *Describe one hardship in your life and how it's been transformative.*

○ Despair is often the nut in which the fruit of resilience ripens. *Describe a moment of despair and how it ended. Describe a moment of resilience and how it began.*

○ We're constantly asked to enter the conversation that difficulty opens. *Name one difficulty you have faced and describe the conversation it opened within you.*

○ Being vulnerable makes us malleable enough to transform, find our place in the larger Universe, and feel the Oneness of things. *Describe your current invitation to be vulnerable and how you're meeting it.*

○ In order to lead a full life, we need to open our hearts, so we can be completed by everything that is not us. *Name one teacher that came from outside of you and what it taught you.*

○ We give birth to everything we look at with love, including our own soul. *Tell the story of one thing you've given your love to.*

○ It's often in the depths of love and suffering and wonder that we touch on the unnameable center. In that moment, we're touching our core, which, felt deeply enough, brings us to the core of all life. *How would you describe the unnameable center of life?*

○ The practice of being a spirit—in a body, in the world—is a practice of returning to our center where we can know the world fully. Returning to center is a form of saying yes to life. *What do you do to return to your center?*

○ It's nothing short of heroic that we are asked to choose life and living, again and again. *Tell the story of someone you admire and how that person chose life and living.*

Spilling Water

One of the rewards for saying yes is deep presence, which opens the vibrancy that exists between all things. For presence is how the soul breathes. And for all the places I've traveled, all the people I've studied with, all the books I've read and written, I'm humbled to say that whatever I've learned has come alive through deep presence, which is only accessed through personal authenticity. Such presence resides in the invisible, charged space in-between: you and another, you and the world, you and the mysterious Oneness of Things. While we're accustomed to use speech to translate and explain who we are and where we've been, presence is a form of dialogue that opens us to the common realm in which we can experience our bond to each other and the Universe we live in.

Authentic presence can enable us to honestly say what we know to be true, another form of saying yes. Saying what we know to be true is often the first surprise in our journey. The very utterance of such truth releases our aliveness and allows our experience of truth to evolve and change. To say yes through our presence is like spilling water on the one seed that will grow into the direction we need to take.

As for me, I only know that I no longer want to *make room* for what's heartful. I want to *be* heartful. I no longer want to *see* the heart in others, but *meet* their aliveness. I no longer want to *make space* for stillness. I want to breathe and *be still*. I can no longer explain myself. I simply want to *reveal* myself through the presence that imbues all life. I want to meet you while saying yes!

A Reflective Pause

○ *In conversation with a friend or loved one, describe in detail a moment in which you felt the foundation of all things. In the days that follow, look for a small item—a shell, a stone, a feather, a bookmark—that can serve as a symbol of this felt feeling of the foundation of things that you can hold from time to time to give you access to the feeling of all foundation when it seems far away.*

JUST THIS PERSON

▼ ▼ ▼

THE GREAT TRANSLATOR Stephen Mitchell recounts this story from ninth-century China. After a long apprenticeship and friendship with his master, Tung-Shan asked Yün-Yen, "After you've died, what should I say if someone wants to know what you were like?" After a long silence, Yün-Yen replied, "Say *Just this person*." Tung-Shan seemed puzzled and his friend put his arm around him and continued, "You must be very careful, since you are carrying this Great Matter." They spoke no more about it. Later when Yün-Yen died, Tung-Shan wandered in his grief through a stream, only to see his own reflection, carried for the moment by the reflection of all things. It was then that he understood what his friend meant. Later still, Tung-Shan wrote, "If you look for the truth outside yourself, it gets farther and farther away."

This is a soul-opening riddle. Imagine these two walking quietly so long ago. Perhaps there was a breeze making the day surprisingly gentle. Perhaps it was that gentleness that made the student stop to ask his master such a question. Perhaps it was the love in Tung-Shan's face that made Yün-Yen drop his shoulders and go to the deepest answer he knew.

The heart of this story is carried in Yün-Yen's reply, "Say *Just this person*." What can this mean? For me, Yün-Yen tells us that the work of being who we are is very particular. The humble master tells us that the noble work of every soul is not to be great or exceptional or like anyone else, but to fulfill the reach of our own aliveness.

Consider how every tree follows its own yearning to be in the light.

No one tree envies another. Each shell in the ocean surrenders to its own wearing of the deep. No one shell imitates the ridges of another. And each drop of rain is unique in how it falls; yet all merge once soaking into the earth. We are so easily distracted by each other and the hardships along the way. Yet under all the maps we make and tear up, we are each born with a particular destiny that we will blossom into more than achieve or arrive at—if we can find the courage to live the life we're given, fully.

▸　　▸　　▸

"You must be very careful, since you are carrying this Great Matter." This is Yün-Yen's other instruction. What are we to make of this? It seems the Great Matter resides in the eternal paradox of the particular, in how the mystery of life as a whole unfolds through the inhabiting of each life; the way spring unfolds for the growth of each seed. The Great Matter depends on how each of us comes alive through our own particular experience. Only through being who we are can we experience the Universal Oneness we are all born to.

More than being led or taught, we need to be held and incubated by love till we mature into all of who we are, an ordinary destiny that no one can steer or rush. We must hold each other with great care, so as not to bend a soul away from its truth. Being held and loved has always been the most powerful form of education, in that such warmth of heart allows us to educate ourselves.

▸　　▸　　▸

In his grief, Tung-Shan sees his reflection in the stream of all things, for love and grief enable us to feel how we're all at heart the same. In love and grief, which is always very personal, the distinctions that separate us melt away. Tenderly, we have only our one life and singular person through which to experience the Oneness of Things. And so, "if you look for the truth outside yourself, it gets farther and farther away."

I don't think Tung-Shan is saying that our individual self is the source of all truth, but that the only way to experience the vitality of life is to meet everything and everyone directly, personally, so that truth can rise from that exchange as it moves through us. Though we can learn from each other and honor teachers and mentors and those we emulate, we are each a living cell in the Universal body, each of us just a person—*just this person*—a specific container for the ounce of Spirit we carry in the brief time we have.

▸   ▸   ▸

I love this story of the two masterful friends stopping on a walk over a thousand years ago, only to stumble into the essence of our journey together and alone. They strolled on a gentle day somewhere in Cheki-ang Province in China, perhaps near Mount Wu-hsieh, where Tung-Shan took his vows. Perhaps they softly looked out at the clouds drifting over the valley after having this exchange. Perhaps the clouds bowed slightly at the sight of these two glowing in their love for each other.

The chapters and stories that follow inquire into this magnificent journey of being who we are, in an attempt to uncover how we can become masterful friends—to our souls, each other, the world, and the Spirit that informs the world. The conversation that unfolds is an attempt to detail the work of living the lives we're given, with an integrity so particular that it delivers us into the Unity of Life.

Perhaps each of us, in the glow of our personhood, is becoming just the person we were born to be. Perhaps the glorious sum of a life is that all we feel and give will ripple through everything, adding to the One-ness from which we come, the way rain enters a lake. This is the Great Matter we are here to inhabit. And the only path to this is to work with what we're given and to be full of care.

....

෴ *The only way to experience the vitality of life is to meet everything and everyone directly, personally, so that truth can rise from that exchange as it moves through us.*

....

A Reflective Pause

o *In your journal, describe without judgment one way in which you aggrandize who you are and one way in which you efface who you are. This is an effort to discover more about your true self.*

o *Put these responses aside for a day or so. When you return, begin to surface and journal the stories of how these gestures of aggrandizing and self-effacing have become part of your personality. Where do they come from? What purpose do they serve?*

o *In conversation with a friend or loved one, listen to each other's responses and stories and discuss what insights or questions have surfaced for you.*

o *After a time, pause and enter the silence between you. Let this lead you into meditation together. After a time, look into your friend or loved one's eyes. Inhale slowly and soften your way to the place they have in your heart. Exhale slowly with all the gratitude you feel for having such a friend or loved one. When you can feel the full presence of the person before you, offer them your open hands. Breathe deeply until you can feel the full presence of all your history together. Take one more full breath and ask of each other Tung-Shan's loving question: "After you have died, what should I say if someone wants to know what you were like?" After you have shared, have a cup of tea together, or stand in the light together, or go for a walk.*

▼ ▼ ▼

In the first section, we explored how we're born glowing in all directions, only to meet blessing and obstacle alike. It's through these inevitable lifts and struggles that we face the life of choices. A love astounds us or a pain consumes us and we forget that we glow on our own. Much of our work is to meet life without muffling our inch of light. Perhaps because it's the journey back to our inch of light that introduces us to the life of our soul. And so, the challenge for each of us is to stay in relationship with our soul and the world, with a heartful commitment to be completely who we are until we can awaken, time and again, to the full beauty and truth of being alive. Everything we experience leads us on a journey to become just the person we were born to be. By meeting our particular challenges, we discover our particular gifts. This is never easy, but uncovering our gifts by living the life we are given is how we begin the work of saying yes.

This is a good time to ask: What does it mean to you to become just the person you were born to be? What is the inch of light that lives in you beneath all the praise and blame you encounter from others? How can you listen to that light more? What is keeping you from meeting your own life? What is currently in the way? How can you look at what's before you directly, accepting that what's in the way is the way? How are your challenges uncovering your gifts? What part of you is irreplaceable? And what part of you has been shaped by others that you need to put down? What can you do today in order to stay in relationship: to your inch of light, to your inborn ability to say yes, to the teacher of experience that won't leave you alone, to those you meet along the way?

Every question we encounter offers us a way to personalize our endless practice of being fully here. Whenever we take one step, other steps become visible. So let's step forward now. From here, we'll explore the troubles of living, the sweet ache of being alive, and our need to always keep beginning. We'll try to understand our kinship with the unending cries of the world and what on Earth to do with all that we feel.

A Dream We're Close to Living

If we hold what has suffered,
we will share in what is free.

—MN

It's hard to see the future with tears in your eyes.

—CHEROKEE SAYING

I was given an insight when young, which arrived one day in the rain as every- thing thirsty in me relaxed. It was an insight about destiny and how, like trees and plants, destiny is more a breaking ground of all that grows within—a manifestation of life from seed to flower—than a foretold timeline of projected desires that we create to keep us from the pain of living.

All these years later, I'm in the rain again and everything—the very build- ings, the people walking with their dreams as umbrellas, the way we all want so very much to look into each other's eyes—everything keeps sprouting from within, destined to grow into what it can. For all our creative gifts and our urge to build, we're going nowhere, just stretching like orchids into our potential.

And though I've achieved a lot, when I ignore this natural sense of destiny, I find I don't grow or mature as a soul. To be productive without growing has made me realize that all the effort to be seen and heard is draining, when it is seeing and hearing that keeps us vital. All the effort to be remembered is ener- vating, when it is the peace of putting the members back together that keeps us connected to everything larger than us. All the effort to run from our fear of failure and the constant push toward some fantasized future is exhaust- ing, when our destiny is simply and profoundly to root where we are and grow toward the light.

Still, it's hard to be here, to grow here, though the journey is made easier when we can accept that the process of living is designed for what matters to come through us tenderly. This destiny from within to without is the heart's dialogue with what matters, the way a flower dialogues with the rain to blos- som.

This is the dream we're close to living.

HEARING THE CRIES
OF THE WORLD

*Perhaps the most important reason for "lamenting" is that it
helps us to realize our oneness with all things, to know that all
things are our relatives.*

—BLACK ELK

*A saint [is one] who does not know how it is possible not to
love, not to help, not to be sensitive to the anxiety of others.*

—ABRAHAM HESCHEL

THIS STORY IS so old we don't know who told it or who it's about,
except that it speaks to all of us. We no longer know if it was a
"he" or "she" at the center of the story. No doubt the story has grown
for every telling. But for this telling, let's call our central character Kwun
and let her be a heroine.

One day Kwun crossed a valley and stumbled on a bloody scene. An
entire village was laid to waste, the people torn apart. Walking among
the bodies, her heart was breaking open, enlarging for coming upon the
suffering. She was drawn, almost compelled, to look inside their bodies
and at the same time repulsed by the violence that had opened them.
There was an eerie silence steaming along the ground. It looked like
the fierce work of a warring clan. Suddenly, Kwun heard a terrible cry

from the middle of the scene. She had to pull a dead man aside to find a woman barely breathing, clinging to her little boy, who was bleeding from the head. Kwun fell to her knees and without thinking embraced them both, their blood coating her.

The cry of the dying mother was as much from her own pain as from her powerlessness to help her son. When she saw Kwun, her cries grew worse. It was clear she was asking Kwun to take her boy. At first, Kwun shook her head, unprepared for any of this. The dying mother clutched Kwun's hand and fell away. The boy was unconscious, still bleeding from the head. Wherever Kwun was going before stumbling into the valley, that life, that plan, that dream, was gone. It was too late to close her heart and walk away.

She lifted the little bloody boy, and though he was unconscious, Kwun covered his eyes as she walked over the rest of the bodies, leaving the village. Carrying the boy, she began to cry, feeling for the mother who had watched her man die and her son be bloodied, and feeling for the boy who, if he woke at all, would be all alone. She began to moan as she walked, keeping the cry of the mother alive.

By the end of the day, Kwun managed to climb out of the valley and, exhausted from the tasks of surviving, fell asleep at the mouth of a cave. When Kwun woke, the bloodied little boy had died in her arms. She didn't know what to do, though there was nothing to do. She held him for a long time, then opened his little eyes, wanting to see what was left within him. And looking there, she began to feel the cries of the world, long gone and long coming. It overwhelmed her as she felt a pain that almost stopped her breathing. But she kept rocking the little one, certain the world would end if she put him down. Without her knowing, she began to hold the broken that would fill eternity, long before they would suffer: the stillborn, the betrayed, the sickly, the murdered, the thousands left to mourn. Letting them move through her began to open her heart like a lotus flower. And the cries of the world, though she couldn't name a one, made her stronger. At last, she fell asleep again. While she slept, Kwun became a source of healing. When she woke, she spent her days touching the wounded, holding the dying, and keeping the cries of the world alive. The cries became a song she didn't understand, other than to know that, as the wind can lift the snow off a branch, the cries altogether can somehow lift the sadness off a broken heart.

Wherever We Go

Kwun may be an ancestor of the Buddhist bodhisattva of compassion, Avalokiteshvara, also known as Kuan-yin, whose name means hearing the cries of the world. We'll never know, but like rivers joining in the sea, stories coalesce and merge over time into the one story that remains, the one we each wake to, surprised it is ours.

Wherever we go, wherever we wake, we are challenged like Kwun to hear the cries of the world very personally. The cries are unending and overwhelming, and our noble charge to hear them—to hold them and keep them alive—is how we keep the life-force we need lit between us. As Black Elk says at the beginning of this chapter, the reason to lament is that it helps us to realize our Oneness with all things, and to know that all things are our relatives.

This has never been easy, for grief is so challenging that it often blinds us to its importance. As the Sufi poet Ghalib says, "Held back, unvoiced, grief bruises the heart." Try as we will, we can't eliminate or solve these cries, for they are the song of existence. When we try to mute or minimize the voices of suffering, we are removed from the life-force that keeps us connected. If we get lost in the cries, we can drown in them. So what are we to do with them? What is a healthy way to relate to them?

I've found that whatever I go through opens me to what others have gone through. This is the gut and sinew of compassion. Our own ounce of suffering is the thread we pull to feel the entire fabric. Having pinched a nerve in my back, I can feel the steps of the elderly woman who takes twenty minutes to shuffle from the bread aisle to get her milk. Having lost dear ones to death, I can feel the weight of grief that won't let the widower's head lift his gaze from the center of the Earth where his sadness tells him his wife has gone. Having tumbled roughly through cancer, I can feel fear arcing between the agitated souls who can't stand the wait in the waiting room. I've begun to meet the cries of the world by unfurling before them like a flag.

I was in college, sitting with my grandmother in her Brooklyn apartment, when she fell into another time and left the room. She'd left an old photo on the table. It was of a young family posing in a studio in 1933. The parents seemed to have the whole world ahead of them. When she returned, I asked. It was her sister and brother-in-law and their small son. They lived in Bucharest. There was a long pause and an even longer sigh, "We saved and sent them steamship tickets to come." She dropped her huge hands on her lap, "They sent them back, and said Romania was their home." They died in Buchenwald.

It was pulling that thread that opened my heart to the cries of the Holocaust and, from there, to the genocides of our time. Those cries plagued me, wouldn't let me sleep. In time, I realized I was opening myself to the enormous suffering of history for no other reason than to feel the complete truth of who we are as humans. This is impossible to comprehend, but essential to let it move through us, the way the cries of the world moved through Kwun so many centuries ago.

Each of us must make our peace with suffering and especially unnecessary suffering, which doesn't mean our resignation to a violent world. For the fully engaged heart is the antibody for the infection of violence. As our heart breaks with compassion, it strengthens itself and all of humanity. Can I prove this? No. Am I certain of it? Yes. We are still here. Immediately, someone says, "Barely." But we are still here: more alive than dead, more vulnerable than callous, more kind than cruel— though we each carry the lot of it.

....

 ∾ *Our own ounce of suffering is the thread we pull to feel the entire fabric. This is the gut and sinew of compassion.*

....

That we go numb along the way is to be expected. Even the bravest among us, who give their lives to care for others, go numb with fatigue when the heart can take in no more, when we need time to digest all we meet. Overloaded and overwhelmed, we start to pull back from the world, so we can internalize what the world keeps giving us. Perhaps the noblest private act is the unheralded effort to return: to open our hearts once they've closed, to open our souls once they've shied away, to soften our minds once they've been hardened by the storms of our day.

Always, on the inside of our hardness and shyness and numbness is the face of compassion through which we can reclaim our humanity. Our compassion waits there to revive us. When opened, our heart can touch the Oneness of things we are all a part of. Then we can stand firmly in our being like a windmill of spirit, letting the cries of the world turn us over and over, until our turning generates a power and energy that can be of use in the world.

Running from the Cries

Sometimes, being alive is so hard that we think it would be better to avoid all the suffering. But we can't, any more than mountains can avoid erosion. And there is a danger in running from the cries of the world. In extreme cases, our refusal to stay vulnerable can twist into its opposite in which we strangely get pleasure from the suffering of others. The German word *Schadenfreude* means just this. Such perverse pleasure derives from the utmost denial of being human, the way running from what we fear only makes us more violently afraid. Severely renounced, the need to feel doesn't go away, but distorts itself. In the same vein, the term *Roman holiday* refers to the grisly spectacle of gladiators battling to the death for the pleasure of the Roman crowd.

This danger is insidious in today's rush of incessant news coverage, twenty-four hours a day. We can be brought into heartbreaking kinship in a second, as with the September 11 attacks on the World Trade Center in New York City or the horrific massacre of twenty schoolchildren in Newtown, Connecticut. And like Kwun in the ancient tale, we can be compelled to look at the raw insides of tragedy to glimpse how tenuous our time is on Earth, while being repulsed by the violence that opens such a stark revelation. But if not careful, the endless replaying of tragedy from countless angles can push us over the line till we fall prey to that perverse pleasure of the Roman crowd.

To view tragedy beyond our feeling of it adds to the tragedy and turns us into dark voyeurs. Yet, just as Kwun's rocking of the lifeless little boy enabled her to hear and feel the suffering of those yet to come, keeping our heart open to one torn life can enable us to hear and feel the cries of all who suffer.

Which side of reality we dwell in determines whether we are offspring of Kwun and Kuan-yin, descendants of those who keep the cries of the world alive, or offspring of the warring clan, descendants of those who gut whatever is in the way, who cheer the bloody spectacle. These twin aspects of life are closer to each other than we think. The seeds of both live in each of us. It is our devotion to staying vulnerable that keeps us caring and human.

True connection requires that a part of us dissolves in order to join with what we meet. This is always both painful and a revelation, as who we are is rearranged slightly, so that aliveness beyond us can enter and complete us. Each time we suffer, each of us is broken just a little, and each time we love and are loved, each of us is beautifully dissolved, a piece at a time. We break so we can take in aliveness and we dissolve so we can be taken in. This breaking and dissolving in order to be joined is the biology of compassion. The way that muscles tear and mend each time we exercise to build our strength, the heart suffers and loves. Inevitably, the tears of heartbreak water the heart they come from, and we grow.

Our fear of such breaking and dissolving keeps us from reaching out, from stopping to help those we see in pain along the way, telling ourselves it's none of our business. But no one can sidestep being touched by life and, sooner or later, the fingers of the Universe poke us and handle us and rearrange us. Running from the cries of the world makes the Universal touch harsh. Leaning into the sea of human lament makes the Universal touch a teacher. Hearing the cries of the world fertilizes the ground between us.

....

∽ *Perhaps the noblest private act is to open our hearts once
they've closed, to open our souls once they've shied away, to soften
our minds once they've been hardened by the storms of our day.*

....

What Are We to Do?

The life of Kwun and Kuan-yin calls, their simple caring in our DNA, though it's never easy to cross into a life of compassion. Since the beginning, we have all complained, when weary or afraid of the power of feeling, that we have a right to happiness. Can't we ever look away? Must we always feel guilty for those who've suffered beyond our control? But guilt is the near enemy of true kindness. It won't let us look away or let us give our heart to those who suffer because our lives will change if we do.

No matter how we fight it, life always has other plans and we are faced, when we least expect it, with the quandary of living softly in a beautiful and harsh world. Under all our goals and schemes is the sudden need to help each other swim in the mixed sea of joy and sorrow that is our human fate.

The truth is: my suffering doesn't have to be out of view for you to be happy, and you don't have to quiet your grief for me to be peaceful. Allowing our suffering and happiness to touch each other opens a depth of compassion that helps us complete each other.

There are always things to be done in the face of suffering. We can share bread and water and shelter in the storm. But when we arrive at what suffering does to us, there is *only* compassion—the genuine, tender ways we can be with those who suffer.

Some days, I can barely stand the storms of feeling and fear civilization will end, if we can't honor each other's pain. But in spite of my own complaints and resistance, I know in my bones that our openness of heart makes the mystery visible. Our openness to the suffering we come across makes our common heart visible. If we are to access the resources of life, we must listen with our common heart to the cries of the world. We must forgo our obsession with avoiding pain and start sensing the one cry of life that allows us to flow to each other.

....

〰 *Under all our goals and schemes is the sudden need to help each other swim in the mixed sea of joy and sorrow that is our human fate.*

....

A Reflective Pause

○ *In your journal, begin your participation in the eternal discussion about the pain and suffering that is inherent to life. How have you been taught to respond to this? What is your own heart's reaction to this? How do you experience the conversation between love and suffering that is constantly around us?*

○ *In conversation with a friend or loved one, discuss what has surfaced in your journal. Ask each other: What do you do with the cries of the world as you hear them? Where do they rest in you? What do they make you feel? How do you live because of this knowing?*

ALWAYS BEGINNING

▶ ▶ ▶

T HERE IS NOTHING more difficult or magnificent than becoming
intimate with the mystery of life. Try as we will to avoid it or
sidestep it, leaning into life and engaging our full humanity is the only
way to be illumined by the aliveness at the center of everything. In a
very real sense, we're always beginning, because beginning without
judgment or conclusion is the way we drink from mystery. Beginning is
the way we are reanimated.

It helps to remember that the word *authentic* means bearing the
mark of the hands. Being authentic—being real and genuine—means
touching and being touched, holding and being held. The living work
of hands is where being and becoming meet, where inner and outer, like
two hands, part the veil of circumstance to reveal Oneness. Through
the life of authenticity, we trip into the heart of things and experience
the interconnectedness of things again and again.

Often, our rigidity and our fluidity affect how close we stay to the
path of aliveness. The more rigid we are, the more isolated we become.
The more rigid we are, the more likely we are to break. The more rigid
we are, the more things have to conform to the shape of our ways for
us to let them in. The gentler we are—the more fluid and flexible—the
more capable we are of letting things enter and move on through. This
increases our chances of being rinsed and cleansed and scoured by life.

If we are to grow, it's important to discern between *steadfastness* and
stubbornness, and between *gentleness* (fluidity) and *codependence* (acquiescence). These are crucial if subtle differences, which no one may ever

notice but you. To be steadfast is to be faithful to what we know to be true, without a need to explain or justify that truth, but to simply live it.

Walt Whitman is a great example of steadfastness. In 1844, Ralph Waldo Emerson published an essay called "The Poet," in which he yearned for and called for a new American sensibility that could break the British hold on our young imagination. While America had stopped being a colony of England almost a hundred years before, he rightly claimed that our imagination and language as a people were still obedient and compliant to the English tradition. Emerson's essay swept America.

Eleven years later, upon reading the first edition of Whitman's *Leaves of Grass* (1855), Emerson was stunned to find that Walt Whitman was the American poet he'd imagined. He wrote Whitman a now famous letter (July 21, 1855) in which he praised the young poet:

> *I give you joy of your free and brave thought. I have great joy in it. I find incomparable things said incomparably well, as they must be. I find the courage of treatment which so delights us, and which large perception only can inspire.*

Emerson and Whitman became fast friends. But in 1860, as Whitman was preparing to publish the third edition of *Leaves of Grass*, he ran into opposition from his greatest champion.

While visiting Emerson, the two poets went for a long walk through the Boston Commons. In his diary, *Specimen Days*, Whitman tells us that the two walked and talked the better part of an afternoon, during which Emerson persistently tried to convince Whitman *not* to publish his "Children of Adam" poems, which revealed his homosexuality. Whitman recounts that he listened for two hours without saying a word. When Emerson was done, Whitman was more certain than ever that he was right—he couldn't hide who he was.

This is a profound example of quiet integrity—staying true to one's own nature and staying whole. Steadfastness, in its deepest regard, inhabits the resolve not to be persuaded or worn down to be something we are not. Stubbornness, on the other hand, is resisting the teachers and lessons we are given that invite or require us to change and grow. The line between the two is often thin and steadfastness can slip into stubbornness all too quickly, while we are the last to know.

The empty king Gilgamesh is an ancient example of stubbornness. In one of the earliest narratives we have, Gilgamesh is an unchallenged king whose refusal to feel or reflect inwardly leads him to break more and more of the life around him. His rigidity isolates him from life and so he creates excitement by inciting urgency and conflict. This leads to the death of his only friend, Enkidu.

In his arrogance, Gilgamesh demands to see the Immortal One, Utnapishtim. The empty king wants Enkidu brought back to life. A long journey ensues. A seer tells him that he will meet a ferryman who will take him across the sea of death, where he can meet the Immortal One. Along the way, he will come upon a set of secret stones that he must present to the ferryman. In his continual stubbornness, Gilgamesh tramples everything in his path, wanting to be touched but not knowing how to meet anything. When he trips on the secret stones, he smashes them in anger. When the ferryman asks for the secret stones, Gilgamesh is surprised and empty-handed and angry at life. Being rigid, Gilgamesh bounces off everything. He seems incapable of receiving anything.

To be steadfast is to be faithful to what we know to be true, without a need to explain or justify that truth, but to simply live it.

Receiving depends on *gentleness*, which relaxes our boundaries. It lets us interact with what comes our way. It lets us lend some of our shape to what's before us. *Lending our shape* in this way allows for a momentary joining, through which we can feel the aliveness that flows between things. When rigid, we close and bounce off each other. When gentle, we open, and are able to exchange energy and life-force.

A mythic example of gentleness is the story of a blind boy who in a dream is told that bowing will open his eyes and let him see. He tries for several days to bow and open, everywhere he goes: in the grass, in the wind, in the soft hands of his mother. None of it gives him sight. He bows his face into the holiest of books, the one his father studies. Still nothing. The dream felt so real that he's now in despair, certain he's misread the gift of this instruction, certain he's lost his chance to see.

In his sadness, he wanders to the shore of a lake, where he wades to his waist. Depressed, he sits in the water. And as a child sinks in a bathtub, he holds his breath and drops into the lake, below the surface of things, below the noise of his blindness. He is surrounded by such softness and quiet that he begins to cry as the water from his eyes mixes with the water of the lake. In the slow, gentle wash of water meeting water, he begins to feel the bottom of the lake. He begins to feel the old fish swimming behind a rock. He can feel the oar in the middle of the lake slipping in and out of the cloud-reflected surface. He even feels a heron circling above, its shadow cooling pockets of the deep.

He returns to the surface and can feel the movement of air against his eyes, and the heat of the sun warming his face. From that day on, he can *feel* with his eyes, as long as he remembers to slip below the surface of things. And though he is blind, from that day on, he carries great vision. In time, he becomes a teacher that others seek out, and through his gentleness, others learn that whatever our blindness, the heart can sink below the noise of its memories and wounds. The sweet blind boy tells everyone who asks that the heart wakes slowly, and only our gentleness—our willingness to sink into the depth of things and wait—will let us see and make our way.

Yet even gentleness, taken to the extreme, has an underside, which we all struggle to avoid. Without steadfastness as our anchor, we can give ourselves away completely, through the dissipation of our center and through overcompliance. In this, *codependence* is the shadow of gentleness. The examples are everywhere and commonplace: not voicing truth to power, always putting our needs last, being nice instead of authentic, hiding who we are instead of expressing who we are.

Remarkably, being human is dynamic, not static, and so we are always beginning, as the maps we draw are out-of-date by the time they dry. We are left squarely in the practice of being human, which requires us to course-correct constantly. As one steering a boat is always adjusting the tiller to approximate the true course—first left to right, then right to left, we have to steer our way back and forth between steadfastness and stubbornness, between gentleness and codependence. Until, drawn as we are to the surface, we sink below the noise of our blindness, where the heart can see.

Whatever our blindness, the heart can sink below the noise of its memories and wounds.

A Reflective Pause

○ *Often, our rigidity and our fluidity affect how close we stay to the path of aliveness. In your journal, begin to tell the story of the most stubborn person you have known, and the story of the gentlest person you have known. Who has your ear these days, the stubborn you or the gentle you?*

TO UNDERSTAND THE WEAVE

▼ ▼ ▼

THERE ARE TWO recurring sins that plague us as we walk through the days. By *sin*, I mean a moment of not-seeing that limits our ability to relate. One is *the sin of literalism*, our loss of the fact that depth and being underline everything. This leads to partial thinking, where we see only the effect and lose all sense of cause. Someone is quiet and unresponsive and we think they are rude or angry with us, when they may be lost in the unseen waters of sorrow or wonder. Like the ocean, the surface of what we're living may be choppy and disturbed, while the depth of life that holds us is calm and deep. When we lose the sense that everything is *in*-formed and connected, life appears chaotic and frightening and we run from the situation we find ourselves in rather than find comfort in the depth that holds us.

The other is *the sin of imposition*. When we lose the humility that lets us wonder and seek life other than our own, we lose sight of the mysterious variety that holds all life together. Then we become insular and preoccupied with making everyone and everything like us. We become *self-replicating creatures*, longing only for that which will confirm our own experience.

How does this happen? Often, in our drive to make sense of our experience, we go too far and assume *our* experience is *the* experience. In our want to find patterns, we often extrapolate what happens to us into a philosophy of life, which in time we think is *the* philosophy of life. We burn our hand on a stove or break our heart in love and then we're teaching others that fire and love are dangerous, not to be trusted.

Soon, the only ideas that have value are those that confirm what happened to *us*. This insulation of conclusion can happen to anyone very quickly. We certainly need to make meaning and form our own direct understanding of life, but only to offer that understanding, that philosophy, as one thread in the fabric of life. To understand the weave, we need to find the other threads.

When stuck in our own experience, we're pressed to quell the troubles and uncertainties of living by finding sameness wherever we go. This is at the heart of all fundamentalism. Yet when we can remember that *our* experience is not *the only* experience, that *our* understanding is not *the only* understanding, then our efforts turn to learning how to weave your experience and mine into something that can help us live.

We all succumb at times to the power of the surface world drowning out the depth world. It's helpful to learn from these moments of not-seeing, helpful to revisit the times we recede into the sin of literalism—into an over-reliance on the surface world. It also helps to understand when we fall into the sin of imposition—into not allowing difference to touch us.

Why is this important? Because without depth and difference, all we can do is self-replicate. It's important to note that in the biological world, self-replication is what allows cancer to grow. A cancer cell is a biological unit that will self-replicate at all cost, even at the cost of eating its host, the loss of which will kill it. Cancer is self-replication gone rabid. And the dangers of literalism and imposition make us self-replicating creatures. They make us look for sameness, not wholeness. They make us look for mirrors that will repeat us to ourselves, when we often need doorways to the world and everything that is not us.

Like the base of an iceberg, what holds everything up remains out of view. When we insist there is only a surface world, we lose access to the depth world, which by its nature remains out of view. The sin of literalism can be despairing because under its influence we don't see or feel how life is connected. And without the connections, the tensions of living are made extreme. Without our connection to the depth world, life appears to be chaotic, ruthless, random, oppressive, and full of catastrophe.

Feeling isolated and disconnected, our over-reliance on the surface world leads us to be over-practical. Starkly, we live in an age where the sin of literalism has made practicality a religion or a philosophy to live by. But practicality, without inner values to fuel it, leads to heartless self-replication and a fear of anyone or anything different. Pragmatism can't replace genuine connection.

....

     Without depth and difference, all we can do is self-replicate.

....

Recurring Blessings

Wonderfully, there are two recurring blessings that lift us when we fall into the trap of literalism and the fear of sameness. By blessing, I mean a moment of seeing that returns us to our Original Presence.

One is *the blessing of shimmer*, the glow of presence that animates everything. This underlying presence is what connects all life. It's always near. Like light, this underlying presence will naturally fill every opening. When we constrict into being literal and imposing, we block this blessing. When we can behold whatever is near—that is, hold our complex histories and judgments open—the being that waits in everything can reach us. Given the smallest opening, the blessing of shimmer will illuminate our depth with its gossamer of light, the way the sun causes any root to grow.

Let's look at this more closely. The unseeable depth world that connects everything is another name for Spirit. The blessing of shimmer is how the depth world that is unseeable emanates Spirit. Everything—the stone in your shoe, the flower that you water, the food you feed your cat, even your laptop computer—emanates Spirit. When we can slow down and give our full attention, even though our eyes are busy seeing, when we can put our planning and remembering down—all of a sudden, things start to glow. They start to shimmer. They start to feel, for the moment, more than three-dimensional.

This is why when we wander into each other's eyes long enough, our hearts melt. Why when we stand quietly on the edge of some magnificent piece of nature, it starts to reveal an extra quality. This is the blessing of shimmer. One reward for being so present is that the unsee-able depth world can touch us completely with its aliveness. When we can open our hearts and lean in, it's the shimmer of Spirit emanating from life that permeates our worry to renew our aliveness.

If the blessing of shimmer is what emanates from all things, how do we receive it? This brings us to *the blessing of inlet*, which is a moment of seeing that rejoins us to being wholehearted. Our ability to receive like an inlet opens our inborn capacity to relax our fears and judgments so that life can flow through us, cleansing our being as it goes. When we can exercise this quiet courage, the mysterious variety that holds life together restores our place in the living Universe. And we become *wholeness-seeking creatures*, longing for anything that will enliven the kin-ship of life we are born into. The blessing of shimmer is how life meets and completes us. The blessing of inlet is how we meet and complete life.

Consider that an inlet is an opening of land that allows water to flow between a smaller body of water and a larger body of water, whether it's a river and the sea or a small bay and the ocean.

To be an inlet inwardly, we're asked to open ourselves so that every-thing we experience can exchange with what's inside us. The easiest way to understand this is how we breathe. We breathe thousands of times a day. When I inhale and exhale, the single breath in me mixes through the inlet of my lungs with the air that is everywhere. Now I can't tell what is my breath and what is the sky. Similarly, when I can stay open and let my soul mix through the inlet of my heart with the Spirit that is everywhere, I can't tell what is my heart and what is the heart of life. When we give ourselves over to the blessing of inlet—when we let the things of the world exchange within the quiet bareness of our soul—we become wholehearted, as we were at birth, and merge again with everything.

Being human, we move between these moments of seeing and not-seeing. Being human, we lose the shimmer of the depth world and trip over the weight of the physical world. Being human, we relax our life open after great pain or love and are deeply reanimated. Being a soul on Earth, we each must learn our own particular rhythm between the skin of things and the shimmer that all things contain. Being a soul on Earth, we must inhabit a personal practice that puts down the imposition of what is familiar, so we can be an inlet to everything that is not us—so we can discover the very pulse of life that wants to complete all its parts.

In a daily way, we live with the challenge to restore our wholeheartedness when we fall into literal-mindedness and a fear of all difference. When struggling with this in my own life, I woke recently with two images of the mind, one as dangerous and one as a gift. Waking this way led to this poem:

An Open Hand

The mind is not a storeroom
with mirrors where we retreat
to convince ourselves
that we exist.

The mind is a livingroom with
windows and more than one chair,
so friends can come and look out
and discuss what they see.

Not a fortress where we frisk and
strip others of what they believe
in order to share our secrets.

More a porch with birdfeeders
and coffee or tea where before
hello, you have to share a story.

Pull the curtains! Open the
windows! Brew the coffee!
Put out a sign: Other Views
Wanted!

This is what all the meditative traditions and practices are asking of us—to pull the curtains and open the windows, to stop making everything in our own image, to let life reach us, one more time.

....

~ *Sin is a moment of not-seeing that limits our ability to relate. Blessing is a moment of seeing that returns us to our Original Presence.*

....

A Reflective Pause

○ *In your journal, recount a time when you discovered that some way other than your own had value and how you incorporated this new view into your life.*

○ *In conversation with a friend or loved one, tell the story of one thing you learned by using your hands.*

THE GOLDWEIGHER'S FIELD

▼ ▼ ▼

I WAS AT an exhibit in New York of those lost at Pompeii. The ash-molded bodies had been sent carefully from Italy. The remnants of one civilization buried two thousand years ago were displayed quietly on Forty-fourth Street in the midst of our civilization rushing about, thinking we're immune to such things.

Pompeii was a wealthy town near the coast, the Roman version of Hollywood or La Jolla. Before Vesuvius erupted on August 24, 79 AD, there was no word in the Roman language for *volcano*. When I told others I was going, some thought it too dark. But it's not the death and loss that draws me, rather the timeless quiet that waits inside all this, if I can outwait *my* fear of death. I feel this need to stand before what life has to offer without removing myself and without drowning in it. We tend to fall to one side or the other: shutting down our feelings for fear of what they will do to us or following what we feel at all cost, fearing a life with no passion.

I wanted to see their last gestures. Of all that was destroyed and returned to the earth, these wisps of tenderness have somehow endured. Such an ironic and lasting tribute to impermanence. A thousand years can vanish in a day and be discovered two thousand years later. Or not. This is both remarkable and devastating. And yet, does this make what had meaning there any less meaningful? Does this make the love accepted or rejected by the particular people of Pompeii whose names we'll never know any less kind or cruel? I found myself compelled to stand before them.

Within twenty-four hours, the entire city was buried under twelve feet of volcanic ash. After the Roman era, no one knew that Pompeii had ever existed until in 1740 a farmer sinking a well struck a ruin. And excavations began. Mark Twain visited the nearby town of Herculaneum in 1867, and tells us that, "in one apartment, eighteen skeletons were found all in sitting postures, and blackened places on the walls still mark their shapes and show their attitudes, like shadows."

I stood before those skeletons arranged in a dark corner of the museum, stood there for a long time. So much like the secret room in our heart where the bones of everyone we ever loved sit with their song of love, unfinished or about to be lived, leaving their mark on our most private walls.

A few days before finding myself here, I met a friend Karen for dinner in TriBeCa. She had invited her mother, Sarah, and her uncle Glen to join us. Sarah and Glen hadn't seen each other in twenty-five years, since Uncle Paul's death. Paul was Glen's partner and Sarah's brother. Karen remembers being uplifted by Paul's kindness to her as a child. The three of them conjured up his presence so profoundly that I feel I know him. It was incredibly tender to see Glen and Sarah take each other in. As the night unfolded, we talked about Paul more and more and it was clear how much Glen still loves this man.

The next day Karen was traveling and Glen was back at work in his small shop in SoHo. And I was wandering through Central Park feeling glad that I had been a witness to such a deep and lasting love, and to the coming together of old friends after twenty-five years, through the love of a child now grown who watched them from the stairs, watched them talk of their struggles when they thought no one was looking. I was wandering the park also feeling sad for all the friends and loves that have fallen away in my life, for the Glen-Sarah dinners I have *not* been a part of. I sat on a bench near a very old tree growing out of stone. I could feel the bones of old loves leaning on each other in the secret room of my heart.

It made me think of my parents, who were frightened by my creativity; made me think of my mother, who is still smoldering, angry at the world, and my father whom I finally embraced last year at ninety.

It made me think of my brother, whose eyes and ears have weakened. It made me think of my first love, Chris, who wrote me in my thirties, wondering if we might try again. I took Amtrak to the city, to these very streets, to see what was real and what was not. We met in her apartment and had some tea. I brought a yellow rose. We sat and talked and she was beautiful and the place in my secret room began to ache. Yes, I still loved her and didn't want to turn away from that feeling. But I also could see who we had each become: nothing wanting, just different. It was then I noticed that the florist had kept the yellow rose upright and open by slipping a wire through the center of it. This made me cry and say good-bye. This was my first time withstanding the tension of feeling both the truth of love and the truth of life, without minimizing either. I admit I've never stopped loving those I've loved, whether it's been possible to journey with them or not.

It was after having dinner in TriBeCa, after everyone went home, after wandering in the park, feeling grateful and sad, that I found myself standing before those ashen figures arranged in a dark corner of the museum. I focused on two who seemed to be falling in or out of embrace. Their moment was burned up but somehow preserved. The longer I stood there, the more I realized that their moment is our moment: the anatomical moment of embrace. Each of us in it, each of us in need of it: Glen and Paul, Glen and Sarah, Paul and Karen, my father and I, the embrace that never happened with my mother, Chris and I saying good-bye, my friend Alan breaking our friendship after thirty years, and my dear wife Susan holding my head unexpectedly after a bad day.

I drifted about the museum, among the ten or so excavated bodies brought all the way from Pompeii. As I met them, I struggled to feel them as themselves *and* to let all my friends and loves rise from my own excavations. I tried to let them merge. Under a spotlight on a barren platform were two friends or intimates, turned to ash as they were reaching for each other. Their bodies were incinerated but their gesture toward each other was sealed forever. Across from them a crouching man with nowhere to go, a dog curled on itself, an infant covering its face to escape the heat. Another poor soul, solidified to ash, had fallen on some stairs to nowhere. Our deepest gestures wait inside to be released, by love or crisis. What gesture waits inside me, inside you?

I left and wandered into the Sixth Avenue Cafe, sat near the door where I could see dozens walking by in both directions, having no idea who was coming or going. I wondered: What is *our* life built on? What gestures curl and reach beneath this sidewalk from another age? After a while, I made my way back through Central Park to find that massive tree, perhaps two hundred years old, its roots bursting through an outcrop of stone, its back arched like Atlas, its arms reaching to the light. It stood in perpetual embrace of the sky, never turning away. Such strength of being. Its uppermost limbs were trees by themselves. It graced the rock that made its beginning hard. I had to touch its folded bark, had to feel where it knit itself to the stone. Why are such teachers mute?

Clouds moved in and I ambled on to the Frick Collection at Seventieth and Fifth, to meet some etchings by Rembrandt. There, I saw *The Goldweigher's Field*, a drypoint etching done in 1651. The title of that etching stays with me. For though the gold of the world is heavy, the gold of the soul is light. And isn't this our challenge: to discern the gold and where it's buried and how much it costs and whether it lightens us or weighs us down?

It's getting toward night and the ashen figures of Pompeii have made me sad, though the massive tree growing out of stone gives me hope. Not hope that we will outrun death, not even hope that we will be remembered. But hope that the Goldweigher's Field is where we coax eternity to rise through us in a flash of life. I'm tired and all this clouds my heart as I ride the E train to the Village, on my way to see Al Jarreau and George Duke at the Blue Note. Getting on at Thirty-fourth Street, a young Asian father sits with his little boy on his knee and, like the tree beginning its way out of stone, the little boy's completely unwritten life leaves a splash of light on the subway walls, as remarkable as the stains of the bodies on the walls of Herculaneum, as remarkable as the songs of our loves staining our hearts. We keep carrying what matters without even knowing it.

Waiting on line, I meet others. Waiting on line, we begin to say who we are, what we do, what we wish we could do. Inside, I sit next to a man from New Rochelle who works with window treatments. He's become expert at how to let light in or keep it out, at how to angle glass so the music stays alive a little bit longer. And the old man against the wall tells us that he saw Jimi Hendrix in a club in the sixties. He says Hendrix was already burning up before he began, like the figure of Pompeii found running or dancing at the moment of his death.

As we eat and talk, all the conversations merge into a clear smoke above us. Everyone's soul flickers briefly. Finally, the lights dim and out they come, two intimates reaching for each other and the music they so love. Al starts scatting in the aisles and the sight of someone being so thoroughly himself in the face of eternity makes me well up. This is what it all comes down to, opens up to: giving our all in the moment we have, coming out of the darkness singing, holding nothing back, like a tree growing out of stone or a spark in the night that no one will know of.

∾ I admit I've never stopped loving those I've loved, whether it's been possible to journey with them or not.

A Reflective Pause

○ *In your journal, describe what currently weighs you down and how it's come into your life. Describe as well what lightens you and how it appears in your life.*

○ *In conversation with a friend or loved one, talk about your history of being weighted and being lighted.*

THE LAST QUARTER

▶ ▶ ▶

I've reached the age of self-knowledge, so I don't know anything.

—WISŁAWA SZYMBORSKA

THERE ARE TIMES when the ground we stand on loosens and shifts. Sometimes we regain our footing. Sometimes we fall and get up. Sometimes what shifts is dramatic and sometimes subtle. Whatever the cause, each shift opens a different stance of being. When this happens, it's important to accept the shift and honor the truth of the new stance. Otherwise we remain at odds with our own existence and eventually something will tear.

I've encountered several of these shifts in my life, each opened by deep, unexpected moments: the slap of my mother when I was fifteen; the silent, slow-motion floating in air while playing basketball in the middle of a crowd-filled gym; the moment my ninety-four-year-old grandmother thought I was her dead husband; waking after having my rib removed; the freefall after leaving a twenty-year marriage; standing on Table Mountain under the stars in Cape Town; being suddenly laid off when fifty-nine; and most recently, bearing witness to my father's slow fall into death at ninety-three.

Each of these unexpected openings has drawn me deeper into life. For sure, I haven't dealt with all of these gracefully. But sooner or later, I found new footing. Each time I was allowed to feel differently, to think differently, and see the same world anew. We can speak of this very personal sequence of new footings as the evolution of our inner self over a lifetime: a migration into the depth of being alive. Over time, our foundation is reshaped the way a landslide rearranges the face of a mountain until a new bottom is revealed on which to stand.

Eventually, we come to the Last Quarter, the final stage of life. I find myself here and, whether ten years or forty, there are more years behind than ahead. How does this change the view? How does this open the embrace of life in the time that is left? It seems that preciousness—in all that is before us—is all we ever have.

I've known for a long time that we slowly become what we seek. Just as we discover the ounce of wisdom we can offer the world, our tongue humbly falls off, the way the lip of a cliff falls after years of erosion into the sea. After a lifetime of seeking, we become a beautiful part of the path by which others seek. Lean into the unknown long enough and we become a small part of the mystery. Though the first taste of this is sad, it's a perfect safeguard of the mystery. Much as we want to spare others the journey, the gift of life *is* the journey, which each soul must take. Our job is not to expose the mystery but to participate in it.

Over the last few years, I've begun to feel the first traces of this vanishing. While I'm strong and healthy and clear of mind, I'm no longer able to track everything, only enter everything. I'm beginning to feel the edges of this mystical erosion, from being a witness of all that is inexplicable to becoming—inch by inch—a part of all that is inexplicable. At first this was troubling, but it has settled as a humble blessing.

I know now that return and loss are gates that swing open to the mystery; sometimes so fast, we don't know what happened; sometimes so slow, we don't think anything is happening.

Each of Us Tripping

This is a story of return. My dear friend George told me about his father, a Hungarian diplomat who came to New York in 1948, just as the Soviets came to power. His father resigned and never spoke of Hungary again. His grandfather, still in Budapest, walked the cobbled streets, muttering to friends, "I'll never see little Georgie." Now, fifty-two years after his grandfather died and six years after his father died, George, who is sixty-five, is overcome with the need to return.

He corresponded for months with his second cousin, Camilla, who was a bassist in the Budapest Philharmonic Orchestra. One week before he went, he sat in the woods where his father's ashes are buried, wondering why his father never spoke of Europe. Wishing his father could go home, he raised the claw end of a hammer and chipped a piece from the marker. He took the small stone with him. And five thousand miles away, he and Camilla searched the old neighborhood till they found the house where his grandfather raised his father. The gate was closed, but George reached his hand through and tossed the small stone near the doorway.

What kind of migration is this, across the years: a yearning for home awakened after decades, a small stone carried across the sea, a grandson returning the son to the father? It takes more than one life to grow a hand back after oppression has cut it off, more than one generation to grow a soul that can love the world again.

I imagine thousands of stories like this, across the globe. Each of us tripping on our own small destiny, without anyone knowing: losing home, dreaming of a way to return, finding home. Each of us sent on our way, harshly or gently, to look for our gifts, only to find we've carried them within the whole time, only to find that the weather of the journey has exposed what matters.

·····

❧ *Our job is not to expose the mystery but to participate in it.*

·····

Seeing Through the Gates

This is a story of loss. I, too, have tripped on my own small destiny: losing home, dreaming of a way to return, finding home. You see, it's been hard for me to return to my life after a week with my father in the hospital. I see him everywhere: shifting in his motorized bed, unable to get up, his arm sore from the IV. And keeping him company has brought me closer to the presence of death.

It was attending a book reception for a dear friend that brought me back to the living. Mingling with others, listening to parts of everyone's overlapping story, it was clear that no one was aware of my father struggling to breathe in his bed a thousand miles away. Nor did I expect them to know. Life is always happening, in all places at all times. My love for my father made me forget this. So I was reminded that the heart's job is not to play seesaw with life and death, with joy and sorrow, with peace and fear. The heart's job is to stay open to all these territories at once.

It's the soul's natural want to keep both horizons in view—the horizon of life always becoming and the horizon of death always undoing. The intensity of our experience will naturally compel us completely into peace or fear, into joy or sorrow, into living or dying. But wisdom rests in holding both horizons open, regardless of what wave we're riding or what wave is crashing in on us.

I now have a felt understanding of the Roman deity Janus, the two-faced god who is always looking—at the same time—to the past and the future. Janus: the god of beginnings and transitions, the seer of gates, doorways, endings, and time. Regardless of the culture or era we're born in, we always live into this knowing: we must keep both the beginning and the end in view at once. In real terms, in a single life, it means not forgetting that my father is struggling to breathe as he lies on his side *and* not muffling the awe in this young girl before me as she hears violin music for the first time. For powerfully, mystically, it's through my open heart that the wonder of first music might reach my father as he struggles in his sleep.

Each day, we're asked to be such a conduit: to keep the heart open to the things that form while bearing witness to the things that come apart; including ourselves, especially ourselves. If we have any chance of being formed by the journey of being alive, we must let the wisdom of ending ground the intoxication of beginning *and* let the freshness of beginning soften the poignancy of ending. We need to bear both faces to the world, not in surface duplicity, in being two-faced, as the modern world would warn. More deeply, keeping both horizons of life in view speaks to an original sense of being *all-faced*, where the completeness we are born with feels and perceives in all directions, like the globe of heart that helps us breathe.

⤳ *The heart's job is not to play seesaw with life and death, with joy and sorrow, with peace and fear. The heart's job is to stay open to all these territories at once.*

Brought This Close

This is a story of mystery. After a month of helping my brother keep my father's head above the tides of death, I had this dream: I'm swimming in the ocean while my wife, Susan, is walking the shore with our dog Mira. I'm at home out there, fascinated with the deep. The swells spread out, get larger, and looking up, I'm alarmed at how far out I've been taken. I'm not sure I can make it back to shore. Then I become aware in an intuitive way that a large whale-like creature will be coming to swallow me. I start trying to swim back to shore, but the current is too strong, going the other way. I realize the drift from shore to where I am has taken my sixty-two years. I'm afraid I will die and start to imagine the moment the great creature from the deep will find me. Will the grip of its jaws kill me or will its pulling me under drown me? Or will it toy with me as it's doing with my father? I'm so far out, I can't see Susan onshore. I'm heartsick not to get back to her. The sun comes out from behind some clouds and the sudden splash of light on the waves and my face makes me relax and forget everything, and I'm at home again treading the deep. Another set of clouds comes in and I'm back in my fear, feeling powerless to escape the great creature on its way and unable to get back to shore. The clouds part again and I'm at home again in the light. It's clear that life has become the deep sway between these two states. It's then I wake.

Clearly, the great creature coming is death, but death of what? Actual death? Eventually. Death of our map of the world? Yes. With each life-changing experience, we're forced to redraw the map of our knowing. Death of our smaller self? Yes. Death of the identity we construct that has served its purpose by carrying us this far. This dream points to a maturation of being, in which we're asked to wake beyond the tension of spending our days swaying between feeling afraid of what lives in the deep and feeling at home drifting in the light.

This sway between light and depth is where the first three-quarters of life leads us. Joseph Campbell speaks of this threshold, of living beyond the story of our circumstance, as the hero's journey. Carl Jung speaks of this as the journey of individuation that cracks the smaller self, letting us swim without entanglement in the Universal Sea. The ancient myth of Jonah being swallowed by the whale tells us that we've known about this process of soul maturation since the beginning of time.

Spit back into life after three days, Jonah is the same but softer and the world he meets is the same but more luminous. What happened to him during those days in the belly of the whale? This dark and potent time symbolizes the mysterious incubator of transformation we each must pass through, once the trials of living break us of the shell that brings us to adulthood. We can't anticipate this part of the journey or prepare for it, other than by staying true to our deepest nature.

At sixty-two, the clouds come in and I get afraid. The clouds clear and I'm at home. Like everyone before me, like my father now, I must have this conversation between being here and not being here. I've had it earlier than most because of my cancer journey in my thirties. But now, it returns in another form, as I hold my father's ancient hand with one that looks just like it, as I see my face in his as he sleeps, as his struggle to bring up speech resembles the pre-speech gasp of heart that has led to every poem I've ever discovered. His words now rest like pebbles trapped under his stroke-heavy tongue.

My father doesn't know of these things, but he's living them all the same. I only know that when brought this close by love, the veils that tell us we live separate lives are torn, and holding his hand until he wakes, I feel the One Life that floods through us all. Everything leads us to this: We're all living One Life, that we each carry as far as we can, and love is the touch, the handoff that relays the One Life into the next carrier. Yet beautifully, while in *this life*, we're thrown together by experience until facing each other and holding each other, the One Life kisses itself. And that brief kiss of Oneness bestows us with a flicker of great peace and great knowing, which lets us feel larger than our trouble, deeper than our dream, and humbled to be part of something uncontainable.

> ∽ *With each life-changing experience, we're forced to redraw the map of our knowing.*

The River of Time

So, entering the Last Quarter, what unexpected shifts await? What disguises will grief and wonder use to bring me closer to the mystery? What will I gain for each thing I lose? What foundations will I find under all that gives way? What small destiny will I trip into when inhabiting the gift I've been carrying since birth? What will I learn that I can't put into words, when I stop seesawing between life and death, and joy and sorrow, and peace and fear?

I only know that life is precious when I can live beyond the story of my circumstance. Strangely, the closer I am to death, the closer I am to life. Not since being wheeled into surgery twenty-six years ago have I felt life and death so closely knit. Still, I feel I'm just beginning. I want to see more and feel more. I'm convinced that what we see and feel is bottomless.

Whenever I've been enervated or winded in my soul, whenever I've felt there wasn't any more to give or find, a great love or suffering has broken me into a new depth. Having endured all the landslides and shifts that have brought me to you now, I believe each new sensitivity is the result of a worn part of us falling away, and what's left becomes more essential. This is the inner process of aging.

This is how the constructs of the mind are worn away. When we stand beside a river, it is we who call behind us downstream and ahead of us upstream. The river is simply flowing in all places at the same time. With ubiquitous clarity, the French philosopher Henri Bergson told us that time is such a river, existing in all places at once. It is always present and eternal. And it is we who call what's before us the present, what's behind us the past, and what's ahead of us the future. These are human distinctions, maintained to help us manage the days. Yet, in spite of ourselves, we keep entering the days, and the longer we're blessed to live, the more these distinctions fall away. Till eternal moments open more frequently, and whenever we exhaust our constructs, the river of time appears to quiet our demons from the past and our sirens from the future.

But these are only heartfelt guesses that rise because my way of feeling in the world has become more subtle. Now I begin farther in. The flash and fire I knew so well, the intensity of meeting others, has settled into the clearness of a lake. It seems that aging is the realm of light, not fire, and what matters is always near. What matters waits for me to stop thinking, like an old, quiet friend, soft as a feather that tells me a bird was here.

Let me say this slowly. The fate of being human is that our spirit is revealed like the arc of a comet. The outer surface of our life is worn away as we move through time, our center getting brighter as we fall through the years. Living through the time we're given, we keep becoming more essential, until all that's left is light.

....

     Whenever I've been enervated or winded in my soul, whenever I've felt there wasn't any more to give or find, a great love or suffering has broken me into a new depth.

....

A Reflective Pause

o *Describe one object that has come into your possession that has a history. Describe this history and how it touches you. Describe one object of yours you'd like to pass into the hands of others and why.*

WHAT DO WE DO
WITH WHAT WE FEEL?

❥ ❥ ❥

Understanding our emotions and working with them and through them has never been more important. Personally, relationally, globally, the maturing of emotion is the first step toward peace.

WITH ALL THE work to open our heart, to be awake, to meet experience and lean into life, what do we do with what we feel? How do we understand what we feel? What does it mean? Do we miss it? Do we mitigate it? Or do we lean further in, even if we don't understand, and start to deepen our relationship with what moves through us?

Human beings have always struggled with the impact of feeling. Mysteriously, to open the heart is major work that can take years or it can happen in an unprecedented moment. In his great poem, "Poet's Obligation," Pablo Neruda ends with these lines:

> *So, through me, freedom and the sea*
> *will call in answer to the shuttered heart.*

He beautifully suggests that the purpose of an open heart is to serve as a conduit between the mysterious Whole of Life and the closed and pained individual. The virtue of being so open and close to the flow of life is that this effort alone connects us to everything. Neruda suggests that the only thing to do with our feelings is to receive them completely. It seems that the sea's answer to the shuttered heart is to open it and reanimate the life that carries it.

A shuttered heart can be imagined in two ways: the heart as a hinged panel that opens and closes, like a louvered shutter before a window, opened to let light in and closed to keep light out; and the heart as a camera shutter, opening and closing like the pupil of an eye, depending on the flood of light or lack of it. We all have the need for light to restore us and the need to tone it down when we feel so sensitive or damaged that the light is overwhelming.

Being human, the heart will open and close in response to particular situations. But under these dilations and constrictions, under our damaged edges, we're asked *to live with an open heart* more permanently, which rearranges our basic stance toward life. In daily ways, living with an open heart shifts our inner geography. The heart no longer widens or closes, but stays open like an inlet. It assumes a permanent edge of receiving. Under all the turbulence of circumstance, the art of living centers, not on the mind's ability to trim and sort the feelings that come through, but on the heart's capacity to hold, merge, and absorb the mysterious abundance of feeling that direct living washes over us.

The River and the Riverbed

The riverbed and its banks can't seize or stop the water that passes through, and yet it couldn't have a more intimate relationship with all that water. The riverbanks soak in the water on all sides and are shaped by it. It's the same with what we feel. We are the riverbed and the water of life is the river. The rush of the river of life moving through us, shaping us, is the life of feelings. We can't avoid the rush of feelings any more than the riverbed can avoid the rush of the river. It's what the riverbed is made for. And to be a home for the life of feelings and the aliveness that it brings is what we are made for.

Learning from what moves through us is what makes feeling a means of perception equal to thinking. Becoming adept at feeling is a way of knowing the Universe and interpreting our human experience. This leads to understanding the energy and practice of being real. How then do we begin to work with the life of feeling, which is always rushing through us?

I offer that like a sponge, we absorb it; like a flag in the wind, we convey it. We let the life of feelings move through us. We bear witness to it. With grief and loss and pain, we have to let it through. We have to let it rearrange us. I invite you to resist being a juggler and sorter of your feelings and to absorb them the way sand absorbs the sea. We need to take time to receive and reflect on what we feel, to listen for where this takes us.

When we can meet and receive what we feel, it's possible to glimpse the truth that, though I'm frustrated, not everything is frustrating. Sometimes, in the midst of sadness, it's possible to glimpse that, though I'm sad, not everything is sad. When we deny what comes through us, it defines us. When we honestly face what comes through us, then who we are grows. Meeting and receiving what we feel is being authentic. When we're authentic, we discover what we already know.

....

⁓ *In daily ways, living with an open heart shifts our inner geography. The heart no longer widens or closes, but stays open like an inlet. It assumes a permanent edge of receiving.*

....

Nowhere Else to Go

There is such an emphasis on happiness in our culture that we're conditioned away from the fullness of the human experience. We get alarmed and skittish when feeling anything other than neutrality or happiness. When things unfold other than we want, we assume something is wrong and pull back.

Yet no matter how we try to distance ourselves, the impact of those we meet and care for affects us and changes our lives. It's been known forever, that to distance ourselves from our experience makes our feelings a liability, while staying in conversation with our experience makes our feelings a resource.

If we want to live, there's nowhere else to go but through the life of feelings. Given this, there are two recurring ways we grow: by willfully shedding and by being broken open. Transformation begins when we can find the courage and support to *lean into* what is opened when we're broken and to willfully shed once there. When broken open, it's natural to recoil and pull in. But after the initial impact, it's just as natural to lean into what's next, the way we inhale and exhale, one after another. This can be difficult, which is another reason we need each other. We can grow and transform through love, creativity, and relationship, as well as through difficulty, obstacles, and life-changing rearrangements.

Avoiding our feelings can be deadly. A form of wound cleaning called debridement is a surgical process that involves the removal of dead or infected tissue that encloses the remaining living tissue. When a wound has sealed over without healing, it must be opened and cleaned out. Dead tissue must be cut away until live tissue bleeds, because only live tissue can heal. If this isn't done, the enclosed dead wound can become septic, leading to a patient's death.

This is a powerful caution against the cost of not feeling, because unfelt feelings don't go away. They seal over as unhealed wounds. In time, they can go septic, which drains the life from the person carrying the wound. Emotionally, this tells us that when we're numb or enervated, we need to cut away the dead tissue that has enclosed our unfelt feelings in order to heal. Such dead skin may feel like cynicism, insignificance, or apathy. I think the epidemic of cutting, where people inflict self-injury, is a desperate way to feel, to bleed, to find a way to the live tissue waiting under a painful but unfelt wound.

How do our feelings become so infected? Though I never physically hurt myself, I felt insignificant when younger and overwhelmed by difficult feelings I wouldn't face. In the midst of my trouble, my pain, my doubt, I feared that who I am in my humanness was not worth the light of day. When confronted with my shortcomings, I feared if I showed who I really am, I'd be ostracized, rejected, and even shamed into exile.

And so, I retreated and the press of secrecy only made my pain and doubt and woundedness worse.

The unexpected truth is that, no matter how painful living with our flaws is, once voiced, once our questions and feelings are put in the open, we're humbled to discover that we all share the same trouble, the same pain, the same doubt. We all have to live with our shortcomings and seed them in the soil of humility, if we are to see how they will grow.

The details of our trouble and pain may differ but our life position is the same. No matter our path, no matter how differently we come to this, suffering and compassion lead us to drink from the same eternal well. And drinking together from the well of life, this is Heaven on Earth. Arriving here, there's nowhere else to go.

Where Old Loves Go

And what do we do with the loss and grief of relationships that end? I've been blessed to be loved by many. Certain relationships haven't worked out. All were painful in their loss, even when separation seemed inevitable and a right course of action. So how do we meet and receive the tender lessons of loves and friendships that have been broken or which burned themselves out?

I believe everyone we ever love has a place in the garden of our heart. I believe all past loves and friendships are tangled in our roots. The question, then, is not how to move past the tribe of our feelings, but what will our relationship with these lifelong feelings look like? Each bears a fruit and fragrance that make life bearable, though the brokenness of these relationships is no longer bearable.

For me, there are too many to name, but just a few: the lifelong estrangement from my mother which has now been repaired by the death of my father; the brutal end of a thirty-year friendship; the end of my second marriage, and the ripping of the circle of friends who couldn't tolerate that their world was changing when we divorced. While it's been over twenty years since some of these loved ones have gone from my life, each has a place in the garden of my heart. I can't rip them from that soil without tearing up my identity. So I must tend them, and not let them overtake the garden.

I was driving today to meet a friend for breakfast, and a very touching song came on the radio. It didn't really speak to my experience, but something in the soft piano and honest voice touched the common place where we all ache for what has come to pass. And so, my former wife came into view. I didn't long for her or for what we had or couldn't live into. I just felt the presence of our journey years ago and wondered where she is at this stage of life. That feeling led to other people now gone. This tender moment rising from a quiet song under the rolling clouds punctured my busyness with the unfathomable history a human life accumulates.

Still, I've learned that feeling something that rises from the bottom of my life, where it touches the bottom of all life, doesn't require me to solve anything. If I feel sad or touched by my mother, who now has dementia, it doesn't mean I need to fix our relationship. At times, *feeling* the feeling *is* acting on it. In these moments, I'm moved to follow whatever presents itself and drift to the bottom of my personality, on into the place where it touches the common pain and joy of being alive. Staying with these feelings opens my heart further. In this way, I have loved many from afar, while honoring the boundaries I need to stay integral with who I am.

So I listened to the tender song and put my hand on my heart with the belief that doing so would loosen the tangled root of care we all carry. Beyond all the grief, I wish them well. Like an underground spring, the one water of life connects and feeds us all. Tears are the water of life rising through an open heart. Oh, I welcome the water of life.

⁀ *We all have to live with our shortcomings and seed them in the soil of humility, if we are to see how they will grow.*

A Difficult Blessing

Deep feelings are often teachers we resist or turn away from because of their intensity. If we can move through our resistance, we're often asked to enter deep feelings the way we might enter a field after a long walk through the woods. Once in the open, it's clear that deep feelings often lead to great openings. In truth, all feelings, when met honestly, lead to the same depth and openness.

I used to feel inconsistent, because my moods would change. I'd want solitude. Then, when alone, I couldn't wait to be with others. I'd want to be still and walk in silence. But once there, I couldn't wait to hear live music and dance. It took years to realize that one mood leads to another. Like trickles streaming from all sides of a hill into a stream, all our feelings fill the river. We need them all to quench our thirst for aliveness.

The end of our initial journey of wakefulness is to thin what exists between our heart and the world. This makes us incredibly sensitive and fragile. If blessed, our heart becomes our skin. This is, at once, an incredible gift and an incredible challenge, because we can no longer encounter life without being changed. We can no longer limit the depth of what we feel. We can no longer resist the great openness all feelings lead us to. Once entering the days with an open heart, it's not as easy to steel ourselves to the suffering we encounter. This is a difficult blessing.

Gold Dust Is Everywhere

Alchemists in the Middle Ages were intent on discovering the philosopher's stone, a legendary substance that could turn iron into gold. Their efforts mirror the timeless attempt of humans to control life rather than face it, by turning what we don't like into something else. In truth, the gold of life waits *in* the iron and *in* the difficulty, no matter its shape. Everything is inherently of great value and we don't have to turn any one thing into anything else. Rather, we need to discover the gold already there. More to the point, we're asked to pan for the gold in our suffering; to sift it through the truth of our feelings in order to discover the many forms of gold dust that every experience carries.

When we resist both things-as-they-are and how we feel about what-is, we pour our efforts into turning things into gold, a misperception that can occupy our energy and worth for years. When we can face what we're given and feel our feelings all the way through, we find the value—*the gold*—in everything and in ourselves. Then we're close to discovering the meaning imbedded in life.

At its best, this want to turn one thing into another is a *resilience of doing*. It taps into our ability to create and adapt, which by itself is a gift that has co-created the world. Such adaptability is at the heart of innovation. But without facing what is true, that same creativity dissipates into reframing what we need to face. When afraid, we rationalize what we're given and our effort turns to denial.

Addiction of any kind is a destructive example of turning one thing into another as a way to run from our fear of death and the substance of living. Like drink, sex, success, exercise, or danger, anything in the extreme can be shaped by our alchemist of fear into something shiny and golden that will keep us from facing that fear. All the while, our *resilience of being* is waiting for us to stop and softly face the fact that we will die. Mysteriously, through that facing, the precious energy of life reveals itself even more.

Often, our attempt to turn what we don't like or fear into something else has us bypass the very lessons put in our path to break our self-centeredness. Often, our attempt to turn our suffering into something shiny and distracting has us skip over the pain waiting to transform us, as we try to paint every difficulty as rosy and promising. When afraid of what we feel, turning one thing into another removes us from what we have to face in order to truly live.

A fish awakened in the rush of the river has nowhere to go but deeper into the miracle of the current. And a soul awakened in the life of feeling has nowhere to go but headlong and heartlong into the miracle of the day.

   〜 *The end of our initial journey of wakefulness is to thin what exists between our heart and the world.*

A Reflective Pause

○ *In your journal, identify a mood of frustration or sadness that you're currently struggling with. Without denying or minimizing your frustration or sadness, let your mind and heart open beyond your struggle and describe, if you can, life around you that is not frustrating or sad. What does it feel like to allow both to take up space in your mind and heart at the same time?*

OUR RING OF FEAR

> > >

Y EARS AGO, WHEN living in Albany, New York, I would jog through the city streets. After two or three miles, I'd wind up on a bench outside a beautifully restored building where my good friend Robert worked, on the fourteenth floor. I'd wait for him to come down and join me for lunch, then jog back. One summer day, I sat on the bench, feeling winded in a good way. The light was beautiful. Just then, a bee started to hover above my arm.

I have to pause to say that I grew up in a small suburban home on Long Island. My parents grew up in Brooklyn and had very little exposure to nature. My mother was one of those people who, if a bug was in the house, life couldn't continue until that bug was captured or killed. For some reason, nature coming in felt scary.

That day on that bench, with the bee hovering above my arm, I realized I had inherited this fear. There I was, sweaty and feeling thoroughly alive from running, when the bee appeared. My first instinct was what I'd been taught—to swat it. I don't know why, maybe because I was exhausted, maybe because the light was particularly strong that day, but for the first time I started to wonder, *Why? Why should I do violence to this bee when it hasn't even threatened me?*

Suddenly, I was below what I inherited. In that moment, I began an experiment. With my arm on the bench and the bee hovering near it, I watched the bee and thought, *Well, let's just see what happens.* The bee hovered a little closer. I had a rush of adrenaline but calmed myself. It didn't threaten me. Finally, it actually landed on my arm. I had another flare of fear and thought, *Maybe that's enough of this experiment!*

But I didn't move. I realized how much bigger I was than the bee. And now, because I'd let the bee get close enough, I could see it more clearly. I could see that its stinger wasn't extended. Because I allowed it to get that close, I had more information. It still wasn't a threat. I realized I could move at any time. I had choices. I could get up, walk away, or shoo the bee. I continued my experiment and the bee eventually lifted off my arm and flew away.

This experience stayed with me for quite some time. The little bee had instructed me. What I came to understand is that each of us has *a ring of safety* that we carry around us. That is, we know that if something threatening, unexpected, or violent should cross that ring, we are experiencing legitimate danger and need to respond in some way—need to protect ourselves.

But we also have *a ring of fear* that often extends farther into the world than our legitimate ring of safety. That is, we often mistake the ring of fear for the ring of actual safety and keep the world farther away than necessary. If something crosses the farther ring of fear, we respond as if it were a true threat when often it's not. When the bee appeared, the ring of fear I'd inherited told me that this was dangerous and I needed to protect myself, even to the point of doing violence, when the truth was, my actual ring of safety was much closer.

In a very personal way, our daily practice evolves around the great question: How do we bring our ring of fear and our actual ring of safety more in accord so that they're congruent? When I'm pushing out my ring of fear, I'm not letting things touch me. I'm keeping life out of reach.

The lesson from the little bee is profound. When we start to fear people and experiences with no real need, we keep life farther away than necessary and begin to feel isolated and disconnected. Once out of touch, we can quickly become disheartened and discouraged. We start to feel insecure and less than. This makes our level of fear increase. Now we move our ring of fear even farther away. Now it's even harder to be touched by life and others. Then we feel even more disconnected. That makes us feel even smaller and more alone. And so we move our ring of fear even farther away until we feel even more threatened and more insecure. We begin to tumble in a psychological doom loop.

All this to say that we each have some work to do in aligning our ring of fear with our ring of safety. On any given day, they may drift apart, and we need to bring them back in accord. It's part of what we do with what we feel. For me, how close or far apart these two rings are is a barometer of my well-being. I know when my fear extends farther than need be, life seems farther away. The dissonance between my sense of fear and safety tells me that my insecurity is agitated and I'm not centered. When more fearful, I know I've stopped moving toward what is precious. I know I'm not outwaiting the clouds within me or around me. I know I'm not leaning into the sweet ache of being alive. When my ring of fear extends too far, I know I'm less awake. Once I finally realize that I'm more fearful than necessary, the challenge is to have the courage to put my ring of fear down—to open my windows, my doors, my heart, and my mind—to let life get closer. When I can right-size the reach of my fear, I can once again recognize legitimate fear when it appears.

When overcome with fear, it encompasses us completely. This is understandable. We feel it everywhere, and for the moment all of life seems fearful, the way a single cloud blocking the sun turns life on Earth gray. But it's only one well-placed cloud that, by its very nature, will move on. Likewise, fear, no matter how gripping, is one well-placed cloud that, though it changes everything, will in time move on.

Being human, we're challenged to outlast the cloud of fear. One way to do this is to develop a personal practice by which we can discern precisely where the ring of our safety ends and the ring of our legitimate fear begins. This is an application of seeing things as they are. Often, it's wandering tensely in the inflated territory of our exaggerated fear that adds to our suffering. When we allow our ring of fear to extend beyond what it truly is, we risk doing harm to others by perceiving threat that isn't real and then protecting ourselves by striking out when there is no need. From a heightened sense of threat, we limit our reach of true experience and possibility by retreating when we are actually safe.

The practice of being human requires the effort to continually know the difference between our reflexive ring of fear and our actual ring of safety, and to always bring those two in alignment. In this way, we practice seeing things as they are. This requires specific personal knowledge.

A Way of Unifying

A tradition that helps us understand the usefulness of right-sizing our fear is aikido, a relatively young Japanese martial art developed in the twentieth century by Morihei Ueshiba (1883–1969) as a synthesis of martial studies, philosophy, and spiritual beliefs. Aikido introduces a way of moving in the world that doesn't resist aggressive energy, but rather moves with it; stepping aside, allowing the mounting energy to exhaust itself. The central aim of aikido is to blend with the motion of an attacker, redirecting the force of the attack rather than opposing it. The term *aikido* translates as "the Way of unifying [with] life energy" or as "the Way of harmonious spirit."

The mental awakening of aikido is a metaphor for how we can meet pain, fear, or worry as they approach us. We can begin to understand the parallel in this way. A man comes at you with a knife, screaming in attack. At first, the threat is everywhere. But the aikido student is asked to let that cloud of fear disperse, so he can see precisely where the knife is coming from. Then it's clear that—of all the space around you—only one precise point holds the threat. Now the range of real choice is known. Now there is a way forward.

The same is true with pain, fear, and worry. At first, they are everywhere, but the practice of being human hinges on our ability to let the cloud of pain, fear, and worry disperse, so we can see precisely where the cause and impact are coming from. Then we have choices.

It's important to emphasize that it's understandable and natural that in meeting any aggressive surprise we will experience a cloud of fear that will consume our entire consciousness. This is how fear, pain, and worry present themselves—sharply and completely, overwhelming us. In that moment of overwhelm, the entire world before us seems threatening and dangerous. However, when presented with danger, the challenge of our wakefulness—mentally, heartfully, consciously—is to outwait the cloud of fear until it right-sizes. Until our ring of fear right-sizes to our actual ring of safety. How long the alarm defines our reality determines whether we remain paralyzed or crippled by our difficulty or whether we can find a way through.

While this is helpful, it's not easy. Just necessary. Of course, how anyone can shrink their cloud of fear to their actual ring of safety when someone is coming at you with a knife is startling and amazing. I leave that to the martial arts and the aikido master.

What we want to learn from this is the spiritual, emotional, and circumstantial use of it. When we enter situations in which a cloud of fear makes everything before us dangerous—whether they be relational situations, work situations, family situations, professional situations, situations of pain, or situations of worry—our personal practice, our pilgrimage of the heart, depends on whether we can outwait that cloud of fear to see what point is actually threatening. This is a powerful way to shrink our ring of fear and bring it in accord with our actual ring of safety.

....

Fear, no matter how gripping, is one well-placed cloud that, though it changes everything, will in time move on.

....

Discomfort

This call to see things as they are is also relevant when faced with pain and discomfort. Legitimate discomfort is the uneasiness of meeting new experience. This involves the disorientation that comes when we enter the unknown, when we feel the lack of clarity that comes with ambiguity. It involves the bump and poke of ordinary experience when we tumble into life.

Going through my cancer journey, I experienced many moments of pain, discomfort, fear, and worry. It was always maddening to hear doctors and surgeons describe what I was going through as discomfort, the medical euphemism equivalent to the military use of the term *collateral damage*.

I want to talk about discomfort and pain and their true difference. When I first entered the hospital, I was terrified of what I would go through. My ring of fear was cast so far out that when anyone approached me, I was already groaning, "Ouch!" Someone lifted me and I said, "Ouch!" I was poked and prodded and bumped and lifted and put down and turned over and stuck with needles and propped up with pillows under my legs. Every time I was touched, I reacted in my fear as if that contact was painful. That's how far away from me my ring of fear was.

As you can imagine, that only made things worse. Anticipating pain with such diligence was untenable, unworkable. It was inwardly debilitating when I was outwardly debilitated. My fear of pain had painted me into an existential corner. There was nowhere to go. Eventually, mostly through exhaustion, I had to make discernments. I had to understand and tell myself, "OK, yes, when my rib was removed and I woke up and tried to turn, that was pain. But when someone came and turned me over in my bed two weeks later, that was discomfort. When someone came to check my blood pressure and squeezed the cuff around my arm, that wasn't pain. That was motion and sensation."

Likewise, whatever we experience, we must learn to distinguish between what is truly painful and what is just uncomfortable; what is just sensation and what are the growth pains of change. Physically, emotionally, spiritually, and mentally, we each need to learn how to see the difference between the sensations of suffering and the sensations of growing.

This is the work of meeting what we feel. To grow, we're asked to differentiate between true pain and awkwardness, between true pain and discomfort, between true pain and unexpected sensation. This awareness can help us endure the unavoidable pains of living and not push off on what will actually help us grow. Disruptive as it is, the bump and poke we experience at the hands of time unfolding isn't always pain, but the stretch marks of how we expand and deepen into our time on Earth. We have very little practice at holding true discomfort long enough to experience the growth these sensations are pointing to.

Chronic Pain

An exception to all this is chronic pain, which is hard to comprehend unless we've experienced a dose of long-lasting pain ourselves. I've had pain that has lasted for months and inside that experience, it's chronic. If we have pain that exists even for a day or a week, inside the experience, it's chronic. Yet any passage like this only gives us compassion and admiration for those who have to endure some form of pain endlessly. The closest I've come to chronic pain was when a rib was removed from my back and when for seven months my stomach wasn't emptying.

During these experiences, I had to learn to find spaces within the pain itself. These difficult times taught me that when in constant physical or emotional pain, within a period of depression or anxiety, or when suffering through loss or grief, we have to outwait the cloud of that chronicness so we can start to discern moments of relief. Just as the stock market goes up and down every hour of every day, just as our pulse and blood pressure go up and down every single minute, we have to discern the peaks and pauses in our pain, so we can take refuge in those moments and build resilience before that pain reasserts itself.

It was Hippocrates who said, "Pleasure is the absence of pain." All we need is a moment of stillness when the pain has stopped. If only for a second, we can help each other find the humility and courage to know that second as a moment of pleasure, of peace, and build on it.

❧   ❧   ❧

If we want to lessen violence in the world, we can start by facing what is ours to feel, so we don't play out our unresolved feelings on others. And we can work to reduce the gap between our ring of fear and our actual ring of safety, so we can lessen our unnecessary defensiveness and aggression. If this seems daunting, we can begin by waiting before swatting the bee, waiting for our fear and sense of offense to subside.

It was the great Hindu sage Ramana Maharshi who said:

Wanting to reform the world without discovering one's true self is like trying to cover the world with leather to avoid the pain of walking on stones and thorns. It is much simpler to wear shoes.

It's clear that reacting to things that are *not* life threatening as if they are is responsible for a great deal of the violence in our society. The American poet Henry Wadsworth Longfellow said, "If we were to truly listen to our enemy's suffering, they would no longer be our enemy."

Sometimes, waiting for the noise of fear to settle is the bravest thing we can do.

....

❤ *If we want to lessen violence in the world, we can start by facing what is ours to feel, so we don't play out our unresolved feelings on others.*

....

A Reflective Pause

○ *In this chapter, we touched on the gap between what is safe and where our fear would have us live. In your journal, describe the gap between your ring of true safety and your ring of fear. Name one step you can take farther into the world to reduce this gap.*

THE TROUBLES OF LIVING

❧ ❧ ❧

It begins in mystery, and it will end in mystery, but what a savage and beautiful country lies in between.

—DIANE ACKERMAN

IN THE IMMEDIATE aftermath of the terrorist attacks on September 11, 2001, a transformational moment opened, not only for the people suffering in New York but for the entire country. It happened again in the aftermath of the horrific massacre of twenty school children in Newtown, Connecticut, in December 2012. In the wake of these horrific losses, the boundaries and differences we work so hard to maintain simply disappeared. Within a fairly short time, that soft and boundary-less time closed, as it always does. But in that brief rearrangement of things, lives changed, worldviews shifted, depths of compassion reached new levels. Hearts were cracked open, never to close completely again. Though there was enormous fear, love stretched many people beyond the shattered edge of life as they knew it.

Though we do our best to stay strong and keep going, it's often the moments we're forced to stop that introduce us to the aspects of life that matter. Though no less devastating, the puncture of tragedy happens to ordinary people every day: a loved one dies, or leaves, a purpose is lost, a life's work is destroyed, our investment in a dream seems wasted when the dream catches fire. Herein lies the mystery of woundedness and its infinite connection to aliveness: life constantly asks us to meet fear and pain with love. Not an easy thing to do. But when we can, it's like dousing a fire with water. In the simmer, we are softened to each other and refined by the air. This is the hard gift that waits in the troubles of living.

I was leading a retreat for students at Notre Dame on poetry and peace-building. In the evening around a fire, we were invoking those who've taught us about the gift of vulnerability. After two hours of stories that brought us into a fragile silence, Kelli felt compelled to tell one more story. She described her roommate who sat with her months after delivering a beautiful baby with birth defects. Over tea, with the deformed toddler sweetly crawling before them, Kelli's roommate uttered with a tenderness reserved for those who endure, "It is often at the intersection of beauty and suffering that we find meaning."

When vulnerable, the sage in us appears. When softened, we often find wisdom in the press of beauty against pain. When humbled enough to put our conclusions down, we find what is true because being vulnerable joins us to the Living Center. Whether we endure defects at birth or endure the flaws we cultivate in the world, whether we carry something irreplaceable only to stumble and drop it on the steps of the temple or whether we're brutish and clumsy at every turn, we're called to this intersection of beauty and suffering so we might feel the quiver at Center.

Even so, we seldom come to this moment of meaning willingly. Often, I trip into meaning. Often, it's the impact of a fall that makes me forget where I'm going, as the impact of beauty makes me forget why I keep building all these walls. In those moments of falling or opening, I start to listen—beyond my discomfort with who I am or have not become, beyond my exhaustion from keeping catastrophe at bay. In those moments, I start to listen, even when no one is speaking, especially when no one is speaking.

And as I listen, I can hear Spirit rush through the many lives on Earth the way wind surprises sleeping trees. I know—it's hard to be here without shutting down. That's why we wait for wind. And winded, it's clear that as we walk with two legs, we live by two divining sights—*the one that keeps moving no matter what is taken away* and *the one that accepts everything as a blessing.*

The Practice of Entering Life

The journey of living requires us not just to understand, but to enter. Transformation begins when we stop watching. To enter requires us to touch and open seeming opposites, the way we would open ancient carved doors, reading the markings of those who've come before. This is the deeper work of experience. Life is full of opposites, contradictions, and painful tensions—full of paradox. And try as we do to sort these tensions, to pull them apart and understand, to solve them, to keep them at bay—none of that works. It seems the only way to open the doors of paradox is with a soft heart. When we receive completely, the indivisible world receives us, the way water accepts whatever falls into it; the way oceans let everything settle on their bottom.

It is often at the intersection of beauty and suffering that we find meaning.

The quiet truth is that things that matter defy explanation. They will let us lose years in the game of circle-and-reason, but will not bestow their gifts as long as we try to pull life apart and watch. Things that matter must be allowed in. What matters won't reveal itself until we show that we are serious and committed, till we enter and accept. Only when absorbed can what matters work its magic.

A mysterious example of a soul who kept entering life is Matsukura Ranran (1647–1693) who was one of Bashō's oldest students and earliest disciples. Having found Bashō in Edo, Matsukura resigned his position as a samurai to devote himself to poetry. We don't know why Matsukura so dramatically changed his life but that he did serves as a koan for the archetypal choices we all face between surviving and thriving.

It helps to remember that in Zen Buddhism a koan is a parable that serves as a riddle, used to expose the limitations of logical reasoning.

The concept of a koan is based on the need for something to jar our surface perception open, if we are to enter the depth of being here.

We all struggle to find the proper use of reasoning. As I look at the snow-covered tree this morning, logic helps me understand the way its branches spray in all directions from reaching for the light. The map of reason lets me understand why this tree is leafless and dormant. But it's the sudden appearance of morning sun between all its snow-covered branches that brings the tree to life. In the same way, reasoning lets us understand the map of the world and how it grows, but it's the sudden appearance of truth and light that brings the mystery and potency of the Universe alive. Surviving is so demanding at times that we become obsessed with the maps of logic needed to get by, and go blind to the truth and light only visible in the spaces in between.

Koans are one way to shift our perception back to the unseeable Whole of Life. In Japanese, the word koan literally means *matter for public thought*. Recovering our perception of the Whole of Life is a matter for public thought, though we often go about our quest for meaning like spies. The troubles of living are matters for public thought, though we're often shy about what's difficult. When conversed with, the troubles of living are koans that can restore our perception of the Whole of Life.

Very little is known about Matsukura's inner process, but his devotion to being a samurai at first and a poet later portray how a lightness of soul can sprout from the depth of the world. What made him change his path? How did Matsukura hold the tension of these divergent ways of life?

Clearly, something awakened Matsukura's need to be more whole, which is the central work of a poet. What did Matsukura enter and accept that made him put down his training as a warrior? Perhaps his heart flapped open unexpectedly after running someone through, and the blood he'd spilled was softer and redder than he ever imagined. Perhaps he could suddenly hear the life of that person pool around his feet. Perhaps Matsukura suddenly wanted to put the life and blood back into this person, and not being able to stripped him of his resolve.

Sooner or later, we all arrive at this soft opening where the steeliness we rely on to do what has to be done is suddenly gone. And frightened that we'll no longer be able to make it in the world, we become less sure, though our heart and mind are so much closer to the quivering truth of things. Perhaps Matsukura stumbled into this moment of undoing, which presented itself at first as a crisis, but which having walked through, offered him a new way of life. How we meet that moment of undoing is at the heart of the practice of entering life. Do we meet our moment of undoing as a crisis to sew up like a wound or as a path opened in the mountain of time?

....

∾ *Transformation begins when we stop watching.*

....

The Staff and the Resting Place

Matsukura died suddenly at the age of forty-seven. Lamenting his student's death, Bashō wrote this haiku (#642):

> *in autumn's wind,*
> *sadly broken,*
> *a mulberry staff.*

What is Bashō pointing to in his grief for his friend? Referring to Matsukura as a mulberry staff, Bashō might be suggesting that the samurai turned poet, grown sturdy by nature, was whittled by life to something to lean on while making our way. It's said that the fruit of the black mulberry, native to Japan, has the strongest flavor. In the seventeenth century, the black mulberry was brought to England for the cultivation of silkworms, whose only food is the leaf of the mulberry. Bashō might be saying that the silk of Oneness can only be spun by those who've steadily eaten of life. How sad that one who could be leaned on for his sweet truth should be broken. The samurai turned poet is a quiet example of a life moved and shaped by the troubles of living.

In Spanish, *descanso* means a little rest, a pause to catch one's breath and gather strength before continuing the journey. Way inside, where we sprout from the same seed, we are all warriors waiting to enter our moment of undoing, so we can restore our perception of the Whole of Life. All of us wanting to pause and catch our breath, so we can begin spinning the silk of our lives. Each of us looking to each other to gather strength before continuing the journey.

Being Perfectly Flawed

Our schizophrenic patient is actually experiencing inadvertently that same beatific ocean deep which the yogi and saint are ever striving to enjoy: except that, whereas they are swimming in it, he is drowning.

—JOSEPH CAMPBELL

The dangers of drowning in the troubles of living are great. We are one bob or gasp from swimming in the beatific ocean of existence or drowning in it, one difficult experience from being wise or being fractured, one moment of undoing from reaching out or becoming merciless. The good news is that we can turn it around in a second, so powerful is our humanity if we use it.

It's important to remember that when separated from our soul, we are separated from life. As a comet is a mixture of dust and ice that for some reason hasn't become a planet, a person cut off from their soul is a mixture of intensity and knowledge that for some reason hasn't awakened. Both the comet and the unawakened person will burn brightly and erratically until they burn up.

The great Irish poet William Butler Yeats speaks to this in his legendary poem "The Second Coming," written in the aftermath of World War I in 1919:

> *Things fall apart; the centre cannot hold . . .*
> *The best lack all conviction, while the worst*
> *Are full of passionate intensity.*

Whether through global wars or personal wars, we're always at great risk of being separated from what matters—of losing our belief in life and getting fevered into an intensity without any care or meaning. Consequently, we must follow love and truth wherever they lead us—whether from being a samurai to becoming a poet or from being a gardener to becoming a reluctant soldier—so we can coalesce again into a person through our return to wakefulness and meaning.

I'm not offering these stark comparisons to bring fear into our thinking, but more to accurately describe the magnificent and acute landscape we walk every day. It's helpful to know where the path widens and where it narrows. So much is at stake every day that we must run carefully alongside truth.

There is a Buddhist saying, "Practice like your hair's on fire." This itself is a paradox. What I take from this saying is that life is immediate and unrepeatable, which requires us to have the urgency of wakefulness in order to be fully alive, but not the agitation of urgency that would have us live constantly in fear. I understand this koan as a reminder that what is obvious must be acted on swiftly and without hesitation.

This acceptance of what is true frees us to live cleanly. Such acceptance of things-as-they-are is what makes the samurai a true warrior and the poet a true seer. What is true lives in each of us, waiting for us to use it as a tool. Over the years, I've learned that holding what is true in our heart incubates the troubles of living until they burst open like seed to reveal the aliveness inherent in all things.

Consider that the word *perfect* originally meant thorough, not without flaws. Somewhere history took a wrong turn and we've had to unlearn ever since. When trying to be thorough, we come close to the aliveness inherent in all things. When trying to live without flaws, we only remove ourselves from the flow of life. In fact, there's a Tibetan belief that we each have a unique flaw, which is the mark where the ultimate bareness of being first kissed us, first seared us, placing us perfectly—*thoroughly*—in the world. The unique flaw we carry is the kiss of divinity, the scar of original being through which divinity seeps into our humanity. It's not to be erased, for it's through our flaw that the invisible and visible meet. It's through our flaw that eternity floods us, through our flaw that the joy and suffering of everyone who's ever lived moves into our hands.

This comforts me. For it's the hole in wood that makes a song of the wind, and the softness in our heart that makes the quandaries of living so human. It's how we falter into silence that makes stillness a sea. My mind may be my greatest flaw, the hole I stare into, as I listen for its song.

So when the dangers of drowning in the troubles of living are near, when feeling separate from your soul and the fear of burning up is heating up, rub the place in your chest where you feel most human, most vulnerable, and you will be perfectly returned in time to a thoroughness that will present the next step.

This comforts me, too. For I can't hold all of this, any more than you, any more than the tops of trees can keep a summer breeze. Like the samurai turned poet who died in the wind, when I finally have something to say, I will settle and become the stone on which you sit to catch your breath and gather strength, as you look for something dear and true to say.

The silk of Oneness can only be spun by those who've steadily eaten of life.

Our work is to stay thoroughly human, not to perfect our way out of it. I admit I've lost years to refining myself when I've needed to deepen myself. I admit I've known the lift of the beatific ocean of Spirit and the crash of the world's great wave. And no matter what is taken away, I try to accept everything as a blessing. I try to put down my mask and sword and keep entering life. But I confess, when I was sick, I refused the teacher and the teacher made me sicker until I could hear. This is how I was forced to learn that experience is the fifth element—insatiable and transforming as fire, clear and saturating as water, relentless and binding as earth, and necessary as air.

Outliving those I love and outlasting things I've built is how I've been humbled to learn that grief is how we listen our way through loss. Opened, like a Russian nesting doll, to smaller and smaller shells I didn't know I was carrying, I've been opened to the truth that obstacles are teachers and emergencies are rearrangers. Now I bless the wisdom in Rilke's line:

> The [dove] that remain[s] at home,
> never exposed to loss . . .
> cannot know tenderness . . .

A Reflective Pause

○ *What is the world saying to you right now? How are you being challenged beyond what is familiar? Where do you sense you are being led?*

○ *This meditation leads to a table question. Put down one urgency you're feeling and go for a walk. See what waits when you can enter a single moment without any expectation. Later on, describe what happens to a friend.*

THE SWEET ACHE
OF BEING ALIVE

When the sweet ache of being alive,
lodged between who you are
and who you will be,
is awakened,
befriend this moment.
It will guide you.
Its sweetness is what holds you.
Its ache is what moves you on.

WE ARE EACH born with a gift and an emptiness, and given a life to be in conversation with them, to have one fill the other. It doesn't matter where the emptiness is in our life or what the gift is, it's always the journey of a life to discover how they meet and complete each other. We waste so much time trying to hide our emptiness, feeling ashamed of our emptiness, trying to eliminate our emptiness, feeling victimized because we have an emptiness, or feeling we're entitled not to have any emptiness, that we're diverted from our soul's journey. This diversion gives rise to the blame game and keeps us from inhabiting the depths opened by the emptiness that can only be illumined by the light of our gift.

In December 2010, I was having lunch with two friends in a small bistro in the West Village in New York City. We were talking about the solid ground we stumble onto from time to time, and the immense empty space that always surrounds us. When I went to speak, I found myself talking about the gift and the emptiness for the first time. This is how insights present themselves, through conversation, when being with others causes me to reach for what I don't know. That night, I explored what came from our conversation and wrote the above paragraph and thought, *When we dig a hole or a hole is dug in us, we become preoccupied with all that is unearthed, even try to put all that dirt back, but the empty depth is waiting for us to shine a light in it.* The relationship between our gift and our emptiness had begun its conversation with me.

A few months later, I shared the above paragraph and its paradox with a group I've been journeying with for a year. I brought it to them, the way a diver might haul something undefined from the deep and dump it on board, so we could marvel and puzzle at it together. Puzzle we did! Several people found the whole idea confusing. Others were uncomfortable that emptiness might be such a significant part of our journey.

Like someone leading a group down a steep climb to a lake, I saw a gentler slope nearby. So we walked and talked a ways further, approaching the same water by stepping closer to the idea that we each experience a sweet ache in being alive. I first explored this notion in *Seven Thousand Ways to Listen* and spoke of the sweet ache as "the tuning fork of my soul. It's how I know I'm close to what matters. In actuality, this deep and nameless ache in the presence of beauty and suffering has been a steadfast teacher and friend." This was something everyone could relate to, much more easily.

Though we found another way in, I kept wondering, what is it about emptiness that scares us so? We have a conditioned fear of openness and space, and a stubborn fear of silence, which makes it uncomfortable to face emptiness directly. Yet emptiness is nothing more than vastness and spaciousness, what air is before it enters the lungs.

The following spring I was leading a retreat at Hollyhock, Canada's

Lifelong Learning Centre, a beautiful, almost virgin setting on Cortes Island, between Vancouver Island and the mainland of British Columbia. I had a chance to explore the gift and the emptiness again. This time, I entered it straightaway by asking about the sweet ache of being alive. I introduced the notion of emptiness once we were rooted in our own personal experience. Still, there were those who bristled to peer over the edge into the vastness known as emptiness.

> *When we dig a hole or a hole is dug in us, we become preoccupied with all that is unearthed, even try to put all that dirt back, but the empty depth is waiting for us to shine a light in it.*

Three Ways In

I'd like to offer three quotes to ground us in our discussion of emptiness. The first came to me as anonymous. I was teaching in British Columbia on Vancouver Island, near the city of Victoria, at a wonderful place called Royal Roads University, a serene, small campus that has peacocks running about. On the second day of the retreat, Cathy gave voice to this thought, which she found handwritten on her grandmother's dresser: "My barn, having burned to the ground, I can see more completely the moon." I have since learned that this is attributed to the Japanese poet and samurai Mizuta Masahide (1657–1723) who also studied under the legendary Bashō.

This perception by Masahide is spiritually useful. Without minimizing the loss of the barn, its coming down opens a larger space. I offer this as a way to introduce our topic of emptiness. For whenever we experience personal emptiness, it first appears as lack opened by loss, an emptying of what we carry or hold dear, a carving out that leaves us bereft. But very often, the thing burning to the ground frees up more of the sky, as our personal experience of emptiness will free us into a Universal bareness of being. Hard as it is to endure, on the other side of whatever life brings down, we find the moon waiting in the sky. And we need each other to endure what is cleared and to make sense of the larger vastness waiting.

The second quote is from Martin Buber, the preeminent Jewish philosopher of the twentieth century whose major contribution comes from his book *I and Thou*. Buber suggests that when we can regard everything we encounter as its own living center, then God appears between us—as unrehearsed, authentic dialogue. But when we act as if we are the sun and everything orbits us, then God seems absent from life. It's obvious that a lot of people put themselves in the center. In fact, we all do this from time to time, because we're human and because pain, worry, doubt, and lack of self-esteem make us self-centered, the way exhaustion makes us clumsy.

As a mood, being self-centered is part of the human experience. It becomes a problem when our pain or neediness makes us install self-interest as a worldview and philosophy to live by. Then the many barns of self-interest block the moon and the sky, and we lose our true relationship to the vastness that some call God.

What Martin Buber offers is a relational sense of aliveness in which there is no one center. We each are a center relative to each other. By honoring such mutuality, we can move through our lonely moments of personal emptiness into a common bareness of being that holds us all.

This is what Einstein discovered when he stumbled onto the theory of relativity: there is no one center. Einstein's first glimpse of relativity happened when he was a boy. He tells us in an autobiography of his mind that, at the age of twelve, he understood Euclidean geometry in a flash of intuition. He understood it completely, and knew that the next day of necessity would be dull.

Profoundly, he suggests that the rhythms of life can't yield one extended peak experience. Light will be followed by gray, depth will be followed by surface, and fullness will be followed by emptiness, because this is the nature of life and the nature of being human.

Once Einstein began to understand the theory of relativity, he quickly realized it as a fundamental principle of being. Grasping this, he essentially said (I paraphrase), "Euclidean geometry is a nice system but since its theorems are based on one central point, the basic premise is flawed because there is no *one* central point." Einstein concluded that "Euclidean geometry is only helpful as far as it goes."

We can say the same about our lapses into self-centeredness. If we install ourselves as the center of all we encounter, it's like building a barn that blocks the sky. It will work for a while but, like Euclidean geometry, it's only helpful as far as it goes, because there is no one center. Life is always larger than our one barn. Buber confirms this and concludes that the presence of the Infinite can only be experienced between authentic living centers that recognize each other as such. Once out in the open, once out of our barn, we have the chance to see each other as essential parts of something larger.

This is a long introduction to the second quote by Martin Buber which reads, "The world is not comprehensible, but it is embraceable." This thought appears like a water lily whose roots remain out of view. So what's under the surface here? What's not seeable beneath this thought? To begin with, Buber implies that the mind can only go so far; that the language of embrace—the language of being touched and held—is deeper and more immediate than the language of the mind. His one sentence suggests that we depend more on the empty vastness than on what we can define or give words to. Even when we think we don't know anything, we still can touch what is before us. And that embrace will inform us about the life we're standing in and the emptiness surrounding us.

The third quote is a stanza from a poem of mine that reads:

> *When everything you've put off is here*
> *When every dream of love is on your lip*
> *When everything you've saved becomes a rose*
> *Open your eyes though they are busy seeing*
> *Open your mind though it won't stop planning*
> *Open your heart though it keeps remembering*
> *Open and focus on the first thing you see.*

By saying "you" repeatedly, it may seem that I'm offering advice. Rather, I received this voice as an instruction that I must learn from. Often, poems come as unexpected teachers. This poem came to teach me that we need to put down our conclusions so we can see directly again. One paradox of consciousness is that we have this amazing ability to put things together. So we stitch experiences together and call the cloth an insight. Then we sow the pieces of cloth into garments we call conclusions. Now we have clothes we call principles and a closet full of history. Eventually, all the insights, conclusions, principles, and history begin to weigh us down as we carry them everywhere. In time, our assumptions and conclusions harden into a screen or wall that stands between us and direct living.

Certainly, we have to gather wisdom—that's one of the gifts of consciousness. But not every conclusion is worth keeping solid and fixed. Often, despite our efforts, our eyes are busy seeing what we've already seen until we don't see what's before us. Our mind keeps planning, keeps gauging, keeps analyzing, keeps judging what's happening; trying to put it into some category of good or bad; trying to say this is a blessing, this is a catastrophe, this is dangerous, or this is advantageous. All this keeps us from opening our mind to what's before us.

Our heart keeps remembering the ways we've been touched and held, until we want that again. Our heart keeps remembering the ways we've been hurt or betrayed or surprised, and tries to avoid that. But hiding in what was good and running from what was hurtful keeps us from experiencing what's right before us.

We all do this. I do this. And so, the importance of developing a personal practice of openness through which we empty what we carry, so we can be present to the first thing we see. Because the beauty and sanctity of life is in every moment, if we can empty what clouds our eyes, what worries our mind, and what weighs down our heart.

The next two chapters explore the nature of emptiness and how we might relate to the depths that emptiness opens. Because if a bird can't open to the emptiness we call the sky, it will never fly. And if we can't give in to courage and let ourselves feel the sweet ache of being alive, our wings will never open.

....

∿ *Emptiness is nothing more than vastness and spaciousness,
what air is before it enters the lungs.*

....

A Reflective Pause

○ *In your journal, describe a time when your experience of personal
emptiness (a sense of lack) led you to experience a moment of
Universal emptiness (the bareness of being).*

THE FLUTE OF INTERIOR TIME

▷ ▷ ▷

WE LIVE IN a modern world where more is better. Fill it up. Top it off. As if the more money we have, the more things we can buy, the more places we can go, the more adventures we can orchestrate will protect us from life's journey. In our all-consuming society, we're constantly looking for ways to distract ourselves from the vastness and emptiness which no one can avoid. This makes us uncomfortable, even afraid, when the things around us or within us aren't full.

This preoccupation with being full leads to more than one kind of greed. For greed is not just reserved for money. There's also *experience greed*. We assume that we're entitled to travel to every place on Earth. To eat, imbibe, and receive every food, drink, and experience we can possibly imagine. It's wonderful to be this open, as long as we accept what the ocean of life gives us.

But when we expect everything, we will be severely disappointed. And entitled disappointment can make us bitter. This want to have it all and our inevitable disappointment at what we're given won't let us experience the gift of being human. Because as human beings we're limited. We're not going to be able to travel everywhere in the world. We won't have the time, energy, or resources. No matter how we fantasize or how hard we work, we won't have all the things we want.

This preoccupation with being full creates *love greed* too. We feel we're entitled to unlimited passion and love, "I want to experience as much love as possible. I want to love as many people as possible." Certainly the heart is infinite in its capacity—to heal, to grow, to love, to move through experience and be resilient. But being in one body, in one life, we're humbled to love the people before us. This is a paradox of being human. We can love the world, but we can't have five hundred lovers.

Rather, we love the people before us. That love ripples to the people they love. This is how love, like waves in the ocean, reaches around the world. While our heart can hold all of humanity in its deepest chamber, in daily life, one person can't care for everyone at once. Simply and humbly, with a love of humanity in our heart, the love that borrows us moves through each of us, one person at a time, each to another. Love manifests in us and through us as we thoroughly give who we are, one touch at a time, one care at a time.

I think that *love greed* and *experience greed* have something to do with the epidemic of affairs in our modern world. Since we are implicitly taught that it's our right to have it all, being free is often misunderstood as the chance to grab whatever we want without any responsibility for our emotional trail.

Our preoccupation with being full and our greed for love, experience, attention, and things—all this fuels our fear of emptiness and the vastness that is our eternal home.

Depth Experience

In truth, we fill ourselves up to avoid our conversation with death, though the vastness that holds even death opens us to a greater understanding of life. We're sorely in need of that vastness and though it calls to us, we fill our time with memories and dreams, our mind with techniques and facts, our days with activities and lists, and our heart with worries and fears. No wonder it feels disorienting when life jars us from our constant filling, as if the floor has dropped out from under us. Yet we're still standing and it's unclear if we're about to fly or fall. This is the beginning of depth experience, which getting close to, we often run from, quickly trying to fill ourselves up again.

The spiritual challenge is that we have little hope of receiving or absorbing anything when so full. There's a very telling story of two scientists who travel all the way to India to present their theories to a respected Hindu sage. They're eager for his perspective. After a long journey, they arrive and are led into his small room where they wait. Finally, he enters and without a word begins to pour tea for them. Calmly, the sage keeps pouring even though the first cup is full. Tea is overflowing everywhere. The scientists are alarmed but trying not to show it, when one tentatively says, "Your Holiness, the cup is already full." The sage, without looking up, keeps pouring the tea as he replies, "As are your minds. Empty them and return, and then we can talk."

We face this challenge every day: to learn and grow and remember what matters, all to empty the cup of our mind, so we can live freshly and directly without the sediment of our judgments and conclusions. This emptying, so we can re-experience the vastness of life, is the work of maintaining a Beginner's Mind and Heart.

Still, on any given day, I can feel empty or at a loss or as though there's nothing left in me. These are legitimate feelings that everyone gets to face and move through. With our own strength of heart and help from each other, we can touch the bottom of these feelings. There we begin to touch that spaciousness when the barn burns down and we see the moon and the stars and the entire Universe more clearly. In this way, personal emptiness starts to open into a Universal spaciousness that can fill us.

⌒ This is a paradox of being human. We can love the world, but we can't have five hundred lovers. Rather, we love the people before us. That love ripples to the people they love. This is how love, like waves in the ocean, reaches around the world.

Unknowable Worlds

As we explore emptiness, it's important to find your own synonym for this underlying quality of life. As with the many names for God, it doesn't matter if you call the immensity that surrounds us mystery, vastness, spaciousness, nature, or silence. Whatever name you give it, when we can put down our want and fear, we begin to create space for a conversation with this underlying quality of life.

For me, emptiness is really a surface term for spaciousness. When we look at the night sky, we can think of the infinite galaxies as an endless void or as an unending display of unknowable worlds. Likewise, there is a largesse of being that exists in everything we regard as empty. That unnameable largesse is what some people call *eternity*, what some people call *God*. It's what some people call *being*. When in touch with that largesse of being, we feel both the particularity of our own life and the universality of all life.

We're always asked to live into the question: What is our relationship to the vast depth of all things, to the empty canvas of life that paradoxically holds everything? Within this larger question, we each inhabit a singular life that has its feelings, pains, aches, and questions. We're committed to that life, of course, because we don't just live in the depth world. We're human beings who live on Earth and we can't help but wake in the visceral kaleidoscope of the daily world. We drink water and cut the grass and pay the bills, while feeling wonder, awe, enervation, and doubt.

Relating to the Whole of Life is not an abstract endeavor; any more than a plant or tree can live its own life without having contact with the soil it grows in. We're left to inhabit this very personal exchange between our own particular life and the ground of all life. The depth world—through the soil of its spaciousness, its emptiness, and its bareness—infuses our particular life with wholeheartedness, a hearted gene of the Whole. This infusion of Wholeness gives us the resources to meet whatever life brings us, the way fertile soil infuses stems, flowers, and fruits with the sustenance to grow.

In the Hollows

Years ago, I stumbled through the bottom of a loneliness into the heart of emptiness and retrieved this poem called:

THE FLUTE OF INTERIOR TIME

If you are never hungry,
how can you know
the contours of your stomach.

If you are never thirsty,
how can you know
the edges of your voice.

If you are never disappointed,
how can you know
the reaches of your heart.

If you are never in doubt,
how can you know
the ceiling of your mind.

If you are never empty,
how can you know
the fullness of your spirit.

If you are never alone,
how can you know
God.

Paradoxically, it's the emptiness of things that lets us glimpse their full capacity. Most musical instruments are hollowed out, because if they weren't, there would be no music. Guitars are hollowed out. String instruments are hollowed out. Drums are hollowed out. Reed instruments are hollowed out. This is a great example of the necessity of emptiness in order to make music. It's true with our lives. Each of us is an instrument that experience hollows out in order to have our souls release their song.

It's the same with the Earth. Open spaces are magnificent. Consider how the Grand Canyon in Arizona was carved out over centuries. It's perhaps the most magnificent emptiness on Earth. People travel from around the world to stand on its edge. Why? Because the mystery and magnificence of life somehow shimmers through the magnitude of that openness. This is why we stand on the tops of mountains and go to the edge of cliffs, or stare for hours into the ocean. This is why we lose ourselves in the night sky. This is why we look into the open hearts of each other and lose ourselves in each other. This is why we climb the edge of each other and peer into the canyon that life and heartache carve out in us. And this process of staring into the great emptiness in each other is a form of true friendship.

While staring into the mysterious depth of the Grand Canyon, which reaches over a mile into the Earth, the fullness of the Universe is palpable. And it's the canyon opened in the human heart that lets us glimpse the Universal love we're capable of. So when you give me the honor of looking into your canyon, we are being intimate. There I see eternity through what you've been through. What greater thing can we share?

I think this is what the great Lebanese poet Kahlil Gibran means when he says:

> The deeper that sorrow carves into your being,
> the more joy you can contain.
>
> Is not the cup that holds your wine the very cup
> that was burned in the potter's oven?

Isn't this why after great heartache and loss, we come to the cliff of that loss to wonder about our place in life as we drop memories like stones into the unseeable bottom of eternity from which we must get up and return? This is why I love to enter every room and theater I speak in before everyone arrives, so I can meet and listen to the emptiness that holds everyone who comes to it. From that eternal cliff, we can meet honestly.

Whether the Grand Canyon or the depth opened by our heartache or an empty theater, the resource is equal to the space opened. Consider how a simple well dug in the ground can only hold as much water as the well is deep. And so it is with us. The digging is always painful, because experience hollows out the instrument that is us. Yet, somehow, the bottom of personal emptiness, if we can reach it, brings us to a common song of being.

By its very nature, this digging, this opening of depth within us, is uncomfortable—even as it opens us to the largesse of being that some call God. Yet if we can endure the emptying, alone and together, the space unearthed is often a resource that can introduce us to joy.

....

Each of us is an instrument that experience hollows out in order to have our souls release their song.

....

A Reflective Pause

○ *In your journal, tell the story of a moment when you had the privilege of looking into the canyon of another's heart. What did you see there?*

THE HARD HUMAN SPRING

▼ ▼ ▼

How do we befriend this emptiness so we can feel it as a resource, so we can know it as a gift? It helps to remember that the personal leads to the Universal. And just as personal emptiness can lead to a Universal emptiness or bareness of being, personal love—love for one person or one thing—can lead to a Universal love, a feeling of love that like air surrounds us and informs us.

Regardless of their tradition, all the saints and sages open their love in a way that's not reserved for any one person or thing. Whether the Dalai Lama or St. Francis of Assisi or Pema Chōdrōn or Mother Teresa or Martin Luther King Jr., their love is no longer dependent on any one circumstance. Though they continue to love particular people and things, their love can no longer stay in its personal container. It becomes a love of life that spills like water on everything. We all have this capacity. In the deepest moments of personal love, we touch into the experience of all love.

From that bare place of love, I've learned that each person is connected to all of existence and the edge between what is personal and Universal is very thin and very close. Yet when I focus on what's emptied out of me over what's opened in me, I confine myself to a private sense of emptiness. This keeps me from knowing the deeper sense of love and makes the journey more difficult. For this private focus creates a sense of lack, which causes me to retreat from both the depth of being and the depth of the world. However, when I can experience what's opened in me by feeling it completely, I can enter the bareness of being that informs everything, a bareness that is very close to love. In this way, my grief for my grandmother, even twenty years after her passing, can let me feel—for a moment—my place in the chorus of everyone who ever lost someone. I can feel their eternal company.

Likewise, my love for any one person or thing, when given completely, allows me the privilege of feeling everyone who ever loved or tried. When stroking my Lab's face as she sleeps after our winter walk, when seeing her yellow lashes twitch in dream, I am—for the moment—loving her in exact rhythm with everyone who ever loved a dog, going back to the prehistoric hunter leaning on the wall of his cave with his coyote-dog asleep at his feet.

The Enormity of Life

Still, knowing all this, how do we live? How do we become intimate with our sweet ache of being alive and all that it opens? Given the difficulty of the journey and the miracle of deep connection that waits inside every difficulty, we're left with the challenge of giving our complete attention and affection to this life; that is, we're asked to hold nothing back until our quiet immersion into life lets us feel the tug of the Universe. Nothing is more central or basic to knowing our aliveness.

Even so, no one can teach us how to hold nothing back. We can only compare notes. For me, holding nothing back is the quiet courage to bring all of who we are to each experience. It's less a forceful act of will and more a surrender into the current of life we're always in. Holding nothing back lets us *be who we are* and not *hide who we are*. In essence, to hold nothing back means to live *wholeheartedly*. It's the presence required to experience Oneness. In such moments, we stumble through the bottom of our pain into the enormity of life.

....

⟳ *In the deepest moments of personal love, we touch into the experience of all love.*

....

The Infinite Part of Our Heart

I believe in the infinite part of our heart. I don't question it. Can I prove this? No. I just know my experience. At different times, I've been beaten up by life, broken, and rearranged, and even when I thought I couldn't go on, something elemental couldn't be broken down or extinguished.

It seems that holding nothing back awakens the unending dynamism of being alive. And though we feel like retreating or protecting ourselves when bombarded by life, very often the deepest lesson is that we need to go the other way. We actually have to open our heart further and lean into whatever life is asking of us.

My experience tells me that in the depth of every moment runs the current of life, which we have to somehow find and follow. When a fish finds the current, it swims effortlessly with the stream. When a hawk or eagle climbs and pump its wings through clouds to find the current of air, it glides. This is the alignment of the part—the fish, the bird, the individual—with the whole—the sea, the sky, the bareness of Universal Spirit. Once we hold nothing back and lean in, we move through the turbulence or clouds to find relief in that spaciousness because we start to swim or glide with the current of life.

Holding nothing back presents itself in many different ways. We can be an introvert and hold nothing back or very expressive and hold nothing back. This has more to do with our internal opening of presence than running headlong with abandon into experience. Holding nothing back means being vulnerable and giving our complete effort. In our culture, we're misguided to think that being unreadable and aloof is a mark of sophistication, when integrity comes from being transparent and giving our all.

During my cancer journey, I was pressed between life and death and had no choice but to hold nothing back. I was surprised to discover that this was exactly what I needed to do to access my true nature and to enliven the resource of aliveness. Because leaning into what I was facing gave me access to the very pulse of life.

When we do hold things back, when we hide who we are, when we make ourselves the center of everything, we inevitably become half-hearted and live a life of hesitation. Of course, no one is exempt from being both wholehearted and half-hearted by turns. I'm not wholehearted every day or every minute. In the same way the heart pumps till I grow tired and fall asleep, I go from being wholehearted to being half-hearted. I go from wakefulness to drowsiness. But it makes a difference which I'm committed to. When devoted to a life of wholeheartedness, I can endure my lapses into half-heartedness.

Inevitably, in moments of holding nothing back, in moments of wholeheartedness—in moments when we can be who we are, when we can reach the bottom of our personal emptiness—we stumble into the sweet ache of being alive.

To hold nothing back means to live wholeheartedly. It's the presence required to experience Oneness. In such moments, we stumble through the bottom of our pain into the enormity of life.

Happiness and the Ache

We've created a culture that is emotionally out of balance. Consider the well-earned phrase in the Declaration of Independence that says we have an inalienable right to life, liberty, and the pursuit of happiness. This stands as one of the most important societal declarations in human history. The notion that freedom is a birthright is, in a secular sense, sacred. Yet, over the past 240 years, the pursuit of happiness has been taken to such an extreme that we feel entitled to happiness. This has made the dream of happiness a refuge to which we run to avoid the rest of the human journey. Frankly, happiness is overrated. I like being happy. But it's a welcome mood and not the basis of a moral code. Happiness is one of a thousand feelings and under it, and all the other human feelings, is the depth of being alive.

On the far side of my cancer experience, I began to realize that yearning for happiness and bemoaning the other thousand feelings kept me from a full and integrated experience of being human. In time, the common depth of feeling at the bottom of any mood, happy or sad, led me to the sweet ache of being alive. Sweet because the sensitivity of being alive is how we know we're here, and filled with ache because the sensitivity of being alive can't reach us when we're numb or shut down. I've come to understand the sweet ache of being alive as the tug of the Universe, when I feel connected to all life on Earth, to everything that ever was, that ever will be. When this sweet ache tugs, I feel a depth that reminds me how precious it is to be here at all.

Being human, we often run from this ache and so miss the sweetness it carries. I ask you to think about your own sweet ache of being alive. When was the last time you felt it? When was the first time you felt it? Think about your own relationship to sadness and emptiness and what the depth of being human opens in you. Now certainly, we can get stuck in the sadness or the personal emptiness or the ache. This is not without risk, but the reward for leaning in and holding nothing back is to be wholehearted which lets us glimpse eternity.

Integrity comes from being transparent and giving our all.

Seeing the Path

The great German poet Rainer Maria Rilke said:

> *I am alone but not alone enough*
> *to make every moment holy.*

It seems a natural by-product of living—the way windows film over with weather, the way leaves cover every path—that from time to time we are alone but not alone enough to meet life freshly and directly. This in-between state initiates a quiet form of courage: to keep cleaning the film of weather from our heart and to keep sweeping the leaves from our path so we can *see the path.*

This is the crossover point in each of us between our personal sense of emptiness (alone but not alone enough) and the Universal sense of emptiness (alone enough to make everything holy). When we're self-contained, that pressure makes emptiness feel lacking, but when we can be alone enough to feel all of life beyond our small container, then the pressure is dissipated and we can feel the bareness of being that's always been and the spaciousness of infinity that always is.

In actuality, we can be opened by the depth of any feeling, if we are alone enough with it to touch on what is holy. We can be opened by sadness. Or an ache. We can be stopped by frustration. Or clarity. We can be stunned by beauty. We can lose ourselves in a piece of music so completely that we come back and are different. We can be renewed by the suddenness of wonder. We can be lightened by happiness. Being embodied in life is being open to the depth of all feelings. You can't exercise without experiencing an ache, even though you feel good afterward. You can't run without sweating. In just this way, you can't love without feeling your inner muscles stretch.

So we must exercise the heart to counter the entitlements of heart we've constructed. Another example of inner entitlement is our sense in the modern world that we have a right to experience only the "nice" feelings, which is actually very debilitating because then we don't trust the full experience of being human. The truth is that whatever we feel doesn't encompass us. We move *through* what we feel and *grow* for it, even though it might be difficult. To stay open to the fullness of the human experience requires us to restore trust in the capacity of our heart to meet whatever life brings us.

❧   ❧   ❧

While this is my view, what is yours? Do you experience a vastness, an acre of silence that holds you, and a gift, an aliveness that touches you? Are they close to you now? Do you experience the thousand moods? Are you aware of your gift and your emptiness and how they inform each other?

It's not easy to break ground as a human flower. There's much to survive in order to bloom. We're each born with a gift hidden in a wound, and many years to birth it, each given a heat to carry and rough seas to calm it, each seeded with a worthiness, and love after love through which to accept it, each called to enter sorrow like an underwater cave, with the breathless chance to break surface in the same world with everything aglow. If we make it this far, we can, on any given day, marvel that clouds are clouds, and name ourselves. We can use the gift born of our wound to find an unmarked spot from which to live. If we settle there, giving our all without giving ourselves away, the heart within our heart will flower and the whole world will eat of its nectar.

A Reflective Pause

o *In your journal, describe the history of your own sweet ache of being alive. Describe a time when your experience of personal love (directed toward a person, activity, or object) led you to experience a moment of Universal love (the unattached love that exists between all things).*

In the second section, we explored the unending life of feelings that are always unfolding around us and within us. It's always been hard to know how to relate to the pain of the world, and even the wonder. But one thing has been clear since the beginning: suppressing what we feel doubles our pain, while expressing what we feel alleviates the acuteness of whatever it is that hurts. Once we feel and express what moves through us, we're allowed to begin again. There's always fear to surround us, to keep us an added distance from the joy of living. And so, there's always the work of being accurate about what we fear, so we don't keep love and beauty and truth out of reach. No matter what we face, the practice of entering life returns us to two divining sights ready to guide us—the one that keeps moving no matter what is taken away and the one that accepts everything as a blessing. Under everything that weighs us down is the sweet ache of being alive, our oldest friend, who lets us know we still are here; flickering with our inch of light, a breath away from who we were born to be.

This is a good time to ask: What do you do when you hear the cries of the world? Do you relate to them or run from them? If you let those cries in, how do they affect you? What do you do with what you feel? How active is your fear? Does your fear interfere with what you can let in? How can you make your ring of fear more accurate? How can you let life get closer? What holes have been carved in you by life and what song have they released through the flute of your being? There's so much to survive in order to bloom as a soul on Earth. What are you currently surviving and how are you blooming? What do you think is the gift hidden in your wound? How can you strengthen your heart by exercising it in the world?

The more we inquire into our personal practice, the closer we are to living the unnameable dream we are born with. The only way to release what we're born with is through the life of our hands: through caring and building, and holding and repairing. From here, we'll explore the authentic path before us, the chance to immerse ourselves, and the mysterious turning point of faith. We'll try to understand how all things are true and how we're asked to seek our way beyond all seeking; little by little, without pause, until we're born of the moment.

The Mark
of Our Hands

You can't step in the same river twice.

—Heraclitus

*Freedom is presence, not absence. Centering is the act
of bringing in, not leaving out. It is brought about
not by force but by coordination.*

—M. C. Richards

In the beginning, the gods interfered with the human journey to occupy their endless time on Earth, until we silenced them, became them. Then it took another thousand years for us to find the god within. Now it is we who interfere to occupy our limited time on Earth, we who pull apart everything we need and poke at everything that is not us, until we fall into the silence that restores what we have known forever but run from: That fame is no reason to do good, and fear, no reason to do bad. Our lungs breathe the sky in every breath. Our heart feels the sea in every feeling. The mind sees beyond itself when it stops insisting it's the thinker. These acts of being have their own continual reward. If we can animate them and let the sky, sea, and all that is beyond us help us and inform us.

There is only one conversation. Each of our lives is a sentence in its story. Loving is the art of putting down our want to be the hero. Listening is the art of threading all the stories. Once threaded, the light in all of us is opened. It is the light of all that matters. Drinking of that light brings us back to life.

TO IMMERSE OURSELVES

▼ ▼ ▼

Nothing else matters but making friends with being alive.

—DON MAREK

WHEN FACE-TO-FACE WITH life or death, the heart will ignore all history—its own and the world's—in order to make friends with being alive. I discovered this in my sixty-second year when sitting next to my mother in the emergency room, waiting for my father to arrive. She and I had not seen each other in seventeen years, deep scars between us. But when her lip began to quiver, my heart ignored our history and I rocked her gently. My heart, which had carried all our grievances like heavy beads, didn't resolve our history or keep it alive. It had been waiting for this moment, which I could never have foreseen, and simply put everything between us aside.

My father is dying. We have entered the end passage, which might come quick or last for months. He's in between worlds. At ninety-three, he had a stroke. He isn't paralyzed but very weak. Then he had the flu, which filled his lungs with fluid. He's repaired from that but can't go home until he can walk on his own. Now the question is which home he will go to.

In the hospital, I watched him be yanked back and forth between life and death, and the yanking is exhausting. I watched him in his sleep bring everything to bear on every breath. Under the oxygen mask, he looked like a boy who'd slept for ninety years in a grown man's body.

I held his hand as his shrinking chest took less and less in and let more and more out. In that moment I realized that in the first half of life, we take in more and let out less, but in the second half of life, we take in less and let more and more go.

This is when Don jumps in, adding, "Until the last breath is a final letting go." I drop my shoulders and pause in my story to my dear circle of men. We have met once a month for six years, just to keep each other company in being alive. We've opened a deep trust and are true intimates. Don is our oldest at seventy-five. He begins to talk about his own death, his own letting go, his own slowing of what he takes in. He stares off and then comes up with this, "Nothing else matters but making friends with being alive."

This happens between us. We fish in the depth that's always under our lives, and being still together, being honest together, the wisdom of the deep, from time to time, will nibble one of our lines and—there—something profound will leap on board. Like now. We look at it slap freshly between us. It seems to say, *No matter what we dream or plan or think we're doing, we're all longing to make friends with being alive—to feel completely here, with nothing in the way.* After we eat of what Don brought aboard, I continue my story, knowing it's all part of one ongoing story.

> ～ *In the first half of life, we take in more and let out less, but in the second half of life, we take in less and let more and more go.*

My father is in between worlds. Being carried on this journey with him, I've discovered another truth: that love allows us to travel between worlds without crossing over. It's my love for him, and my brother's love for him, that has us swimming alongside. Our love will let us tread water with him till the end. But the rush of the in between world is changing us.

Like the appearance of first love, or the loss of first love, or the moment we realize all thought is inherited, or the moment we remember there is nothing between us and life itself—like all seminal passages, the death of a parent, no matter the quality of the relationship, is a passage that alters our landscape. I'm feeling my way into this terrain.

Despite everything we aim for, and scheme for, and work for, the heart just waits, so infinitely patient while it labors through the days, for those few openings where it can put all history aside. I'm learning—this is when we truly live.

I finally stop talking and the five of us stare into the in-between world. George says, "It's sad" and Don says, "When I die, I'd like you to throw a party and tell some stories." We smile and accept each other.

Driving home, I recall when my father was asleep, that he looked like his mother. I held *her* hand as she dozed in her wheelchair twenty-five years ago. It was just as tender, just as much a privilege. I look into the snow and whisper, "Grandma, your boy is coming. Can you soften the way?"

The last morning with him, my father squeezed my hand, in short, repeated squeezes. When watching TV or in the movies, I've always done the same with Susan. How does this happen? I didn't know he did that. We never talked about it. What beautifully strange gestures bind us.

After leaving him that day, I wandered the hospital lobby and cried. I think we're given heartache and loss along the way to rehearse our grief, so we can have the strength when faced with the death of a loved one. I watched my mother, my brother, and my niece walk down the hall and into the elevator—three generations walking out of sight.

....

No matter what we dream or plan or think we're doing, we're all longing to make friends with being alive—to feel completely here, with nothing in the way.

....

My father will go, this year or next, and we will grieve and miss him dearly. Then, after another year or two, someone I've just met will ask why I'm so melancholy on a certain day. I'll stare off and tell his story and they'll listen for a while, then feel the press of their list of tasks. They'll try to glimpse their watch without being disrespectful.

This is yet another truth—life keeps happening, and once we've lost someone who can't be replaced, we carry this world *and* the next, with us always. And someday after my brother and I are gone, no one will know of my father and his love of the sea. While tossed in it, this is sad, but putting the history of my own sadness aside, my heart tells me it's also perfect. In time, we all become the earth on which others sit and search for meaning. It makes this inch of light we call today everything. There is nothing but to immerse ourselves in it.

Befriending life is the art we must stay devoted to, though we will never master it. Showing up, putting our history aside, listening, feeding each other, watching each other sleep, celebrating our flawed majesties and telling some stories. It would be the life of mythic gods, if it weren't so ordinary.

A Reflective Pause

○ *In your journal, explore what it means to you to make friends with being alive. In what ways are you doing this? In what ways are you resisting it? Name one small gesture you can act on today that will bring you closer to your own sense of being alive.*

○ *In conversation with a friend or loved one, tell the story of a moment when your heart put the history of a situation or relationship aside, bringing your heart more into the open.*

A TURN IN THE PATH

▶ ▶ ▶

ONE DAY, AGAINST all odds, when no one is looking, when the clock won't set or the car won't start, we realize how rare it is to be alive. In that moment, if we don't close too quickly, we meet the insurmountable mystery like salmon in the throat of all that water. It's so overwhelming that sometimes we back down and make a race of things, thinking it easier to run alongside each other than to face what's coming. But when blessed to fall beneath our plans, we might return to the is-ness we were born with.

Along the way, we hinge shut like salty clams when it's the ocean coming in on us that lets us grow. But eventually, we lose our grip and, like a clam that can no longer close its shell, we're bathed, against our will, in the brine of the deep.

So one day, while running from life—from a fear we can't control, or a pain we can't avoid, or a limitation we don't want to accept—we're stopped by the early light on the dew-heavy chrysanthemums. Though we're late and feel a need to keep going, we stop and stare at one full drop, like a hidden jewel now freely everywhere. Though something tells us to hurry up and rejoin the race, it seems the flower-drop full of light is some kind of mirror, and there's nowhere to go.

Let me tell you a story. I was in New York. It was spring. I was walking the edge of Central Park. I like to walk the edge of things. At a turn in the path, a mime was blowing bubbles. They were glistening and floating away. I was following one, when I saw a little girl, maybe five or six, across the path. She was following the same bubble. And just as the bubble burst, our eyes met. Surprise and wonder filled her face. She pointed at me, as if a friend were hiding in the bubble. She giggled. I pointed back and began to laugh. Her mother smiled and took her hand. I waved and watched her enter her life. I wonder now when the burst of a bubble became a sad thing, when I stopped finding friends along the way.

In Japan, *kintsugi* is the art of filling cracks with gold; because it's believed that the cracks and wear of life make things more beautiful, not less. As wise as this is, I believe it's not *filling* the cracks, but *entering* the cracks that *reveals* the gold. We carry what matters inside and experience waters that seed until the soul sprouts *through* our cracks into the world.

And one day, against all odds, when no one is looking, we drop what we're carrying—alarmed as it falls, afraid we will lose it, pained by how much it cost. Sometimes, whatever it is—a dream we're close to living, an injustice almost resolved, a cracked sense of worth filled with the gold of our choosing—sometimes, whatever it is breaks like an egg on the floor. And we watch the yolk of something we care for run its bright colors into everything. I don't know how to say it or explain it, but this is the journey: not the race we make of things, or the filling of cracks with gold, but how the bright colors run into everything.

> ᗡ *Sometimes we make a race of things, thinking it easier to run alongside each other than to face what's coming. But when blessed to fall beneath our plans, we might return to the is-ness we were born with.*

A Reflective Pause

○ *In your journal, describe a part of you that seems to be in mid-birth, a wing of your being that is half carved, and try to name one truth or obstacle that is chiseling you free.*

BEYOND THE OLD
PROTECTIONS

▌ ▌ ▌

You never listen—
You never ask—
You're always undoing the peace I find—
It's the only way I can get your attention—

LET ME TELL you a story. Two people meet and fall in love. When the aura settles into the realness of days, as it always does, one is afraid or not strong enough or not encouraged enough to stay an equal partner. From that moment on, the relationship is out of balance and keeps tipping to one side. Until one partner dominates the other. Or the one withholding who they are, at some crucial point, feels suffocated and pushes the other away to save themselves. If balance is restored, the relationship grows. If not, the two, no matter how much in love, will probably separate, way inside, whether they remain living together or not.

For those who leave the relationship, some never try again. Others, if blessed, find another possibility of love. And there, a deeper struggle begins. For inevitably, the same patterns will show themselves. It's a psychic law that keeps presenting us with the same initiations until we master them. So, scarily and blessedly, we get the chance to do the same things differently.

Now, this time around, one of the partners will be challenged not to repeat their role and not to reactively assume the opposite role. Having been submissive, we need to resist the urge to take over, doing to someone else what was done to us. Likewise, having been domineering, we need to resist the self-inflicted penance to serve equal time as the recipient of our domineering ways. A balanced, heartfelt respect is the house being built, not a rearrangement of the psychic furniture.

This story offers one possible pattern among many. Yet, regardless of the patterns we endure—which are at work in same-sex relationships, as well as in friendships and family dynamics—we can stumble, even against our will, into the realm of equal partnership. In this realm, being who we are and not hiding who we are is what keeps the love growing.

Having been in relationships that failed, I know that it's natural enough to retreat in new situations and put on old protections like familiar clothes. But often, it's precisely the old protections that made the original relationships fail in the first place. For old protections harden into stubborn encasements: such as judgment and withholding (on the domineering side) and acquiescence and a high need for approval (on the submissive side). Ironically, the fear of falling back into untenable situations can trigger us into old ways that will only make a repetition inevitable.

The weight of old patterns and old protections brings us back to the challenge of staying in relationship in order to break the modern myth that the only way to truly be yourself is to be *by* yourself. In contrast, the real work of love is to be who we are *everywhere*—alone, in relationship, at work, and in public. Lacking this, we slip into a self-reliant fantasy of what we think love costs, which can manifest as something like "If you have to change at all in order to know love—run."

The potent and often unwatered seed in all this is a working faith that love will protect us; a faith that says we can be loving *and* honest, loving *and* equal, loving *and* all of who we are. But we're so trained by our wounds and educated in distrust that we retract who we are in order to protect ourselves from further wounding. Understandable as this is, it's only by being who we are *and* letting those we love be who they are that we can break our fear-based patterns. Then, we wake in a sudden clearing where another story begins.

Not Hiding Who We Are

*Almost all our faults are more pardonable
than the methods we resort to, to hide them.*

—LA ROCHEFOUCAULD

*You can avoid reality, but you cannot avoid
the consequences of avoiding reality.*

—AYN RAND

Earlier, we spoke of being yourself and losing yourself, referring to our ongoing challenge to be clear enough and sound enough to stay close to all that matters, while at the same time, loosening our certainty and rigidity so we can be touched by life and grow. Here, we explore the more worldly dynamic of this struggle: being who we are and not hiding who we are in the face of others.

This is worth more conversation. We often think that holding back will keep us from suffering, keep us from being hurt. We often think that hiding who we are is the safe thing to do when being who we are is our greatest strength. Though the tides of life are rough enough to make pulling back just good sense, withholding who we are often hurts us more. When life presses, there are times when it's crucial not to put ourselves in harm's way and times when it's important to bring ourselves fully forward or some essential fiber of who we are will wither. Everyone who's ever lived has had to face this choice, more than once: when to show up and when to pull back.

Beyond any one crisis or blessing, the way our path unfolds depends on which voices we listen to. Do we honor the teachings and expectations of others or the voice of life wanting to express itself through our humanity? Do we stay loyal to the voice that's mapped our journey to a doctorate in comparative religion or to the one that admits en route to class that we love cutting hair, that we only want to cut hair? Do we, like Albert Schweitzer, give up a tenured professorship in philosophy to start a hospital in Africa before we've even gone to medical school? Or do we immerse ourselves like the Renaissance artist Lorenzo Ghiberti, who worked for twenty-five years to sculpt the bronze *Gates of Paradise* in the doors to the baptistery of the Cathedral in Florence, in which figure after figure appear to break surface after swimming in a sea of gold?

Whether we stay our course or use one course to find another, the core question is: Why do we sometimes hear our soul whisper and sometimes ignore its shout? Humbly, as the great Chilean poet Pablo Neruda says, we are many. We each contain a tribe of affections, each of us waiting on our own feisty congress that can't agree on anything. But one thing is certain; it's harder to hear your soul while hiding.

It's human to be confused and human to wait for that confusion to clear. In our confusion, hiding who we are is often predicated on a strong fear of what might happen (If I show the truth of myself, a part of me will be rejected or damaged, I will be hurt). In our clarity, we remember and re-see that being who we are is often the result of a truthful feeling that won't let us escape the moment at hand (If I muffle this feeling, if I *don't* speak my truth, a part of me will be damaged or even die).

How do we know when to pull back and when to bring ourselves forward? How do we know when to come out of hiding? No one really knows. But one truthful voicing leads to the next and the reward for speaking our truth, even when alone, is that such authentic speech clears an inner path by which we can discover and build our "hospital in Africa" or our "Gates of Paradise." Over time, being who we are leads us to the one thing we can love completely enough to work on it for years.

Not hiding who we are is a personal spiritual practice grounded in the everyday choices a human life will inevitably encounter. All we can do is try, one choice at a time, one voicing at a time. All we can do is take the risk to come out in the open and listen to the wind.

···

    ᔛ *The real work of love is to be who we are everywhere—alone, in relationship, at work, and in public.*

···

A Reflective Pause

○ *In your journal, describe how guarded you are with others. How did you learn this? How does this help you? How does it harm you? When is it safe for you to relax your guard? How can you visit that safety more often?*

STAYING IN RELATIONSHIP

❧ ❧ ❧

Staying in relationship is the challenge of our age,
the work of our times.

PROFOUNDLY, THE MORE we go through together, the closer we are. The more we can hold each other without judgment, the stronger our bond. The more we can accept each other's love and pain, the more we see of the Universal Fabric. To feel close, we need to uphold a vow to see each other through. Though we seldom think of it, the same vow is needed to stay close to life.

Our understanding of relationship grows out of our sense of how things are connected. Often, in our effort to understand, we pull life apart and break things down, though it's essential to never forget that life doesn't appear in dismantled segments, but as a whole. We learn about the chemical elements by studying the periodic table, in which 118 elements, like calcium and magnesium, have been isolated and detailed in clean, small boxes. But these elements are integrated in life; found together in mountains, in rivers, in plates deep in the Earth. We learn about the laws of physics and the principles of aerodynamics, one concept at a time. But in a single sweep of day, birds chase light in windblown trees without a thought. We learn about the neuroscience of the brain and the psychology of the mind. But in a sudden sweep of circumstance, love and courage appear in inexplicable moments of wholeheartedness.

To *feel* Oneness, we have to stay in relationship. In trying to *understand* Oneness, we often suffer our want to over-analyze. And while this ability to dismantle things to understand them has given us incredible knowledge throughout the centuries, the disadvantage of breaking things down comes when we become so enchanted with the parts that we forget to reassemble them into their wholeness.

Consider how we all know the shapes of the fifty states. We can even outline Texas or Florida in a minute on a napkin. But something is lost when we forget that those boundaries are man-made, when we forget the majesty of the one complete and magnificent continent that exists under our delineations.

To understand how things go together is not the same as being in relationship with those things. In school, we can study the life of the soul and the life of the world, as if they have nothing to do with each other. But it's bringing what we learn back into the wholeness of our journey that keeps us in relationship to what matters.

Eventually, being in the world requires the integration and embodiment of our being and doing, so who we are can author care in the world. Along the way, we often live a split existence—practical doer by day, spiritual seeker by night. Understandably, the weariness of existence can make us keep these destinies separate. But as two lungs enable us to breathe, as two eyes enable us to see, we must bring our inwardness and our work in the world together, the way birds must use both wings in order to fly.

When the practical and the spiritual are kept separate, we become suspect of what we know to be true, as if our larger understanding of things has no value in guiding us through life. Nothing could be farther from the truth. When I trust my sense of aliveness, I'm led to my work in the world. When I realize how rare it is to be alive, the fact that all-we-have-is-now leads me to want to know you. When I face my suffering, my vulnerability opens me to the depths of a nameless compassion for everything.

The Unity of Life

Throughout history, people have strayed and returned to the sacred Wholeness of Life. Most early cultures held the Unity of Life as an unshakable mystery to be honored. In our age, our ability to perceive wholeness has been muffled, though the Unity of Life remains intact and complete. When we can't see the moon, it doesn't mean the moon has ceased to exist, but that we've turned away from it. When our sight dims because we squint, it doesn't mean the light of the world has disappeared, but that we've narrowed our view.

Over the last two hundred years, we're accountable for how we've advanced our minds without advancing our hearts, a phenomenon that has diminished our comprehension of the Whole. Even our language has been enervated of its unity. The word *intellect* originally meant the integrated faculty of both mind and heart. The word *daimon* originally referred to both a guiding presence and a challenging one (both inspiring), before it was split into *angel* and *demon*. And the word *genius* originally meant an attendant spirit (which everyone has) before it denoted a particular brilliance of mind or skill, reserved for the exceptional.

Yet, despite our want to break things down, the Unity of Life remains the foundation of all relationship. In the Yoruba language, spoken in West Africa, there is one word for being and doing, *iwa (ee-wah)*. The word means all that informs your existence. Beauty is part of your *iwa*, and relationship and community are part of your *iwa*. If I were to say, "I know your *iwa*," it means I know your history, your dreams, your strengths, and your frailties. It means I know what waits under your words and between your hesitations. It means I know the unity of your life. *Iwa* refers to an all-embracing way of relationship. *Iwa* evokes a quality of care that connects us to everything.

Isn't this the aim of all relationship: to know each other intimately and comprehensively, to know each other's history and dreams, to know each other's strengths and frailties? And given how we're tossed about so harshly by the storms of experience, our challenge is to see our way through so we can know the unity of our own life, of those we love, and of life itself. It remains a mythic passage: that no matter the size of the storm, our work is to stay in relationship to the stream of life, the way a tired fish thrown from a waterfall relies on the current to receive it and carry it along.

> ◡ *The disadvantage of breaking things down comes when we become so enchanted with the parts that we forget to reassemble them into their wholeness.*

The Spot of Honest Living

Under all our burden and joy, there is a safe, interior place that feels like home. This safe place is the spot of honest being that we arrive at by being who we are. It's here that we're informed by the very aliveness of things, when we risk enough to let that aliveness touch us.

Sometimes, we're called to stay in relationship with that fundamental aliveness when the situation we find ourselves in doesn't honor or support who we are. Sometimes, when the covenants of a personal connection harden or erode, we're required to stay in relationship to the Source that feeds our soul. This requires repotting ourselves.

Many have left me along the way and I have left many. Most of those journeys needed to end, though many were needlessly clumsy and hurtful in how they ended. Sometimes, it's too painful to simply say: *I don't know why, but I've grown in another direction. I don't know why, but who I've become has frightened you and you've pushed me away. I don't know why but I still love you though I have to move on.* To reveal our vulnerability in this way is staying in relationship to truth.

Being human, we forget and drift from what is true, or out of fear and pain, run from it. Yet underneath our coming and going, our awakened kinship with others depends on our return to the common depth that gives us life. Whether we leave or stay, we're always asked to stay in relationship to something fundamentally true.

It's hard work to be who we are *and* stay in relationship—to ourselves, each other, the world, nature, God. It's always easier to fall in love than to stay in love, easier to be intoxicated with the search for truth than to build our home on a foundation of truth. The real work of relationship begins with the rigor of heart by which we stop retreating from life, and the rigor of mind by which we stop giving ourselves away for the sake of belonging. These are not easy tasks.

Yet one of the most intimate things we can do is to ask an honest question and one of the most intimate ways we can answer is to admit we don't know. Then a tender and resilient journey begins—our friendship with the unknown.

How I long for these moments of complete relationship—*to anything*. This is why we love.

....

 As two lungs enable us to breathe, as two eyes enable us to see, we must bring our inwardness and our work in the world together.

....

A Reflective Pause

○ *In your journal, describe a time you were left and how that changed you. Describe a time when you did the leaving and how that changed you. Where do these lessons live in you?*

○ *This is a meditation. Sit quietly, when you can. Start with where you are and slowly allow your heart to sense what else might be unfolding at the same moment everywhere else on Earth. How does letting in the presence of other life affect you?*

IF JUST FOR A MOMENT

❧ ❧ ❧

IN EVERY AGE, we devote our lives to serious ambition with little chance of achieving acclaim. Why do we this? Of course, we believe that we will be the exception, that we will find our place in history. So we press on until, if blessed, we wake and ask: What is all this striving for? Even then, if we endure the harsh blessing that has us put down this striving, what makes us continue with the work? Perhaps the same impetus that makes a falling star streak its light across the face of eternity. Without ambition or intent, a star gives its all to part the darkness briefly. In complete irony, without ever knowing, its entire life keeps casting its light long after it's gone. Giving its all is in the star's nature, as being fully present is in our human nature. When we can give our full, anonymous presence to what we touch, life-force glows through us and the work is fulfilling by itself. This is what it means to be immortal: not to live forever, not be known forever, but to live completely, if just for a moment.

Being Seen and Heard

At birth, we have no sense of being seen or unseen, no awareness of being heard or unheard. But somewhere in our development, the longing for recognition, celebrity, and fame starts to define us. Eventually, our deep need for validation can become relentless, hardening into a want to be permanently remembered, which undermines our capacity to face the dynamic impermanence of life and the lift and drop of eternity.

Beautifully, we're born unknown and filled with curiosity, a good place to start. Once we're given love or have it withheld, we strive to be seen and accepted. In time, we learn a trade or craft, whatever it might be. If blessed, the work itself fuels us. But often, the work stops being enough and our need for acceptance and our need for fulfilling work get entangled. Soon, we find ourselves dreaming of some form of permanent acceptance, which we fantasize as our place in history. Now we feel compelled to build something that will last or do something that has never been done. We secretly hope our name and reputation will last forever. All the while, the wisdom of experience wears our pride down till there is less between us and life. All the while, the constant abrasions of life humble us till we accept that we and all we do will *not* last. Many of us live in the twist of these crosscurrents. Yet, if humbled into honest living, our efforts can open us to the timeless forces that *do* last. This can shift our quest for worth, from inscribing ourselves in history to releasing what is eternal by living a life of care.

Though this journey unfolds for everyone, it is pronounced for artists of all kinds. Revealing the power of the nameless forces that last is often the impetus and terrain of those called to create. And yet, most artists suffer a great loneliness for being nameless. To be clear, artists have no special gift for negotiating these crosscurrents of time. The struggle we all face is simply more starkly in relief in the journey of the creative.

Countless writers, musicians, painters, and sculptors have toiled for years, even lifetimes, in total anonymity. Some are found and celebrated after their death. Like Paul Cézanne who was ignored during his life, only to have fifty-six of his paintings shown in Paris the year after he died. Like the great, humble poet of the Tang dynasty, Tu Fu, unknown in his time, whose last poem includes these lines:

> *The moon bobs in the Great River's flow.*
> *Fame: is it ever to be won in literature?*
> *Office: I should give up, old and sick.*

Floating, floating, what am I like?
Between earth and sky, a gull alone.

And poignantly, others, as remarkable as any master you can name, are buried in the sediment of history without a trace.

In the Great River's Flow

We are all part of this cycle, seeds of life that won't last, carried in the Great River's flow which will last. Artist or not, each of us floats like a gull between earth and sky. While some of us might be recognized and accepted by others during our lives, others will be discovered in a hundred years. Many of us won't be seen or accepted at all. None of which has anything to do with the value of the work we do while here. In three hundred years, most of us will be forgotten. In a thousand years, the witness of history itself may vanish, as the moon continues to bob in the Great River's flow, and the beautiful, mysterious cycle will start again.

Seen from the insecurity of a single life, the abrasion of time can be discouraging, even devastating. But from the perspective of the Unified Life that holds us all, the power of erosion, including human erosion, is mysterious and beautiful. When we can slip through the rise and crash of acclaim and anonymity, a deeper, more resilient set of truths appears, as close to us as our fear of disappointment. So, given that we carve out names for ourselves which will be worn away, how are we to understand this, beyond the plus and minus of tangible achievement? Given all this, how are we to regard the effort we make in the time we have?

The Press of the World

My own experience with striving and waking, with acclaim and anonymity, is very telling. Like any young writer, I wanted so badly to be published and recognized. I began writing in earnest when I was eighteen. It took nineteen years to place my first book. During those years, I struggled, like most young artists, to keep my flame of worth from going out. I constantly felt the tension between trusting my own direct knowing of life and succumbing to the tenuous vacuum of not being seen and heard. I kept trying to forge a proper understanding of my own authority of being, relying on an inborn sense that the essence of who we are is independent of the web of relationship we need.

I worked hard during my late twenties, getting my doctorate and finishing my first manuscripts, steadfast in my vision when immersed in the seeing, insecure when surfacing into my want to be seen. Then in my mid-thirties, I was taken under by cancer, and life and death came so much closer. I was bobbing in the Great River's flow. It was then, in February 1988, in a punctuation of suffering and grace, that I received word, while in the hospital recovering from rib surgery, that my first two books were accepted. After all my yearning, I was happy, but not overjoyed. It wasn't quite as I imagined or as important. Waking up and swallowing orange juice was suddenly the poem of life. Surviving changed everything. For sure, being seen and heard and understood continues to be a great gift when it happens, but almost dying made it no longer essential.

Blessed to still be here, I became a perpetual student, challenged to believe in everything. And so, for twenty-five years I've devoted myself to the common center of all spiritual paths and to listening to that nameless center where we are all connected, the life-giving center revealed to each of us through great love and great suffering. During these years, I carried a tense, but growing balance of solitude and community, as my work slowly became more and more known.

But it was being seen and heard by Oprah Winfrey in 2010 that brought my work more fully into the public eye. With Oprah's heartfelt support, *The Book of Awakening* made its way around the world and has now been translated into more than twenty languages. A small level of fame has gathered. And this has been a teacher as well.

To begin with, as good as it feels to be well received and as difficult as it is not to be received at all, neither has anything to do with the eyes beneath our eyes that we are born with. Neither acceptance nor rejection has anything to do with our direct experience of aliveness and the truth we wrestle from that experience first-hand. This doesn't mean that being centered or true makes us immune to the pain of rejection or the insecurity that comes from indifference.

I'm grateful for my entire journey: the good, the bad, and the mysterious fragility that uncovers our deepest resilience. All parts of living are necessary. For me, the early struggle of being unknown opened the gift of anonymity and the spaciousness it provides, though the pain of feeling invisible had to be endured. Now, as I learn the push and pull of being known, the press of the world takes up more space, and I have to work harder to open the spaciousness that being demands for truth to appear.

The image I've come to is this. If you find yourself walking headlong into a strong wind, you need to lean forward to offset the wind, and lower your center of gravity to ensure solid footing. This is the stance that helps us endure the invisible winds of being unknown. But if you're blessed to experience a shift of winds, you may find yourself walking with the wind at your back. Now you need to lean back to offset the wind helping you along, though you still need to lower your center of gravity to ensure solid footing. This is the stance that helps us endure the louder winds of being known and the expectations that come with it.

The winds change direction again and again, for no reason and with sudden force. And whether we're struggling with the vacuum of anonymity or with the press of the world—within a circle of friends or a certain profession or on some corner of the world stage—what's most important is maintaining our center of gravity, so we can find sure footing.

In truth, the degree of recognition or invisibility doesn't matter. It doesn't matter if you're famous the world over or revered in your family. It doesn't matter if you're an obscure genius or a bright child ignored at home. The dynamics remain the same and each of us is challenged to navigate them, in order to stay close to what matters. Under all our very specific and private desires, what continues to rise is our unending want to find the center of our aliveness.

....

Honest living can shift our quest for worth, from inscribing ourselves in history to releasing what is eternal by living a life of care.

....

The Truth of Our Common Life

I'm continually humbled by the kind souls who seek me out to say that this or that in one of my books has been helpful in their journey. I've come to see that under all these kind remarks, genuine as they are, is the soft and enduring truth that moments of being completely who we are let others see their own possibility. When fully here and fully me, I'm able to open the truth of our common life. And my job, when it's my turn to be awake, is to give these kindnesses back. Whatever light you see in me is only mirroring the light you carry that you are close to knowing. I'm coming to understand that this is the proper role of fame: to undo itself in praise of the worth of everyone who needs to see their possibility in others, before finding it in themselves.

I confess: I've spent a good deal of my life being who I am in the face of *not* being seen. Now, through a cascade of unexpected blessings, I'm challenged to be who I am in the face of *being* seen and *mis*-seen and *half*-seen. This is the inevitable work of living in the open, the work of being who we are while in relationship. Known or not, our constant effort is to break the masks and walls our habits of heart create. If alone in the darkness of our own doubts and wounds, we need to break the mask of insignificance that keeps us from feeling the sun on our face. If known for our strength of character or voice, in our hometown or across the globe, we need to break the oversized mask of public goodness that keeps us from feeling the life around us.

I've always been an anonymous servant of the mystery, even as a child. This is the covenant I keep as a spirit trying to live in the world. The irony is that this is why my work is known. Over the years, the call and press of life has affirmed for me that poetry is the unexpected utterance of the soul. The words are just the trail of that inquiry. Like many others, I began by wanting to write great poems. Then life humbled me into the need to discover true poems that would help me live. Now I want to *be* the poem, to stay as close to life as possible—if just for a moment.

Our struggle with how to be here never ends. But no matter the difficulty or press in our lives, we can always return to the freshness of direct living we are born with: the experience of full presence without a need to name it or position it. When feeling less than, we can immerse ourselves with honest effort one more time, until the work before us re-emerges as fulfilling by itself.

....

~ *Under all our very specific and private desires, what continues to rise is our unending want to find the center of our aliveness.*

....

A Reflective Pause

○ *In your journal, describe an earlier self and how you have evolved from that into the self you are right now. After a time, discuss this with a friend or loved one.*

THE MOST DIFFICULT
TWO INCHES ON EARTH

▼ ▼ ▼

WHEN LEARNING TO swim, it's natural enough to resist our initial sinking in the water. We seem to be going down. And the more we struggle at the surface, the stronger the pull seems, wanting to take us under. But when we can relax into the water, we settle a few inches into the miracle of buoyancy. Amazingly, the unseen depths hold us up.

This moment reveals the essence of faith. Forget all the definitions and debates. It's as simple and difficult as swimming in the ocean of experience and learning how to trust the unseen depths to hold us up. We don't have to name that depth or send messages to it or pray in the dark to it. We simply have to surrender enough to feel its buoyancy. Yet these are the most difficult two inches to travel on earth.

I experienced this literally once when I was swept out to sea. I wasn't paying attention but the tide was going out and I was mesmerized by my glide through the waves. As I tired, I realized how far I was from shore. Then I panicked. Afraid of drowning, I kept fighting being brought below the surface. Yet this resistance only made my struggle worse. Only when I exhausted myself did I surrender; enough to feel the buoyancy of the ocean cradle me in its ancient hammock. Finally, I was able to rest and slowly make my way across the current, back to shore.

Since this experience, I've seen that our challenge is to surrender into the life we're given. Such surrender opens us to the inexplicable buoyancy that holds up all existence. In this, we need the inherent intuition of a duck. And through duck eyes, I can now see that failure, loneliness, and suffering are the forms of drowning which the modern world loves to fear. We spend so much of our lives fighting failure, loneliness, and suffering that we miss the mysterious truth that, if we could only give in to gravity just a little, we would cross our inner boundary of fear and discover the endless world of being, buoyant enough to carry us through.

Consider Rilke's poem "The Swan":

> *This clumsy living that moves lumbering*
> *as if in ropes through what is not done*
> *reminds us of the awkward way the swan walks.*
>
> *And to die, which is a letting go*
> *of the ground we stand on and cling to every day,*
> *is like the swan when he nervously lets himself down*
>
> *into the water, which receives him gaily*
> *and which flows joyfully under*
> *and after him, wave after wave,*
> *while the swan, unmoving and marvelously calm,*
> *is pleased to be carried, each minute more fully grown,*
> *more like a king, composed, farther and farther on.*

For all I've read of Rilke—and I have wandered through his work as through a familiar garden—I had not met "The Swan" until recently. It seems particularly useful here. Isn't this sense of experiential faith released whenever we can let ourselves sink ever so slightly into that mysterious water we call life? What waits for us if we can die to whatever voice of inadequacy is pressing on us in our moments of panic? What happens if we can die to our ambition, or die to our willfulness, or die to our need to measure up, or die to our need to keep score, or die to the dominance of our fear, or die to the machine of our doing? When courageous enough to let go at this level, we're carried by the imperceptible tide that runs clear and deep beneath and around us. And still, these are the most difficult two inches to travel on Earth.

All the traditions speak in different ways about our fear of drowning in the demands of living and about this buoyancy that waits just below our fears. All speak of a need to surrender into experience until life itself lifts us up. All suggest that staying awake is synonymous with faith. Not blind faith, but an *open faith* in the current of life that precedes, encompasses, and outlasts us; the kind of open faith that allows us to be rejuvenated by awe and wonder. As the theologian Paul Tillich describes it, "Faith is the state of being ultimately concerned. [It] is the most centered act of the human mind." It is our abiding and unrestrained concern that keeps us fully alive and connected to life itself. Still, it is a struggle at best and we often lose our way.

The medieval Sufi master Muhammad b. Fadl Balkhi (854–931) was a terse teacher who offered small pills of wisdom, seldom lingering to explain or dilute their meaning. He spoke directly about what puts us to sleep: "One may lose faith in four ways: not acting on what one knows, acting on what one does not know, not seeking to learn what one does not know, and keeping others from learning." Often, in clinging too hard to what is familiar, we lose our wakefulness. So wherever you are, as you read this, whatever your life situation, consider your relationship with what you know and what you don't know. Consider the condition of your ultimate concern.

In order to remediate the ways we lose concern, the Jews of Eastern Europe encouraged a daily taste of holiness. They believed that living keenly, openly, and authentically enlivened what they called the *neshama yetherah*, the additional soul, the soul below which restores the soul in the world.

In truth, everyone alive struggles with how to stay awake. While there are no answers except to stay concerned, there are small clues. One comes from Goethe who says, "Every object well contemplated creates an organ within us." What a startling shift. He suggests what sages and lovers have known forever; that beholding anything with ultimate care makes it come alive *within* us. Put simply, *embracing the world animates our being.*

The courage comes in letting go of our understandable resistance to being drawn into the depth of things. Yet if we are to fully live—that is, to let our love outlast our fear—we must die to everything that would keep us from animating our ultimate concern. And still, we must not be harsh with ourselves, for these are surely the most difficult two inches to travel on Earth.

Our Depth of Practice

For me, the purpose of faith is to be buoyant in the ocean of all there is. I'm no longer interested in faith-in-what, but simply faith in everything larger than me. I'd rather experience this than name it. And being human, there are always cloudlike veils that drop between us and our direct living. Sometimes, we have to part the veil with the clarity of our mind. Sometimes, we have to let the rush of our heart billow the veil away. Sometimes, we need the love of others to pull the veil aside. Parting the veil is a working act of faith; an act of ultimate concern; an act of bringing all of who we are to bear on opening ourselves up when we're shut down. For when we're shut down, we tend to sink. When we're open, we tend to meet that buoyancy and rise.

Given all this, how can we meet our additional soul, the soul below which holds up the soul in the world? When not fighting the pull of the deep, I've learned from hours of swimming that it's easier to move just below the surface. But we can't live in the deep alone. Nor can we stay on the surface only. Too close to the surface and we are prey to the constant turbulence. So we must find our own *depth of practice*, just below the surface where we can glide close to the truth of things.

In daily life, depth of practice means that we try to make decisions based on our love of life rather than out of our fear of death. In daily life, depth of practice means trusting that life will hold us up. In daily life, how close we stay to our aliveness depends on what we do when we feel broken.

Beholding anything with ultimate care makes it come alive within us. Embracing the world animates our being.

What Do We Do When We're Broken?

Though no one likes it, each of us will find ourselves broken at some point in our journey. When we find ourselves there, what do we do? I've been broken many times—through illness, through the loss of a job, through the derailment of a dream, and most recently through the death of my father. For all of this, I can offer a mysterious truth that life has given me: that we are stronger, gentler, more resilient, and more beautiful than we imagine, and that the resource we call life is never far away.

I know this because every time my heart has been shattered, I have felt certain it could never be put back together. And every time, without exception, not only has my heart mended but it has become larger, stronger, and more loving for the breaking. The mysterious and unfailing journey of how this happens is the ordinary art of staying awake. It involves the deep and continuous act of being present in all ways in all directions. Being present in this way is the practice of holding nothing back.

Feeling broken can be debilitating and hard to move through. A few steps we can take to refind our wholeness include the effort to:

1. *Accept the weather.* Realizing that we will be broken is not a pessimistic view, but a wholehearted acceptance of the unfolding nature of life. Being tossed and turned by circumstance is part of life's weather. You may trip on obstacles, hurting someone you love. You may find yourself alone, without the person you thought you'd spend the rest of your life with. You may become ill.

   How do we meet these challenges? For me, I try to remember when breaking that every crack is an opening. No matter how harsh the experience, something is always opened in us, and what is opened is always more important than what breaks us. We might experience cruelty or unfairness or indifference or the brutality of chance—all of which are difficult and life changing. And while cruelty and injustice are never excusable and need to be rectified, we must not get stuck in our list of legitimate grievances, or we will never be able to enter the depth that becomes available for being opened.

2. *Lean into the tender place.* Very quickly, when broken open, we're exhausted of our differences. When broken open, we don't try so hard to keep up needless boundaries and are forced to realize we are the same. Things we thought that mattered don't, and this allows us to touch and be touched more directly. I know once my heart is opened, I can find the courage to lean into the place where I am broken, to lean into that opening—letting life rush in and touch me there, even though that place is incredibly tender. I've discovered over time that the rush of life into the tender place where we are broken is the beginning of resilience.

3. *Ask yourself: What kind of part am I in what kind of Whole?* Beyond all our good intentions and hard work, not getting what we want and working with what we're given can lead us to realize and inhabit a larger geography of being. Despite our resistance, we are led to accept that we are a living part in a greater living Whole. Now we can begin a deeper part of our journey by asking, "What is my relationship to the Living Whole?"

    It's hard to keep this deeper understanding of life in view when in pain, when in fear, when confused and worried. But this is the nature of being broken. It limits our view, for the moment. One of the purposes of love is to help each other *not* stay limited in our view of life. Like a surfer who, when catching a wave, is for the moment at one with the swell of the ocean, when helping each other move beyond our limited view of life, we are for the moment at one with the Unity of Life, which lifts us back into a feeling of health.

4. *Look beyond the broken.* To be broken is no reason to see all things as broken. This notion has been a profound teacher for me in meeting difficulty. Though it's understandable to

be consumed with what we're going through, it's essential to remember that all of life is not where we are. In fact, this is when we need the aliveness and vitality of everything that is *not us*. When closed, we need to open. When fearful, we need to trust again. When feeling lost, we need to remember that we are in the stream of life, which is never lost.

I've come to believe that we were all broken from the same nameless heart, and every living thing wakes with a piece of that original heart aching its way into being. Along the way, we are broken open like seeds that bear fruit, so we can meet each other and be touched by each other; so we can remember and inhabit the one precious life we're given. And when broken of all that gets in the way, we suddenly know each other below our strangeness. This is why when we fall, we lift each other, or when in pain, we hold each other, why when sudden with joy, we dance together. Life is the many pieces of that great heart loving itself back together.

....

〜 *In daily life, depth of practice means that we try to make decisions based on our love of life rather than out of our fear of death.*

....

A Reflective Pause

○ *In conversation with a friend or loved one, describe a veil that you experience between you and life. What do you imagine would happen if you could part the veil? What might part this veil for you: your mind, your heart, the presence of a loved one? What small thing can you do today to begin this effort?*

SHINY THINGS FROM THE DEEP

▸ ▸ ▸

Like a diver who out of breath brings up all the shiny things he can from the deep, I return with a handful of insights I'm trying to understand. I consider them anonymous teachers.

We All Begin with a Trust in Being Here

Then things fall and break, or something's taken away, then something unpredictable shows its face, and now our time on Earth truly begins. Now we're asked to deepen or distrust what we know or what we don't, to enter years of trying love and losing love, of building dreams and losing dreams—all to regain the trust we were born with. From the math of ordinary time, it seems we falter repeatedly, always off course. But this is how life uncovers us. It's a beautiful journey that no preparation can avoid, that no learning can imitate. We begin with an irreplaceable trust and are sent into the amazing race the world has to offer, thinking there are more valuable destinations we can't live without, only to land where we began. We keep running till we exhaust our plans, and ourselves, falling into place, into the handless hands of the beginning, where the ease of all that light quietly thaws our tightness and distrust.

It's the Exchange That Brings Us Alive

My whole life I've waited for the Oneness to show its glow, to be in its aliveness, to bear witness to it, to love it out of others. The only true family I know are those who have loved it out of me. This is our deepest challenge: to love the Oneness and aliveness out of each other, despite the resistance we face and create.

Following the glow in everything while being deterred by my own resistance, I've lived countless journeys of doing this and that in order to be loved. Only to learn that love comes to us and from us like air— nothing to be given and nothing to be taken away. It's the exchange that brings us alive. I live to give my all to that exchange.

So imagine the vast world in each of us, imagine it in everyone whether acknowledged or not, or explored or not. Imagine all the fisher-men repairing their nets by the water, whether the farmer a thousand miles away ever visits the sea. It's not possible to comprehend all that humanity, but in feeling where my own depth touches the Oneness, I can feel the breath of everyone living. And that breath sustains me. It gives me strength beyond what I have, strength to *be* vulnerable, to *stay* vulnerable, to have the face of my heart kiss the face of your heart.

....

     We begin with an irreplaceable trust and are sent into the amazing race the world has to offer, thinking there are more valuable destinations we can't live without, only to land where we began.

....

We Float Through Many Worlds

The trick: how to be alive to everything we touch without becoming everything we touch. I don't want to be polished by you or judged by you. I want to feel the tug of your roots, not what's packed you in. I want to feel your light. I want to feel the one certainty on which your life stands, so I can have the courage to show you mine. There's such an inexpressible geography within, it's amazing we can share anything. Yet if we don't try, what lives forever in each of us will fall away from the world into a bottomless dormancy, out of reach. So essential is relation-ship.

We Are Carried

The aliveness of life is like a clear sea we move through. It gathers and glows, crests and crashes. We call its waves, days. With no awareness of this, we ascribe too much authority to our own actions. Like thinking fish can resist the tide that carries them, or thinking birds glide without the wind. We go here and there, with this in mind and that, but everywhere we are carried by the aliveness.

For me, individuation has been a journey of getting closer to this aliveness, a feeling process by which the little boy in this man's body has slowly become a hand fitting a glove. For too many years, I feared being abandoned or betrayed and the things I did along the way to guard against this, well, at times I betrayed and abandoned myself. The beauty of seeing this from the perspective of all life and not just my life is that the unfolding we all meet is revealed as a series of initiations and not wrong turns. Everything we go through opens us to a greater sense of being, if we don't linger in the ruins.

I only discovered my gift when I stopped trying to fit some need in the world, and I've begun to discover my strength once getting out of my own way. Waking in this body that has carried me all these years, I can finally say, I want nothing. Only this day, and tomorrow if it's there. To close my eyes, so I can see the sun within, and to open them to sun without. To open my long history to the spot where there is no history, opening my mind to the waterfall of aliveness that allows me to perceive. With all this, there is no room for want.

Yet none of this prevents the grit and humanness of our journey. I open up, I close down. The smaller my view, the more annoying things are. The more intense my goals, the more I run into bad timing. The larger my view, the more things go together. The more I become aware of, the less language there is. The more I hear, the more silence there is. The more I feel for others, the more they live in my heart. This is how I feed their better selves. Doing all this feeds *my* better self. In truth, everything is one orchestration. Unexpected events come in like cymbals, right on cue. Meeting you is the opening of the next movement.

....

◠ *This is our deepest challenge: to love the Oneness and aliveness out of each other, despite the resistance we face and create.*

....

Strong Currents

While fish born near a strong turn of current learn to swim and compensate for the water coming at them, this is not the nature of all water. This is a profound teacher. For everyone is born into a turn of current, into a particular sweep of life's circumstance. It may be kind or harsh or tiding back on itself. It may be chilly or suffocating. Whatever it is, it is *not* the nature of *all* life. Part of our initiation into being fully here is the process of understanding the current we're born into *and* the nature and variety of *all* currents. Too often, in our pain and patterning, we project the turn of our initial current onto the world and miss what life has in store for us.

A threshold of individuation and spiritual maturity is crossed when we begin to look beyond the *players* in our entry to the world and understand the *geology* of our entry to the world. For me, the harsh but loving player was my mother, but the ground I come from is beneath her and of my own making. I'm just now, at the age of sixty-two, coming to understand this. A slow learner? For sure. It's the only way we internalize what we learn. Humbly, my experience is one more testament to the unhurried journey life holds for us, if we can keep moving through the sweet and painful openings we're given.

We're asked along the way to do *both*: to psychologically understand the *people* we come from, to hold them and us accountable for how we land and what we do with how we land, *and* to spiritually understand the *ground* we come from, so we can eventually be free from our patterning, free enough to regain a fresh and direct tasting of life. I'm still learning.

The Testing Ground of Courage

Of course, the patterning continues. And there are times the fires meant to keep us warm flare out of control and burn us. In our darkened tenderness, these fires can burn long after they go out. Worse is the fear of fire and dark places that follows, for no one can live without fire and no one can grow without moving through dark places. Perhaps this is the testing ground of courage, our initiation into wholeness: that we must summon who we are to move through what has burned us, so we might reclaim the full use of our heart. But how to do this in a daily way—to discern what's too hot to hold and hot only in memory? It seems so simple: we open the door and walk into the day, only to stumble through a thousand choices between the car and the store that determine how alive we will be.

Everything we go through opens us to a greater sense of being, if we don't linger in the ruins.

Through the Pinhole of My Fear

Who will we be once we truly listen to each other? What will shine through when we prune our expectations and judgments? Who will I be once I truly listen to myself, once I cut back my stubborn growth, which chokes my view of the sky? This is not a pruning to be done with shears, but by letting the warmth of our heart do its work. I want to put my oldest patterns down, so my heart won't have to work so hard. I think I can fulfill my trust in Oneness, if I can move the center of my being through the pinhole of my fear. I'm not sure what this means, other than to let my soul, the carrier of my being, emanate in all directions like the sun, till it softens and transforms the small, tight circle that is my fear. It doesn't matter what I have attached that fear to or what I like to blame it on. Only the light of my being, found in the trust we are born with, the trust we return to—only that *is-ness allowed to glow* can break the pinhole trance that fear holds on me, on you. For fear keeps its control by blocking everything else out, by making us believe that the world is limited to the canopy of our fear. Being washes that falseness away.

Ease of Heart

These are the shiny things I've pulled from the deep: *We all begin with a trust in being here. It's the exchange that brings us alive. We float through many worlds. We are carried by this aliveness. Whatever our turn of current, it is not the nature of all water. Moving through what has burned us is the testing ground of courage. I can fulfill my trust in Oneness, if I can move the center of my being through the pinhole of my fear.*

By listening and waiting, I've stayed in conversation with them. By listening and waiting, I've learned that patience is the ease of heart that can heal everything. So the question is: how to *be* the patience, not just watching as time goes by, but how to *inhabit* patience? How to *inhabit* this ease of heart? What does this look like? What does it mean to bring my full attention to *not trying*, to let being expand over all my agitation? With this kind of patience, it might be possible to have the sea of being erode the shore of fear.

Oh, I'm so grateful to still be a work in progress. Isn't this the revelation we all forget in the busyness of living: that the Universe itself is still a work in progress, like everything unsaid between us, like nature rearranging its face for the millionth time. I'm grateful to be in such eternal company.

A Reflective Pause

○ *In your journal, tell the story of a moment you fell into that was too deep for words. In what language other than words did this moment speak to you? How would you describe the importance of what lives beneath words to a child?*

ALL THINGS ARE TRUE

▼ ▼ ▼

W HEN I FINALLY tire of pursuing what I think is important, a
paradox keeps whispering to me. It's always there like a breeze
that shows me the underside of leaves. What I keep hearing is that *all
things are true*, which doesn't mean that all things are just or fair or even
acceptable. But all things *contain* truth: who we are and who we're not,
what we want and what we're given, how we're loved and how we're
hurt, what we know and all we don't. All things are true and only an
open heart can make sense of how they go together.

When we keep choosing between right and wrong, we spend our
energy sorting life rather than living it. And the winnowing of everything that's not like us makes our sense of truth too small. Somewhere
along the way, we're taught to uphold only what we think is right as a
desired state of perfection, as if a world that is only like us will protect
us from the hardships of living. But the quest for perfection only narrows to an uninhabitable point while the Wholeness of Life widens to
include everything. Ultimately, which is a healthier home: the loneliness
of our attempts at perfection or the messy company of Wholeness?
Experience keeps leading me to an all-encompassing sense of truth,
filled with resources that rush in from life in every direction. Only from
the Wholeness of Life can we see how to navigate this mystery with all
its hardships and blessings.

Our Argument with Life

No one can leap over the pilgrimage of the heart by which we're worn of all that's not essential. No one can escape the questioning of life that comes through pain and loss. No one can bypass the wrestling with God by which we try to make sense of what seems at times unbearable. At some point, everyone has an argument with life, which we're given to move through in order to find our place within the Unity of Things. We struggle with the unfairness of life, the harshness of circumstance, the fragility of our own nature. We struggle with the unanswerable whys of being alive. Often, we try to play that argument out with others, to replay that argument with our damaged history, to recast that argument into our imagined, secret destiny, or to project our frustration with that argument onto strangers.

During the life of our argument, we stumble through many learning positions: hero, victim, rescuer, martyr, scapegoat, abandoned one, abandoner, the promise breaker, and the promise keeper. Sometimes, these positions are so painful, we spend many years trying to maintain or break these identities. But insisting on any one view, any one way, any one side of things and laboring to turn everything we experience into support for that argument can be violent and exhausting.

Coming to terms with our argument with life is an apprenticeship in the art of acceptance. One of the constant challenges of intimacy is not to abandon a loved one while they're entangled in their argument with life, and not to become the battleground for that argument. The rigors of intimacy and friendship demand that we stay in authentic proximity, letting our loved one wrestle with life directly, while not becoming a surrogate for the argument. In deep, important ways, being there for each other means supporting each other through the unfolding of our spirit, not diverting each other from the nameless angel we each need to wrestle for its blessing.

Eventually, if blessed, the pilgrimage of the heart exhausts our argument with life so we can enter the realm where all things are true. Being worn of our stubbornness is how our life blossoms, an acceptance at a time.

....

∽ *Only from the Wholeness of Life can we see how to navigate this mystery with all its hardships and blessings.*

....

All-Encompassing Truth

No matter what we're going through, the opposite is happening somewhere else at the same time. This bespeaks the law of Wholeness. That all things are true means that we are called to honor everything. That all things are true doesn't mean that we muffle who we are because of what others are going through, but that we open our hearts and expand the reach of who we are to join the waterfall of life happening in each moment. That all things are true doesn't mean that we begrudge the good fortune of others because we are slogging through hardship, but that our honest reckoning of hardship grounds the heart of those near us into an open sense of relationship. That all things are true doesn't mean that we lessen our love and joy because others are suffering, but that our awareness of both allows our love and joy to flow to those who are suffering.

In essence, the awareness that truth exists beyond our personal circumstance doesn't minimize our own experience but allows a medicine of Wholeness to inject itself into the larger truth of any given moment. At times, the influx of more than we can understand can seem harsh, the way a rip in the curtains we've drawn seems to violate the privacy we so wanted though it's only letting in the light of the world.

So truth is not just what we believe. Truth surrounds us beyond our understanding; the way air surrounds the Earth beyond the reach of our breathing. As something is breaking, somewhere something is being joined. As something closes, something opens. Where there is dark, somewhere there is light. When things go clear, somewhere things are thickening into confusion. And when people are agitated, others are calm.

I don't understand how this works. But as something is taken, something is given. And when something cruel is poised to sting, somewhere someone is being kind. Then someone is lost, as another is finally at home. And some are aware of this, while others are not. The way things break and join at once, the way people are cruel and kind at once, the way life constantly opens and closes, how there is light and dark in every soul, how we're clear and confused just behind our heart, and lost and at home in every breath—this is the river we're born into, turbulent at the surface, swift in the deep. This is what we try to make sense of and live through, feeling it's all too much but needing more.

Nothing is separate. The wind through the Spanish moss tells me that this has always been. I must keep my heart open long enough for all things to mix until the alchemy of Oneness softens my time on Earth. If you take my hand when I'm like this, we will know each other in a way that will never leave us. Dipping our face in each other's heart, as we would a stream, makes the tribe strong. Enough to build something out of nothing. Enough to love what-is back into just what it is. So lift your head and steady your heart, knowing, as you're swept along, that Experience is the face of God.

One of the constant challenges of intimacy is not to abandon a loved one while they're entangled in their argument with life, and not to become the battleground for that argument.

The Aftertaste of Oneness

The things that matter swim together just below the surface. I was in the chair before my dentist whose "How are you?" twice a year is a small reference point in my life. I hadn't seen him since my father died. I was about to say so, as I had to everyone, stranger and friend alike, during the last month, when something deeper told me, *No, this will be the first time you don't say he died.*

I didn't feel my father any less, but life was moving on. The great whale of his life was going back into the deep. During his last year, I had been in this liminal space, tethered to his process of dying. During this time, I felt underwater myself, struggling to see, struggling for air; his life and death in the foreground everywhere I went.

A few weeks after my visit to the dentist, I held a memorial service for my father with my men's group. There was no funeral when he died because it was too hard for my mother. The day he died, she quivered, "I can't bear a funeral. Is this wrong? I don't think your father would have wanted one. Is this all right?" Though I wanted a service, needed one, I took her hands and said, "There's no one way to do this. Whatever you need is fine." All things are true.

For the service I held, I had some photos blown up, gathered some of his tools, brought two wooden bowls he'd spun on the lathe, and a handwritten notebook from 1937, which held his first notes on pattern-making when he was sixteen. I put together a makeshift altar. The first thing we did, quite naturally, was gather around the low table. I invited everyone to touch what he had touched, to leaf through his notebook, to hold his worn tools, to feel the mahogany and walnut curves in his bowls. I told a few stories, read a few poems, and wondered out loud about the ache of losing him.

After everyone left, I sat in front of the beautiful remnants, feeling thankful to have known him so sweetly near the end. George came back to see if I was all right and we sat for a while together. He said good night and I slowly put everything away and stared at the empty table, just a table again.

Ever since that night, I've felt lighter and deeper. This is why we have ritual, why we honor the dead and bear witness to how hard it is to continue. The affirmation of those we lose and the expression of what the loss is doing to us is what enables us to go on.

I realize now that the rough and tender ride alongside my father is over. Now the great whale of his life glides somewhere in the deep just below my wakefulness. Sadly, beautifully, poignantly, our entire life goes back under, as if we never happened, only alive in the hearts of those we touch.

And we go on. We know a talented woodworker. Susan has asked him to make a desk for me. But before he begins, I want him to know about my father and his love of wood, his skill with wood. Yet what should I say? What can I say that will bring my father up from the deep, so others might know him?

We're no different than Gilgamesh, the ancient king in the Assyrian tale who, after years of mourning his dear friend Enkidu, kept calling his name everywhere. Many thought this the ravings of an old man. A few stopped and said, "I don't understand." And one kind soul paused to ask, "Who?" And even then, poor Gilgamesh, an avatar of grief, couldn't find the words or summon an image to bring the life of his dear friend into view.

Like the sad old king, I don't know what to say to our young wood-worker, other than "My father loved wood, too." I can feel the great whale of his life swimming just below and the aftertaste of Oneness is in my mouth. From the other side, my father seems to say, "Go live your life. I am near."

Beyond all my attempts to find what matters, my deep amazement at simply being here drops into the ocean of the moment like a golden ring dropped into the sea, drifting by its own soft weight to add to the bot-tom, to add to the treasures waiting to be found by the next generation of seekers, who will sense that the truth of all things is just within reach.

⌒ At times, the influx of more than we can understand can seem harsh, the way a rip in the curtains we've drawn seems to violate the privacy we so wanted though it's only letting in the light of the world.

A Reflective Pause

○ *This is a meditation that leads to a table question with a friend or loved one. Whatever you're feeling in this moment, open your heart to it completely. Now open your heart completely to the fact that the opposite of what you're feeling is happening somewhere else. Try to imagine both and let the feelings merge. In the next few days, try to describe this experience to a friend.*

BEYOND SEEKING

▼ ▼ ▼

It's the sides of the mountain that sustain life, not the top.

—Philosopher Robert M. Pirsig

There is the transition from sacrificing yourself for someone to the simple self-sacrifice, which is not a noble giving up of things or a performing of any task for anyone, not even for God, but just a making holy (or making whole) of yourself— the utter simplicity you speak of.

—Helen Luke, letter to Sister Judith, April 1961

As human beings, we're asked, more than once, to choose if we're striving for perfection or fullness. When striving for perfection, we think we have to get somewhere. When working toward fullness, we know we have to open our heart to where we are. While excellence is an admirable and useful reward for our effort in the world, our immersion of heart into whatever we're doing leads us past excellence, beyond all seeking into the experience of Oneness.

If blessed, all our seeking undoes itself, the way a taut harness snaps. At first, it's disorienting not to feel the pull of a goal or the tug of something keeping our nose to the plan. But the fragrance and bareness of things as they are gives rise to an unexpected calm, from which we can try on anything with sincerity and wonder.

To be led beyond seeking doesn't mean we remove ourselves from doing or participating in the world. It means we're drawn to things rather than driven to them. My own awakening to this came after the heat of my cancer journey. Before getting ill, I was a driven artist, determined and focused to learn my craft and follow my call. I was a strong river rushing to the sea, making a lot of noise as I scoured my banks. The rush of my creativity was how I knew I was alive.

When all my loved ones went back to work, it was frightening to wake one day, alone in my bathrobe, wondering what had happened to me. My drive was gone, vanished. I feared I'd lost my creativity. I was disoriented for months. But rushing in our own river, we never imagine what happens when the river finally reaches the sea. It joins the deep and all the noise it made along the way submerges. Our rush of aliveness goes deeper, joining the currents of life. And so, my creative energy was just as present, but in a deeper sea and less visible.

In truth, I'm freer, drawn to things in wonder, less obsessed with getting there—wherever that is—and more called to experience the variety and mystery of life as I meet it. I work just as hard but with less certainty about where my effort is taking me. This unexpected shift from being driven to being drawn has something to do with life beyond seeking.

Though this is never easy, it's inevitable, the way small trees grow out of the tops of mountains, only to be bent and shaped by the endless winds that seem to come from nowhere. This is our small destiny, to be co-created by time and experience, beyond all intent, into something that will shade other weary travelers, who are stunned to discover that the peak is no different than the valley in which they begin.

> ∾ *When striving for perfection, we think we have to get somewhere. When working toward fullness, we know we have to open our heart to where we are.*

Water Lessons

The World can be compared to ice, and Truth
to the water from which this ice is formed.

—JÎLÎ

Jîlî's metaphor helps us understand the nature of existence and every-thing unseen that informs it. With this image, he shows us the impor-tance of love. Abdul Karîm Jîlî (1366–1424) was a Sufi mystic, the author of more than twenty books, the most famous being *Universal Man*. From all his work, these two lines crystallize like a jewel that held to the light reveals so much.

We all know that ice is the solid form of water. Thick enough and it will hold us up, thin enough and we'll fall through. Jîlî suggests that everything in the world seems separate and solid, but if held with warmth, everything will return to its common flow, the one water, the one truth from which all forms rise.

Of course, ice is cold. In our hardened positions, so are we. You and I may be hurt, go through difficult times, and feel guarded against the harshness of the world. We may seem separate in how we make our way. We may even push off of each other. But warmth turns the ice of world back into what matters. Warmth turns us back into the one truth we share. Jîlî suggests that the one sure way to dissolve our separate-ness—to break our hardness and undo our coldness—is to behold each other with care and love until that warmth thaws our differences and we refind the water of truth.

Jîlî tells us that the surface world is always more than it seems and the warmth of care and love and wonder is the best way to penetrate that surface. This has helped me lean toward others when the coldness I encounter pushes me away. I try not to withhold my presence, so my warmth can contribute to keeping truth in the world. While telling the truth is always important, we're asked as well to serve the truth by not withholding the warmth of our presence.

Six hundred years after Jîlî retrieved this metaphor, the great Spanish poet Juan Ramón Jiménez (1881–1958), who won the Nobel Prize in 1956, wrote his striking poem, "Oceans":

> *I have a feeling that my boat*
> *has struck, down there in the depths,*
> *against a great thing.*
> *And nothing happens! Nothing . . . Silence . . . Waves . . .*
> *Nothing happens? Or has everything happened,*
> *and are we standing now, quietly, in the new life?*

A quiet and profound harmony is struck by these two voices across all these years. Jiménez tells us that from time to time we rush along in our surface lives, only to strike upon the one truth in the deep, unsure what has happened. So deep, so moving, so subtle is this type of transformation that we're seldom sure if nothing has changed or if everything has changed. The world seems different and we're asked to loosen our mind-set, to put down our lists, to stop answering our calls, long enough to feel how the one truth is rearranging us. Often, the only thing that can make us open in this way is exhaustion, the weighty gift we resist that relaxes our face and unfists our heart long enough for what matters to re-enter us.

Only then, can we realize that we just may be "standing now, quietly, in the new life."

Life in the Container

There's much conversation and consternation about the nature and purpose of a self. In the West, the individual is considered sacred and self-reliance and independence are seen as ultimate virtues. In Asia and Africa, the communal web is considered sacred and the preeminence of the individual is seen as an impediment to harmony and peace. In deep ways, we need the interdependent weave of the individual and the larger living fabric it's always a part of. How we hold all this affects what we work toward while we're here.

In the Hindu worldview, there's an ancient trinity of intrinsic forces that bring us in and out of the life of forms. Brahma is the creative force of the Universe always rushing its way into the world. Vishnu is the god of forms, providing infinite containers that can carry the creative force of life for a time on Earth. And Shiva is the transformer, the force that takes the forms apart, allowing the energy of life to return to Brahma, so the eternal cycle can begin again. In essence, our individual self is one of life's many forms, the container for the portion of Spirit we're each born with.

It's often reported in the West that Buddhism tells us we have no self. We need to clarify this. The term *anātman* in Sanskrit means the illusion of a self. Along the way, this has been more widely translated as *no-soul* which can be misleading. Though some sects of Buddhist thought clearly reject any idea of a self, other sects suggest there is no permanent self, no central or fixed center of individual consciousness that can retain its singularity, its particular history or preferences from one life to the next. The self is regarded as a temporary container whose spiritual essence disperses back into the Universe, once the container has come to an end.

While we're here, the self is our container, our vessel, our soul carrier. Our self is how we relate to the essence of things we carry in our time on Earth. So what kind of relationship is this for you? What kind of conversation do you have with the essence of things as it moves through you? This is worth giving attention to as it enables our resilience and aliveness.

A Never-Ending Practice

We're all small boats on a mysterious sea. This brings us to another water lesson, the use of a *rudder*, a vertical steering device hinged in the water at the aft of a ship. The handle coming from the rudder into the cockpit is called a *tiller*. Moving the tiller left or right will cause the rudder to move and this will begin to steer the ship. Long oars were first used as rudders on Egyptian riverboats as far back as 3100 BC. In the Zhou dynasty in China (1050–256 BC), models of ships had steering oars as rudders.

I remember working the tiller on our sailboat as a boy, a job I loved, one I could get lost in, especially in the fog. My father would tell me the direction. He'd point to the degree on the compass and trust me to keep her steady. I quickly learned that steering a rudder toward a point on a compass is never fixed. The compass needle never stands still. It constantly moves a little to the left, then to the right, and the effort is to keep steering as close to the imagined destination as possible.

I raise this because the self is both the vessel that carries our spirit *and* the rudder by which we steer our way through life. What does this say about the unending practice of caring for the self? First, without a self, we have nothing to carry our spirit in the world. And when we forget or deny that the self is a container for Spirit, we think our container is everything and become self-centered, losing all connection.

And just as our effort to steer to a point on a compass is never still, but always veering to the left and the right, as a person, we're always inflating who we are and deflating who we are, always a little over or under as we steer our self toward through the fog and choppy sea. Knowing we will always veer, we need to constantly return to center—a never-ending practice—to assume our authentic, full stature; no more, no less.

This is the self's journey through life, veering into inflation and deflation, always coming back through steady effort to our authentic center. Regardless of where we think we're going, the journey is the reward. And when we die, our container wears away and we rejoin the living Universe. The recycling of spirit is how our unseeable essence returns to be carried by another container.

Intention and Surrender

Given all this, how are we to hold the seeming opposites of intention and surrender? At first, they seem so far apart, the way the peak of a mountain and the ravine at its bottom seem far apart. But from across the river, a mile away, the top and bottom of the mountain are very close, their connection at the base obvious. It's the same with intention and surrender. When standing between them, they seem to stretch us in opposite directions, but from an eternal perspective, they are kindred ways of being.

What keeps intention and surrender far apart, at least in our minds, is our insistence that our intentions matter. Oh, they do, but not as sacred manifestations of our will that we must slave toward. Rather, intentions are kindling, small parts of our desire gathered and thrown into the fire to keep us close to what matters. They're only important in how they're used up, how they're burned as fuel to keep the fire going. We must intend them into being, only to surrender them into the fire of our aliveness.

It's the same with our dreams and ambitions, which are just a deeper form of intention, a deeper form of kindling. Our inborn need to be kinetically engaged with life makes us formulate dreams to reach for. When we become fixed on the dream, ambition appears as a way to manifest that dream at all cost, as if our happiness depends on it. In truth, our happiness depends on the aliveness our dreams carry us to. It's not the dream, but where it takes us, which we can seldom foresee. When we can remember that dreams are a *way* to aliveness, not the *keeper* of aliveness, intention and surrender work together.

Imagine a fish born in a fast current, with barely any time to learn how to swim. As it swirls out of control downstream, it sees a bed of rocks ahead and its only dream, out of fear, is to find refuge from the current in those rocks. Landing in those rocks becomes its dream. Steering toward those rocks becomes its intent. But as the fish nears the rocks, the current grows even stronger and it's swept beyond the rocks into the rush of a magnificent falls. The fish has no choice but to surrender to its flight down the falls, which is the most terrifying and exhilarating journey of its life.

Beyond its dream of those rocks and beyond its intent to hide in the rocks was a life it couldn't have imagined. Before the life of the falls was in view, intent was necessary. But once the life of the falls came into view, surrender was necessary. At the bottom of the falls, the fish found its version of Heaven on Earth: the calmness of a deep and clear pool, where it lived the rest of its days.

So it is with the transformative journey of a soul on Earth. Our intentions and dreams are only important so we can nose our way toward the unknown Unity of Life that waits beyond whatever we might hide in. Once that Unity of Life is in view, our surrender is paramount, if we are to know the ride of our life and find the calm, deep pool from which to live the rest of our days.

....

　　⌒ *Regardless of where we think we're going, the journey is the reward.*

....

It's a hard journey for each of us to learn that if we can touch one thing completely, it will give us access to everything. We run all over the world, trying to achieve as much as possible, to love as many people as possible, to go as many places as possible, to have as many conversations as possible, to save as much as possible or spend as much as possible. But sooner or later, beyond all seeking, we run into some obstacle or light, are stunned, knocked down. And once on our knees, we finally stop, our face toward the Earth, to touch where we are, to feel where we are, to know *we are here* and all that this means.

A Reflective Pause

　○ *In your journal, describe a time when your heart was exhausted open and what you saw or felt through that opening.*

BORN OF THE MOMENT

Joshu asked Nansen: "What is the path?"
Nansen said: "Everyday life is the path."
Joshu asked: "Can it be studied?"
Nansen said: "If you try to study, you will be far away from it."

—THE GATELESS GATE

Every [person] has the right to risk [their] own life in order
to preserve it. Has it ever been said that [someone] who
throws [themselves] out the window to escape a fire is guilty
of suicide?

—ROUSSEAU

WHILE MOMENTS OF great openness allow us to glimpse the Wholeness of Life, these moments are not sufficient by themselves. They're doorways to living more wholeheartedly. More than grasping moments of truth or beauty, we're asked to *enter* moments, so we can *come alive.*

Once blessed to be awake, we're challenged to return there when we stray. And we all stray, because we're human and this is what humans do. Yet the smallest moment can return us to what matters by catching the break in our heart. And just as trees, plants, flowers, and fruits all grow from seed, the gifts of being human are born of the moment.

When lost, what we need is never very far, though our access to it can seem a continent away.

The Buddhist word *hecceitas* means *this-ness, the ever-fresh unfolding in the next moment*. Following the this-ness or life-force that waits like a shimmering atom in the center of each moment is the path of everyday life. Any task when fully entered leads us here. Inhabiting such elemental presence is both simple and elusive, because of our immense capacity to run from where we are and to complicate where we are.

Awakening the conscious heart means entering the moment we're in while not being a prisoner of the past or the things that have shaped us. The gift of Now is to begin again each moment; a task as simple and repeatable as breathing, if we didn't have to see and hear through our wounds and ideas. The challenge of Now is to feel all that has shaped us while knowing that these things no longer shape us.

When a cup is fired in a kiln, it's transformed. The shape created by the fire determines what it holds, what it carries, what it pours, and how we drink from it. In just this way, what we carry, what we pour, and how others drink from us is determined by how we're transformed in the fire of experience.

We can't will ourselves to be something useful but only live into it. The journey of living authentically is a slow fire that shapes us into something useful. Over time, the this-ness of each moment, truly entered, begins to wear away what thickens between our inner life and outer life, between our being and becoming, and slowly, we become useful cups. This is how the conscious heart awakens.

We're left with the recurring commitment to live moment to moment, but not with the God-given innocence of animals. Sacred as that is, we will never be allowed to inhabit that innocence completely. As humans, it's our lot to bring the full awareness of our being—all we've been through and all of our possibility yet to be—to bear and flow into the moment at hand. Like an awakened Sumi painter, whose every sweep of brush is fresh, uncorrectable, and final, our every stroke and gesture in the canvas that is the world is both a commitment and a surrender.

⌒ More than grasping moments of truth or beauty, we're asked to enter moments, so we can come alive.

Surprised by Care

Try as we do, the things that matter, the things that enliven us and shape us can't be prepared for, only met. Ultimately, preparation is more about being centered and present than anticipating every possible outcome. How does a bird prepare to fly? It lets go of the rim of its nest. How does a fish prepare for the waterfall? It swims headlong over the edge. How does a heart receive and send blood? It keeps pumping. For us, meeting each moment means letting go and swimming over the edge while our heart keeps pumping. And when we can stop anticipating life and simply meet life, we're surprised by care.

Often, we get lost in over-preparation. If not careful, our endless anticipation can hood us from the moment at hand. We can become so mired in our plans and their alternatives that there's very little left in us to meet what actually comes our way.

The distraction of being over-prepared is beautifully captured in this wonderful haiku about baseball by Cor van den Heuvel:

> *the batter checks*
> *the placement of his feet*
> *"Strike One!"*

The endless practice swings and digging in the batter's box are legendary in baseball, an apt metaphor for the jittery way we try to prepare for everything. The lesson of this haiku is as quick as the pitch, and can be as easily missed. For all his readiness, the batter, finally at the plate, checks the placement of his feet one last time, just as the pitch is coming. While he's looking at his feet, he's pulled out of the moment and a perfectly hittable pitch sails by—Strike One!

Whatever task we face, whatever decisions or turning points we approach, there will always come a time when to re-check our stance one last time will pull us out of the moment we've been preparing for and we'll miss our small or large destiny. In such crossed moments, we're challenged to trust our preparation rather than go over it one more time.

In actuality, trusting ourselves and our work is the culmination of our preparation. No one ever told me that the mastery of preparation is to put down all the planning and enter with trust the moment prepared for. No one ever taught me how to do this. But clearly—whether entering a moment of surgery or love, or being washed over with a wave of creativity or winded by the sudden death of a loved one—the truth that helps us live waits like a clear pool for us to dive in, a baptism born by entering the moment at hand.

Ultimately, preparation is more about being centered and present than anticipating every possible outcome.

For This Time Only

We were in New York City in summer. After dinner, we strolled back to the hotel with Robert and Ellen along Central Park, the soft air filtering the light, making everything touchable. That night, I dreamt again of Grandma Minnie. In the dream, I'm on my way, en route to complete a task, when I see her in her kitchen reaching for a strainer for tea. She's in her body when she was seventy. There's a large age spot on her cheek. I call to her. She surfaces and sees me. I'm as I am now, sixty-two. She knows I'm still living. She wipes her hands on her apron and says, "Look at you." We gently embrace for a long time. I say, "I so loved being with you." She smiles quietly and replies, "Time closes and opens your life at the same time." I rest my head on her ancient shoulder. She rubs my head, as she did when I was a boy, and says to no one, "Time closes and opens us, till part of us blooms and part of us falls away."

Up early the next day, I wandered the edge of the park, watching birds swoop between the old trees and skyscrapers. What to make of such a dream and her profound koan at the end?

I reflected on this for months when I came to learn that *ichi-go ichi-e* in Japanese is often translated as *for this time only, never again*, or *one chance in a lifetime*. This notion was taught in depth by the great tea master Sen no Rikyū (1522–1591) as a framing awareness with which to perform the legendary tea ceremony; a ritual-based presence practiced to enter all of time through the moment at hand. Rikyū's teaching brought me back to Grandma's koan about time in the dream. What was confusing started to become clear: each moment closes and opens us at the same time in an effort to strip us bare. And lining the simplicity of a single day is the truth that life is not our continual movement from here to there, as the thousand tasks would have us believe, but a depth experience in which part of us blooms and part of us falls away. The closing and opening and the blooming and falling away makes us more essential.

For this time only, we're born through whatever we touch and whatever touches us. And time closes us and opens us at the same time so we can be more real, more present to the fact that every breath is one chance in a lifetime, never to happen again.

Who would have thought that Grandma and Rikyū were kindred spirits? I'm boiling water now for tea, smiling to imagine Rikyū crossing eternity to stir the leaves for Grandma in her Brooklyn apartment when she was alone, for this time only.

To Improvise Our Way

We are left with the one art no one can master—
the art of living the unrehearsed moment.

The jazz legend Herbie Hancock says, "Improvisation is a higher form of intelligence." What kind of preparation and letting go does this invoke? And what does it mean to improvise our way through our lives? Regarding the inner life, improvisation involves the application of heart and mind in unrehearsed situations that enliven us. Improvising our way through our lives requires the practice and discipline of various skills without knowing how we will use them until what is asked of us is born of the moment. This is the jazz of our days.

Let me share two telling examples of improvising our way. The first speaks to where our true calling lies. The jazz saxophonist Ken Morgan tells this story about his first music teacher whose devotion to music shaped Ken's life. As a young man, Ken's mentor wanted to become a priest. One day while studying scripture, he heard George Gershwin's "Summertime," the classic aria Gershwin composed for the 1935 opera *Porgy and Bess*. The young man was opened so completely by this song that he went straightaway to play it on the church organ. The playing of that tune so awakened his heart that he knew he had to be this close to music to stay awake. And so, he left one form of priesthood for another and became a music teacher.

While we can dream and train to make that dream come true, the unexpected impact of life can lead us from where we look for God to where God finds us. I take this as an example of the exchange between Joshu and Nansen at the beginning of this chapter that reminds us that everyday life is the path, and if you try to study it, you will be far away from what matters.

The second story comes from my dear friend Bob who, though a talented photographer, no longer takes pictures. When I asked why, he chuckled to himself and told me of an unexpected outing thirty years ago. He was in the Vermont woods in autumn. The light and foliage were magical. He roamed for hours with his camera and fell into an extended mood of Oneness. Time opened as he stood in utter amazement before different thatches of color. He patiently looked through his camera until an incandescent sense would rise. Only then would he slowly click the shutter. Frame after frame glowed with a mystical edge.

Later he discovered that the edge of the film hadn't caught the sprocket, so it never advanced. There were no pictures on the film. Yet, after his disappointment, he realized that this time alone in heightened concentration in nature was clearly his most complete experience of photography. Bob shook his head. The question remains: Did he take the pictures or not? What does his experience in the autumn woods say about capturing life or entering it? What does it say about the sincerity with which we take things in? Is being a photographer taking the pictures or entering the pictures? Is any act of care defined by having something to show for it or is the entered experience itself what matters? Is being an artist producing the art or living it?

We all arrive at the same threshold of living the unrehearsed moment. Sooner or later, having broken or lost things we once thought indispensable, the erosion of time wears our mind open and we see what's truly possible. Then air itself is all we need and thirst itself is rewarding. Improvising our way through burden to renewal, we can find the strength to put down all that is not life-giving. Humbled into the open, we can stand in a place of this-ness that no one keeping score can see.

Returning to what matters by entering the ever-fresh this-ness of each moment, rediscovering our elemental presence through the slow fire of authenticity, awakening our conscious heart by improvising our way and staying real—these practices describe what happens when we're genuine enough to feel alive.

When wholehearted, we are, for the moment, as the great Taoist Chuang Tzu says, conduits and not containers. He describes this moment of having life move through us in this way:

> To be poured into without becoming full
> and to pour out without becoming empty,
> without knowing how this is brought about . . .

To be a live conduit for the forces of life requires a different kind of preparation. As a jazz pianist diligently learns scales, tones, and chords so he can receive the music of the spheres and improvise without hesitation, we learn skill sets to negotiate life, so we can meet life without hesitation and inhabit the depth born of the moment. As Pissarro, Monet, and Picasso had to master realism so they could open the surface world in order to find the light within objects, we have to face things-as-they-are in order to find meaning in between the facts and pain of our days. And as quantum physicists looked so thoroughly into matter till they discovered that nothing is solid, that all is ineffable, we're challenged to move through the hard surfaces of experience to discover that everything carries the mystery and luminosity of being.

> ᐸᐳ *The unexpected impact of life can lead us from where we look for God to where God finds us.*

The history of a single life is always about to be reshaped in the moment at hand, and entering the moment before us, we are most alive. But the moment doesn't last, can't last, and we're always asked to bring our entire aliveness forward. Everything into the next moment.

Like salmon swimming upstream, bringing their muscled glide through the water to the instant they break surface and seem to fly, only to re-enter the water and continue on.

Like walking, as we push off everything we've known to begin another step. Until lifted, we're off the ground, with nothing behind and nothing ahead. Only to land where we are. And from that simple foundation, we lift again into the new life that each step holds.

Like breathing, as we take everything in to fill our chest and, for the moment, we're complete and still. Only to empty ourselves, as we add something from within us back into the world.

We dive, we surface, we dive again. We push off, we lift, we land, we push off again. We take in, we feel complete, we empty, giving of ourselves, and take in again. We have this basic rhythm of being to return to that never fails us. The worm inches through soil. The bird pumps and glides through air. The fish wriggles and noses through water. The soul breaches into life, moment by moment.

When chancing there, when stumbling there, when surprised by care, I feel so alive, I need more senses.

A Reflective Pause

○ *In conversation with a friend or loved one, tell the story of a small moment that returned you to what matters and how it affected you. Have your friend share such a moment. What do these moments have in common?*

○ *At another time, tell the story of a moment when life suddenly felt complete, with nowhere to go and nothing to work toward. What led to this moment?*

LITTLE BY LITTLE

*As sticks were rubbed prehistorically to start fires,
the rubbing of our humanity against the daily
sparks the spiritual.*

I THINK THE purpose of the human experience is for the soul to
blossom in human form here on Earth. Little by little, the way the
hundredth drop of water opens a seed, the rub of what is human against
the days releases what is Divine. Within this journey, I plod some days
like an ant so focused on the grain above my head that the next step
holds all of life, and I feel in the lineage of slaves pushing the next stone
up an unfinished pyramid. Then, without reason, life billows with an
unearned ease I can't describe. When it leaves, like a breeze of Spirit,
I feel renewed and certain that God is in both the moment of lift and
the moment of ease, in the moment of pain and after. So I've given up
wishing for ease and running from pain. Everything on Earth moves
by this inching between ease and pain. It's how we grow. And praising
both, surrendering to both, accepting both is the work of love.

Little by little, the way an amoeba pulses under a microscope, the
soul of a human being pulses like a faint star throbbing in place. Our
spirit seems to emanate as our psychology constricts. The contrast
makes us glow and shimmer. It's useless to want to bypass this journey. For it's only by inhabiting it that we chance to know Eternity, not
as some far-off place reserved for saints, but as the Numinous Delta

in which the very marrow of life forms and re-forms. To live in this unending dynamism, between being and becoming, is the path of transformation. More than finding Heaven on Earth, we are asked to release Heaven by living here on Earth.

A Ground for Practice

Yet how do we release Heaven on Earth? Little by little, a step at a time, an honest self-reflection at a time, a pinprick in the monolith of falsity that keeps us from each other, one puncture at a time. And how do we strengthen our trust in what matters and find our resolve? Little by little, for as daily exercise strengthens our muscles, doing small things with love, one gesture at a time, will strengthen our heart and let us uncover the lesson that every obstacle carries.

How do we begin? The Tibetan Buddhist Jennifer Fox suggests that:

> [Our] understanding emerges and evolves through practice . . . maintaining a ground in yourself that the teachings can soak into, which would remain abstract if there was no practice.

And the therapist Barbara Thompson says, "Letting go of what gets in the way of loving is a practice all by itself."

Can it be that the work of everyday life is to let go of what gets in the way of loving while loosening our grip on what we think and feel so our mind and heart can soak in everything we learn?

Recently, I spent an entire day talking about love with people I love and, little by little, it became clear that honest care leads us to the rim of what we know. We all ride this tension of building a home in ourselves, while trying to climb out of ourselves. And it seems quite natural that loss and suffering and question and surprise rush us to and from our edge. When we can risk our way beyond what hurts us, we discover that love is the fifth element.

Yet, having inched, a day at a time, into the depths of honest loving, and having fallen back, a pain at a time, into my worry and fear, what would I offer to anyone who would listen? Not in the way you might listen to a teacher, but more as you would stop and listen to an old tree creak about its years of standing in the wind. If you should listen that way, I would whisper that each step in being alive—in dreaming, in suffering, in wakening—takes us out of our image of ourselves and tosses us into the very stuff out of which all selves are made. There, aliveness and woundedness become our ground for practice until the murmur of life sings quietly and completely.

Unlocking the Gate

We must accommodate time the way
the eye learns to see in the dark.

—JOEL ELKES

The Japanese Zen master Shido Bunan (1603–1676) was a gatekeeper until something happened in his forties, which awakened him to the life of a poet. It's unclear what changed his way of meeting the world. Perhaps keeping things out exhausted him. Perhaps when all alone he turned one day and looked through the gate from the outside and realized he was as much in exile as those he sent away. Would it help if we could know what opened him?

It seems Bunan's journey is the path that awaits each of us. The gate we guard and keep may be very different. It might be the gate to our truth that we show no one. Or the gate to our wounded heart. Or the gate to our lack of esteem. It might be the gate to our fear. Whatever the entry point, we're all gatekeepers waiting for something to happen that will force us to open the gate or even take it down. How can we transform ourselves from being a gatekeeper to being someone who crosses a threshold? How do we soften the stubbornness that makes us fear the life we're born into?

How do we open the gate of our mind that, unless a servant of the heart, will take over and run our lives? No matter how well intended, a gated mind will narrow what comes to it. A gated mind is a judging mind that doesn't allow people or things to assume their true nature. A gated, judging mind will scoop a bucket from the sea, have us dip our feet in it, and claim that's what it's like to swim in the ocean.

As our journey unfolds, we all are hurt and we all do the hurting. No matter how hard we try, each of us will be stubborn and not truly hear or misunderstand or force our views on someone we love just as they are about to form their own. Our trespasses seem intended by our nature; all so we can have the chance to understand our very human flaws and own them, make amends, and repair what we have done. This is as important as doings things well in the first place. Perhaps even more important, because when aiming, missing, and stopping to help repair the damage—our damage—more lasting relationships unfold. By unlocking the gate, no matter what we thought we were keeping out, we let life cleanse us and complete us, as we try to live more honestly from day to day.

Ultimately, unlocking the gate means listening in all directions. When we listen, we open and expand. And what we listen to grows for our listening. There's no question: being seen, heard, and loved opens the inner eye, while remaining unseen, unheard, and gated closes the inner eye. When listening in all directions, affirmation, respect, and love expand everyone's capacity to be aware and see more—both for the seer and the seen, for the hearer and the heard, and for the lover and the loved.

....

     The work of everyday life is to let go of what gets in the way of loving.

....

Heartwork

What does it mean for you and me to stop being a gatekeeper? How do we stop keeping watch? Little by little, by recovering our openness of heart. Little by little, by retraining the heart like a fist to open instead of close. And how do we undo the old habits that close the heart? This brings to mind another simple teaching. I learned this by taking our dog, Mira, to do nosework. Nosework is how dogs are trained to be search and rescue animals. We bring Mira simply because she loves to use her sense of smell. Nosework engages her completely.

The way dogs learn to track scents is called "pairing." For the first two weeks, every dog is given the scent of a treat. The food is hidden. The dog finds the treat and is rewarded. In the middle sessions, the food is paired with a scent of anise or birch. Now the dog learns to associate the scent with the food. In the final weeks, you take away the food, and the dog simply goes for the scent. Once finding the scent, the dog is rewarded with the treat. Eventually, dogs will track whatever scent they're given: drugs or clothing, if they're helping to find people who are missing.

This is a great metaphor for the heartwork of slowly replacing limiting habits with more authentic responses. When I have an old behavior or dysfunctional pattern that's triggered, when I have a button that's pushed, when there's something I do that doesn't work well but I've done it forever, how do I correct these dark reflexes? How do I put them down?

Like nosework for dogs, we can make ground in our heartwork by "pairing" the old habit with a new one. We stymie ourselves by trying to exile old behavior outright, thinking, *I'm never going to do that again.* It might be better to pair an insecure feeling with a moment of being fully seen so that every time the insecure feeling comes up, it's paired with an authentic replacement. Eventually, over time—the way a dog drops the treat and looks for the scent—we can minimize our insecurity in favor of a more grounded sense of being. Eventually, through our heartwork, we can couple and pair the habitual with the authentic, until we can replace what drains us with something that will sustain us.

For example, there are times that I suddenly feel small. An old wound is bruised and I'm triggered into feeling less than. Instead of telling myself I should know better, which only makes me feel worse, I now try to pair that enervating feeling with a moment of assuming my full stature. When feeling small, I follow up by standing tall, not larger than I am but just as I am. I find the pairing of heartwork right-sizes my sense of smallness as I slowly pick up the scent of self-esteem. When feeling less than, I keep my heart to the ground and follow the scent of being.

∾ When we can risk our way beyond what hurts us, we discover that love is the fifth element.

The Murmur of Life

That the heart can receive and hold anything *and* that the intensity of feeling so deeply is too much to bear is a paradox we can only live into. Under what is both unbearable and endlessly uplifting is the murmur of life.

I hear this murmur wherever I turn: when sweeping the grains of coffee from the counter, when picking up the stray bottle in the parking lot, wondering about the one who drank it, when watching a frightened child being squeezed in the back of a crowd erupting into violence. I feel the glow that lifts things further into life; the way wind blows pollen down the field when no one is looking. I feel the breeze of light that lifts a bruised, tired head after the weight of great pain. I feel the thing in life that won't let us stop growing, no matter how difficult the circumstance.

As a bluebird needs a small, enclosed house propped in the open where it can nest and give birth, the heart is our enclosed house propped in the open, in which the soul nests, as we wait for some small song within us to be born.

And still the heart, by its very nature, is destined to be smaller than what it needs to fill it. For the heart is a powerful incubator. And we're left with the agitation of always feeling more than we can digest, make sense of, or handle. It seems the heart needs to heat up, so what it's incubating can pop out of us with its hungry beak reaching for the sky. Our most precious moments of aliveness arise when the heart, propped in the open, is brimming with more than it can contain. Our job is to be a trustworthy birdhouse for the hatching of mystery. This is how life awakens the soul.

....

⌒ *More than finding Heaven on Earth, we are asked to release Heaven by living here on Earth.*

....

Born to Give

The more you know, the more you bend.

—AN OLD KOREAN SAYING

A tiny, tender wave of love rocks the boat of life.

—MAHARISHI MAHESH

Under all the harsh noise of the world coming in on us, this is how the things that last move: a small wave from the deep moves us on and the more we're moved, the more we bend and bow and reach for each other. Our very life is the ground of practice by which we struggle to unlock the gate and let life in. It's the murmur of life that fills us with another chance. Little by little, it's the courage to assume our full stature one more time that enables us to do the heartwork that always makes us come alive. It's the turn from hiding to giving that releases Heaven on Earth.

I have a dear friend whose niece, when eighteen months old, would offer everyone a bite of her food before eating herself. This was all the more striking, as this little one's great-grandmother, Nana, used to do this in her immigrant journey from Italy to America. Nana taught her daughters to do the same. Such generosity became a trait passed on in the family. But how does an infant innately know to do this?

Can we encourage the heart's want to give? Can we greenhouse or irrigate the heartwork that brings us together? Or, try as we will, is it every bird's impulse to fly that extends the flock's path of migration further and further each year? Either way, when kind, we're not just helping the person before us but evolving the heart of humanity. Little by little, nurture can become nature. Every inch of kindness matters. A kindness earned can become inborn. This is the deepest education, one that lives in our bones.

So take the sweetness and ache of where you've been and plant it wherever you go, in soft and hard places alike, and watch as strange and beautiful things take root.

A Reflective Pause

- *In your journal, tell the story of a time when your heart felt more than it could contain, a time you couldn't quite make sense of, and try to describe what was incubated in your heart during that time.*

- *At another time, describe a recent moment of ease and a recent moment of pain. What is each opening in you? If your ease and your pain are extensions of your being, hands of your being, what might you build or lift with them?*

- *At yet another time, ask yourself, are you looking at something in life in too narrow a way? How can you expand the way you're relating to this?*

WITHOUT PAUSE

▼ ▼ ▼

T HEY SAY THE legendary hitter Ted Williams could see the seams of the ball as it came out of the pitcher's hand. All of his practice, swinging the bat for hundreds of hours, enabled him to discern in half a second that the pitch coming was a curve and not a fastball. This shows us the true relationship between practice and living. All practice is preparation for the integrated act of unrehearsed living. All practice yearns for a chance to apply itself in real time. Here are two indispensable teachings about the integrated practice of living. They come from the life and work of the gifted Irish writer Oscar Wilde and the great composer Ludwig van Beethoven.

Our Alchemy of Spirit

In 1894, Oscar Wilde (1854–1900) wrote a prose poem called "The Artist" in which a sculptor is moved to create *The Pleasure that abideth for a Moment* in bronze. But there is no bronze left in the world, except in the image of *The Sorrow that endureth for Ever* which he himself created and set on the tomb of someone he loved.

Finally, the artist

> took the image he had fashioned, and set it in a great furnace,
> and gave it to the fire.

> *And out of the bronze image of The Sorrow that endureth*
> *for Ever he fashioned an image of The Pleasure that abideth*
> *for a Moment.*

Three years later, Wilde, who was openly gay, was put in prison for "gross indecency with other men." We can only look back at such hostile prejudice the way we must face the horrific stories of slavery. He was prosecuted along with Alfred Taylor. I speak of Oscar Wilde's journey because we can't talk about *The Sorrow that endureth for Ever* or *The Pleasure that abideth for a Moment* without bearing witness to the life behind the story.

At his first trial, Wilde spoke his truth:

> *Prosecutor Charles Gill:* What is "the love that dare not speak its name"?
>
> *Oscar Wilde:* "The love that dare not speak its name" in this century is such a great affection of an elder for a younger man as there was between David and Jonathan, such as Plato made the very basis of his philosophy, and such as you find in the sonnets of Michelangelo and Shakespeare. It is that deep spiritual affection that is as pure as it is perfect . . . There is nothing unnatural about it . . . [But] the world does not understand. The world mocks it, and sometimes puts one in the pillory for it.

The jury of the first trial couldn't reach a verdict. But when the second jury returned its verdict of guilty, the presiding High Court Judge, Sir Alfred Wills, a well-known mountaineer and president of the Alpine Club, made this statement:

> *Justice Wills:* Oscar Wilde and Alfred Taylor, the crime of which you have been convicted is so bad that one has to put stern restraint upon one's self to prevent one's self from describing, in language which I would rather not use, the sentiments

which must rise in the breast of every man of honor who has heard the details of these two horrible trials . . . It is no use for me to address you. People who can do these things must be dead to all sense of shame, and one cannot hope to produce any effect upon them. It is the worst case I have ever tried . . . I shall, under the circumstances, be expected to pass the severest sentence that the law allows . . . The sentence of the Court is that each of you be imprisoned and kept to hard labor for two years.

Oscar Wilde: And I? May I say nothing, my Lord?

The court adjourned without giving him any say and Oscar Wilde was sent to prison where he suffered greatly. During his term, he wrote a fifty-thousand-word letter to his lover, Lord Alfred Douglas (1870–1945). In this letter, called *De Profundis* (in Latin, *The Depths*), Wilde writes:

When first I was put into prison some people advised me to try and forget who I was. It was ruinous advice. It is only by realizing what I am that I have found comfort of any kind . . . To reject one's own experiences is to arrest one's own development. To deny one's own experiences is to put a lie into the lips of one's own life. It is no less than a denial of the soul.

Wilde was not allowed to send his letter, but permitted to take it with him upon his release. He spent the last three years of his life ill and in poverty, dying in Paris on November 30, 1900.

With his small prose poem "The Artist," written before his trial and time in prison, this gifted and persecuted spirit leaves a hidden jewel for us, not as well known as his only novel, *The Picture of Dorian Gray*, or his masterful play *The Importance of Being Earnest*. But quietly before his triumphs and tribulations unfolded, he affirmed a timeless truth that helps us turn sorrow into joy. Not by minimizing our sorrow, not by denying the pain of our journey or the gross indecency of injustice, but by putting our sorrow and the pain of our journey into the heart's fire, to melt *The Sorrow that endureth for Ever* down to its essential element. By meeting life and not running from it, we can mold and recast what we've been through into *The Pleasure that abideth for a Moment.*

Oscar Wilde surely knew both *The Sorrow that endureth for Ever* and *The Pleasure that abideth for a Moment.* Whether or not we can succeed in this alchemy of spirit, each of us is an artist looking for more bronze in the world, only to discover that *our own experience is the bronze.*

Glimpsing Eternity

Being deaf, Beethoven could hear the music of the Universe, unheard by the rest of us. The String Quartet No. 14 in C# minor, Opus 131, played without pause, seems to gather the slow and steady rise of the sun, mixing it with the unyielding turn of the Earth around the fire in its center. He somehow weaves the discord of all the roots on Earth gripping further in the ground with the harmony of the winds that swirl through the mountains and over the oceans. Within this is the slight pump of all the hearts stunned to be here. Listening to a performance of this quartet, Franz Schubert, a contemporary of Beethoven, remarked, "After this, what is left for us to write?"

Completed in 1826, Opus 131 was considered groundbreaking, offering seven movements instead of the traditional four. Beethoven's compositions for string quartet rush players into dynamic and intimate relationship, the way we can only know the wisdom of experience through actual relationship, learning how to play the music of life together.

This is the inspiring lesson of Beethoven's Opus 131: it mirrors the non-stop demand of life to have us make music of what we're given, not knowing what will happen next. Inevitably, having to play seven movements without pause, the instruments will go out of tune. With no time to re-tune their strings, musicians have to adjust and improvise within the structure of the music. In this piece, Beethoven insists on allowing both the harmony and discord of life to be present. He challenges musicians to see the movements through, even out of tune.

Likewise, we are challenged every day to say yes to the movements of life, to see it all through, without pause, staying in relationship to the music of life and each other, adjusting as we go, not knowing what will happen next. Yet even out of tune, this messy and magnificent practice, so essentially human, will let us hear—briefly—the music of the Universe being the Universe. To hear this larger music while grinding out the smaller music of our lives is what sages of all traditions have called *glimpsing eternity*.

So, though there are times to rest and times to rehearse, the blessings and resources of life rush into the flawed and raw openings that come when we keep playing without pause, reaching for ways to find the unknown harmonies between us. For all his brilliance of composition, Beethoven's strength of heart confirms that a moment of meeting life completely is more rewarding than an ounce of perfection. It's inspiring and helpful to realize that saying yes when we feel depleted and out of tune wakes the sleeping genie of our soul who smiles to say, when looking at our trouble, "I've been waiting for this. You have everything you need."

▼   ▼   ▼

Just how do we do this? How do we wander so honestly and tenderly in the pilgrimage of the heart? How do we uncover a personal practice by which to restore our trust in living as the original art? How do we take the sorrow that endures forever—because every one of us will have our share of it—and find the courage, support, love, and skills by which to melt it in the furnace of our heart, so from that everlasting bronze we can shape the pleasure and peace that abides in a moment?

And how do we tune as we go, without pause, making amends for our clumsy missteps and making music with what we have?

I don't know how to do this, but by God, I'm devoted to try. I'm devoted to learn. I'm devoted to journey with you and others to discover how. Because this is why we were put on Earth—to hold our turmoil in the fire of transformation until it emerges as peace. Who would have imagined? It's through our humanness that we glimpse eternity and work our alchemy of spirit, never knowing what will happen next.

A Reflective Pause

○ *Begin separate journal entries with each of these beginning phrases: My suffering comes from ... My joy comes from ... My work going forward is ... Explore what your suffering, joy, and work going forward have to do with each other.*

○ *In conversation with a friend or loved one, tell the story of a time when you had to meet life without pause. In what way were you stretched out of tune? How did you adjust? Did adjusting reveal any unknown qualities to you?*

In the third section, we wandered beyond the old protections we all carry into the persistent drift born of each moment, where just for a moment, we need nothing to be happy. Stumbling onto such a turn in the path, we're faced with bemoaning that such moments don't last or letting such nourishment sustain us until the next shiny thing appears from the deep. Being a spirit in a body on Earth is such a simple and difficult journey, which requires that we learn how to move toward what is precious and how to restore our trust in life, when fear and anxiety and other forms of suffering make us lose our way. Mysteriously, all things are true and only an open heart can receive and make sense of them. When we can accept this, we open our hearts further and receive each other more deeply. When we can accept that life is the master teacher, we begin to discover, little by little, that more than finding Heaven on Earth, we're asked to release Heaven by living here on Earth. Humbly, we keep everything connected by letting the light of our soul join with the light of the world.

I'm moved to ask: What is your history with immersion? What are you immersed in now? What is your daily rhythm between the surface and the deep? Which is more difficult: diving or surfacing? What sustains you during periods of confusion or pain? Can you describe a moment of Heaven on Earth you've known? Little by little, how are you learning to listen to both your gift and your emptiness? Without pause, how are you learning to tune your heart as you go?

Ultimately, it's the exchange of aliveness that keeps us vital. From here, we'll explore that exchange and the courage not to waste our gifts, the oasis of reliable truths we can return to, and the magic of peace. We'll enter the tender and resilient practice by which we take turns at the edge of the world, wanting to give up and needing to carry on. We'll speak about the One True World that holds us and our inextricable place in it.

THE EXCHANGE THAT
BRINGS US ALIVE

▸ ▸ ▸

On this ever-revolving wheel of being
The individual self goes round and round
Through life after life, believing itself
To be a separate creature, until
It sees its identity with the Lord of Love
And attains immortality in the indivisible Whole.

—THE SHVETASHVATARA UPANISHAD

There is always a practice before the practice; a sitting before the incomprehensible long enough to feel and sometimes understand the mystery each instrument and craft is designed to invoke.

In Japan, before an apprentice can clay up his hands and work the wheel, he must watch the master potter for years. In Hawaii, before a young man can ever touch a boat, he must sit on the cliff of his ancestors and simply watch the sea. In Africa, before the children are allowed to drum, they must rub the length of skin stretched over wood and dream of the animal whose heart will guide their hands. In Vienna, the prodigy must visit the piano maker before ever fingering a scale, to see how the keys are carved and put into place. And in Switzerland legend has it that before the master watchmaker can couple his tiny gears, he must sit long enough to feel the passage of time.

Starting this way enables a love of the process that is life-giving. The legendary cellist Pablo Casals was asked at ninety-two why he still practiced four hours a day. He smiled and replied, "Because I believe I'm making progress."

It is this sort of deep progress that saves us.

WHAT MORE COULD I ASK FOR?

▼ ▼ ▼

THREE MONTHS AGO, my father died. Like aftershocks of an earthquake, my grief is jagged, then subtle and deep. I keep trying to hold on to his face and voice, though it fades like a mask dropped in water, sinking out of view. I keep trying to remember our last real conversation, which happened in the hospital in January, when he took my hand and said, haltingly through his stroke-laden tongue, "Thank you for having the courage to find me again." What more could I ask for?

Most days, I'm just below the surface in a heavy melancholy. I sense him out of the corner of my eye, but when I look—nothing. His whole life gone, a brilliant sea at sunset eaten by the night. I feel death's whisper everywhere. Does anything matter? So unlike me to dwell in the dark nothingness, but riding alongside him to his death has saturated me with the vanishing of all our effort. Yet, there's still so much to learn.

Once things settle, though they never settle, let's find each other, over coffee, and spend a long moment together in the swell of this mysterious sea. You must tell me if you have ever been saturated with the dark, if you've ever fallen into a cave along the way.

My friend Sandra tells me, "I remember digging my heels into time in the weeks after my father passed. Each day that separated him from me felt like an assault as time pulled me farther and farther away from his face, his voice, the warmth of him."

She reminds me that *dayenu* in Yiddish means *it would have been enough*. It was enough to hold his hand as he was slowly leaving. It was enough to kiss his forehead as he slept. It is enough to finger his tools now that he's gone. And it isn't.

My father's spirit left his body when he died and joined the sea of light, no longer contained or nameable. And yet, once home, in my study, my first sense of him without a body came in the pour of morning light through the high, thick branches of the oak beside our house. Somehow the essence of my father poured through the leaves and branches that hover over my study, until like water filling a hole, that nameless sea of light filled the hole in my heart, until a sense of him flooded my one window, making me stop, feeling bathed in the part of him that had no words.

Beyond the trees and living forms on Earth, my father remains indistinguishable from all the other particles of light, but the mystery of the heart's unending gravity is that, as certain flowers draw certain insects to pollinate them, our grieving hearts open like those flowers to draw the particles of spirit we love to us. It's what the Universal moves through that makes it personal; the way river over stone makes water sing, the way each stone makes the water sing differently.

My friend George, kind, wise George, listened to me when I ran out of words the other night. Then he took my hand and said, "We can love despite what happens to us, when we see both sides of life, when we see the paradox of life, when we've lived enough to see that nothing is static, when we're not stuck, when we can be vulnerable, and because life exists beyond our ability to make sense of it."

What more could I ask for, than to have friends like these. I know what he says is true. Yet I feel stuck. And being stuck is part of the journey. I might be stuck for a day or a decade. The challenge is for my stuckness to invoke my compassion, not my judgment. Often, I remain stuck because of my willfulness. But, just as often, I remain stuck because of the unexpected harshness of the weather of experience. And compassion—to ourselves and others—allows us to help each other move through the stuckness that incubates us while we grow.

What more could I ask for, than for the wisdom of experience to reveal itself in the continual journey we make from partialness to Wholeness.

Yet I am drifting in this dark sea of grief, day by day, which I can't deny or simply leave. Always when I feel exhausted or out of balance, with nothing left to say, I know I need to take things in, to learn something new. Not to distract myself or avoid what I'm moving through, but to enlarge the mix, to open myself to the swirl of mystery I'm always a part of, so the acuteness of the one life position I'm overwhelmed by can evolve.

I was in such a mood when I was interviewed by phone by a thoughtful young woman from Idaho who was asking genuine questions, the kind no one can answer, the only kind of question worth entering. I was in my study, where my father's spirit poured through the trees, when she asked about the dream we all carry to become an artist of some kind.

I believe we are already what we seek. It waits like a seed to be loved into blossom. It was then I began to talk about the ancient story of Aladdin and his lamp. Later, I realized that, though I've known this story since I was a child, I didn't know where it came from. So I went searching.

"Aladdin's Lamp" is a Middle Eastern folktale, one of the most famous stories in *The Book of One Thousand and One Nights* (*The Arabian Nights*), though the story was added to the collection by the French translator and archaeologist Antoine Galland, who was the first European to translate *One Thousand and One Nights*. He published it in twelve volumes between 1704 and 1717. Galland first heard the tale of Aladdin from a Syrian storyteller from Aleppo. On March 25, 1709, Galland records in his diary that he met an Arabian scholar, Youhenna Diab, known as Hanna, who was brought to Paris by Paul Lucas, a celebrated French traveler. I can almost see Galland on that early spring night in Paris, transfixed by the strange storyteller as he spun the old tale in a dark parlor by a flickering light. What was Galland like? What was Hanna like? Who did they love? Who did they grieve? Galland couldn't stop thinking about the story and translated it during the following winter.

The story takes place in China and begins with Aladdin struggling in poverty when a sorcerer from Maghreb (Northern Africa) takes him under his wing. While feigning kindness, the sorcerer uses Aladdin to fetch a magical lamp hidden in a cave. The lamp is home for a powerful genie that will serve whoever rubs, caresses, and cares for the lamp. A trouble-laden journey unravels to possess the lamp, so the owner can have access to the powerful genie. But, like so many anonymous tales told and retold through the centuries, the unconscious lesson is that *we* are the lamp and the powerful genie lives inside each of us. Despite all the travails and misbegotten adventures, no one can possess the lamp or trick the genie. Only the authentic care of our deeper being can bring forth the abiding spirit that lives within us.

After tracing the origins of the story, I could see that I'm stuck in the cave of my grief, holding the lamp of life, of my life, the lamp of my soul, close to my chest. But I've forgotten how to make the genie appear. The word *genie* comes from the word *genius*. As I mentioned earlier, in its original form, genius was not reserved for the brilliance of a few, but first meant *attendant spirit*. And everyone has a genie, an attendant spirit. We could call the spirit that attends and guides us our soul, our *ātman*, our Buddha nature, our Christlight, our center point of being, the swirl of the living Universe enlivening us, or the current of the Tao moving us along. Whatever name you give it, we all have a genie, an attendant spirit that we hold close to our chest, especially when stuck in the dark cave of our journey, when surrounded by pain or fear or grief.

Like me, now. Is this all part of the incubation of experience that births something deeper each time we make it through? Is this what the great Irish poet William Butler Yeats means when he says, "Genius is a crisis that joins that buried self for certain moments to our trivial daily mind"? Isn't the dark weather of circumstance the hothouse that joins our depth with our surface, that causes us to endure the rough, transformative process of becoming more whole?

What is it in me that reaches for something new when questioning if life is worth living? What is it in me that, when stuck in the dark, lifts my sorry head to search for a way out? What authority of being, what lamp in the chest, says—take this old story and see where it comes from? Time and again, I learn that it's only the mark of our hands, the tending and caring of what's before us that lets the lamp of the soul guide us out of the dark.

Three months ago, my father died, and in my grief I'm led to discover that the story of Aladdin's lamp unfolds the timeless truth that when we can tend and care for the small light we carry—in an authentic way—our inborn gifts will show us our genius, our attendant spirit. And working our gifts in the presence of our attendant spirit will guide us to become who we were born to be. Often, this journey begins in the dark cave of our trouble when we finally trust that the small lamp we carry will transform us and show us the way out.

What more could I ask for?

....

∽ *We are already what we seek. It waits like a seed to be loved into blossom.*

....

A Reflective Pause

○ *In your journal, explore what kind of space your heart needs to do its job. What steps can you take to create this space?*

○ *In conversation with a friend or loved one, describe one way you have been bent by kindness and one way you have been softened by suffering. How have these experiences shaped you?*

THE COURAGE NOT
TO WASTE OUR GIFTS

*No one can construct the bridge upon which precisely you
must cross the stream of your life, but you.*

—FRIEDRICH NIETZSCHE

EVERY SINGLE BEING has an amazing, unfathomable gift that only
meeting life head-on and heart-on will reveal. And we can't fully
know our gift alone. We need each other to discover the gift, to believe
in the gift. And then, to learn how to use it. The challenge for each of
us is not to discount our gift because of the indifference of others, and
not to abdicate our gift because of the various weights we're forced to
carry.

What does it mean to have a gift? For the lamp, the light it was
shaped to carry is its gift. Without a light, a lamp has no purpose. For a
person, we are shaped by experience to reveal the light we carry. For a
person, how that light comes through us is our gift. We could say that
for every hand, the heart it was shaped to carry is its gift. And a life cut
off from the work of its heart has no purpose. Our call in the midst of
our days is to discover the gift that connects our heart and our hands,
to discover the light that fills the lamp of the life we are given. Once
discovered, our work is to never let the light of our gift go out.

The gift can come through us in any way: cleaning the snow off a neighbor's car, clipping your dog's nails, reading books to blind children, helping a retired couple refinance their home, or through devoting yourself to Beethoven's violin concerto. As a lamp can light any patch of ground, the hand filled with heart can light anything it touches. The gift is what fills our hand. The various skills of the world are how the gifted hand moves.

Through our gift, we bring our portion of life-force back into the world. Each of us is born a heart's length from everything that ever lived and from everything yet to be. Every being on Earth is created to be a conduit between the Universal Life-Force and the moment coming alive. Being such a conduit is our birthright. When the gift of life moves through us, we are enlivened to be completely who we are. Whatever form it takes, being completely who we are fulfills us *and* makes us an instrument of Spirit in the world. Inhabiting our gift and giving it freely is how Spirit renews the world. Like a lightning rod, it's through our authenticity that the Creative Force of Life informs and grounds the world. It's opening our heart to the Whole of Life while living in the particular rush of life before us that makes our gifts shimmer and show themselves.

In an evolving interview with the psychologist James Hillman that spanned a decade, Tim McKee came to understand that:

> [Hillman] believed each individual has a purpose or calling in life that reveals itself in childhood and reappears, often as a set of so-called symptoms, until it is heeded. Harnessing this potential is what he considered the great mortal, and moral, challenge. [Hillman] once said our duty is not to rise above life but to "grow down into it."

Paradoxically, we're born with a sense of Oneness but we have to move through the days to understand and realize it. For all the dreams we dream and goals we work toward, we often stumble into a moment when what waits inside our dream somehow shows itself as already true. Not wasting our gifts means trusting the signs of potential we sense along the way that, if listened to, will lead us to our inborn nature.

Growing down into the heart of things is how we find our voice, the one note of truth that remains true under all our trouble, even when we can't give words to it. How do we know when we're hearing that voice? No one but you can say. For me, I've known my voice when I feel like a fish who's found the current, or a bird who's opened its wings to glide. When listening to my soul, I feel like my heart is opening to its native trust of life. When I can follow my heart into the vast waters of being, I feel like a turtle who loses the burden of his shell once slipping into deeper water.

Finding the ways our soul can breathe cleanly and completely is our career. Where that happens is our occupation.

To Live Out Loud

Forget conventionalisms: forget what the world thinks of you stepping out of place; think your best thoughts, speak your best words, work your best works, looking to your own conscience for approval.

—SUSAN B. ANTHONY, painted on a newspaper vending machine

It was the French novelist Balzac who declared, "I am here to live out loud." From all accounts, he was flamboyant and overflowing. But what he invoked raises more than just being the talk of the party. To live out loud has more to do with presence than noise. More to do with exposing our quivering center than with being verbal. Living out loud remains our best chance to shed a muffled existence and to know things directly. In truth, I can be hidden or revealed in a crowded room without saying a word, without making a move, and no one will ever know except me. So living out loud depends on finding the quiet courage not to hide from life. This is a crucial step in not wasting our gifts.

In Japanese, *kenshō* means seeing into one's nature. By investing time and care into our wonder, curiosity, creativity, and compassion, we stay in conversation with our inborn nature. And whether we're a shoemaker, surgeon, plumber, or pastor, inhabiting our inborn nature is what enables us to manifest skills that contribute to each other's lives and to the world.

When we let these qualities wither, an important part of us goes voiceless. If we experience love without wonder and compassion, we wind up touching things without care, thinking the world a cold and lifeless place. The painful irony, of course, is that no matter how muffled we are, the need to live out loud and feel doesn't vanish. It just intensifies as we look for what we need in all the wrong places, like fleeing to the desert in search of water. The inability to feel leads to violence as a last attempt to feel. That we live in an age where sexual assault and abuse are rampant is a haunting indictment that we've created a culture that keeps divorcing its citizens from their inborn nature.

To live out loud is to allow ourselves to be tender as we feel life directly. Only the tender can be shaped and transformed. Only when tender does the gift move through us.

....

As a lamp can light any patch of ground, the hand filled with heart can light anything it touches.

....

Never-Ending Assignments

He was locked in jail, but the bars were a yard apart and he could have walked out whenever he wanted.

—FRANZ KAFKA, from *The Prisoner*

It's natural enough to circle a difficult decision, to chew on it until we're strong enough and clear enough to move forward in our lives. The decision might be to leave someone or to find someone or to follow a dream or to begin again. But often, we ruminate so hard and long that we think the struggle to decide is our home. In this regard, becoming transfixed with diversion is an insidious way to waste our gifts.

An old story that speaks to the power of diversion is part of the great epic poem *Khamsa,* written by the Indo-Persian poet Amir Khusrau Dihlavi (1253–1325). In this small tale, Solomon occupies two ambitious demons with never-ending assignments. He tells one to fill the sea with sand and the other to fill the desert with water. Driven by their ambition and their fantasy of reward, they spend the rest of their lives trying and so are kept from doing harm to others. Tucked within this small encounter is a great deal about human nature and how we can easily slip into squandering our talents by occupying our gifts rather than facing the hard work of releasing them.

At first glance, it seems rather clever to occupy these demons forever. But part of Solomon's consciousness will forever be tied to monitoring the whereabouts of these demons and making sure they're still occupied. The harder task is to quell the voraciousness of our ego, which makes aspects of ourselves demonic and ambitious in the first place.

Let me translate this personally. Before I had accepted my small place in the scheme of things, I suffered great insecurity and couldn't find the bedrock of my own self-worth, a common malady, to be sure. So my twin horses of ego set out to be great and well known and I was able to occupy them with the endless task of seeking validation and recognition from people who didn't know me. This was very much like trying to fill the sea with sand or to fill the desert with water. And regardless of whether my demons were successful or not, my gifts were being squandered in the private industry that was necessary to keep searching for a sense of worth that no one could bestow but me. Whatever my workhorse demons brought back, it was insufficient because I viewed it with unworthy eyes.

The demons take many forms but two recurring names are ambition and the need to be accepted. Now there's nothing wrong with wanting to work toward something or with wanting to be loved. These longings become demonic when the ambition is seen as a way to jump over the work of being human—to be famous as a way to solve feeling unworthy, for example—and when the cost of being accepted is giving up who we are instead of entering true relationships that can affirm and enrich who we are. These quandaries never go away and the challenge, constantly before us, is to make a difference among the living, while not being intoxicated by the hubris that we can change the world.

A Story and a Song

Too many of us go to our grave with our music still inside.

—OLIVER WENDELL HOLMES

If we hide long enough, we forget what we are hiding or that we our-selves are hidden. Among the Kannada people of India, there's a fable about a quiet yet troubled housewife who knows a story and a song. But she keeps them to herself, never telling anyone the story and never singing the song. Feeling imprisoned, they slip out of her mouth one day while she's sleeping. The story takes the form of a pair of shoes and the song becomes a coat. When her husband returns, he becomes suspicious, "Who's visiting?" The housewife replies, "I don't know." Thinking she's betrayed him, the husband goes to the Monkey Temple to sleep, where he overhears the lamp flames gossiping that his wife knows a story and a song. But she never tells the story and she never sings the song. He runs home to ask her about her story and her song. But she has forgotten them. "What story, what song?" she says.

Implicit in this old fable are the questions: Do we know our story and our song? And do we trust those we live with enough to tell our story and voice our song? If not, our gifts won't tolerate being hidden. Feeling suffocated, they will find a way to leave us and be free. For a story is for telling and a song is for singing. So you don't have to hide whatever God has given you. You don't need to apologize for what you love. That you love it makes it sacred. In truth, your love makes the sacred show itself, the way the sun makes flowers open. The missteps we make and the ways we hurt each other can be ugly. But from inside the vantage point of love, nothing is ugly and no one is ugly. From inside, there is no bad music, no bad voicings, no trite expressions. Near the pulse of what matters, the only standard is vitality.

That which is thoroughly alive defies critique. In this, Spirit is like electricity. It flows through clean connections. When the connections are broken or severed, the vitality is out of reach. And without Spirit, vitality, and love, things can turn ugly. Too often, we cut our connection to the sacred by *critiquing what matters* rather than *taking in what matters,* which is like rejecting manna because it has no salt. But beneath the muffling of what we know, beneath our fascination with diversion, beneath our endless critiques, love leads us to our gifts. As in all eras, gone and to come, the wind carries too many songs not to try.

∽ *Finding the ways our soul can breathe cleanly and completely is our career. Where that happens is our occupation.*

Being Kind and Meeting the World

I am not bound to win, but I am bound to be true. I am not bound to succeed, but I am bound to live by the light that I have.

—ABRAHAM LINCOLN

To make use of our gifts, we have to give. With no rhythm of kindness in our lives, we move through the days very close to death. But in any given moment—*any moment given over to*—meeting the world with kindness will rejuvenate our soul. When we return to being kind—*being open, receptive, and respectful to the life that comes our way*—we are brought alive. Giving is the atom of daily resurrection.

When we exercise our heart—*walk it, stretch it, reach with it*—being kind restores our authenticity and openness. We become a conduit through which life-force flows. No matter what we give or the amount we give, the giver receives as much, if not more, in *spiritual resurgence* for offering such care. Kindness is a continual necessity, like breathing. We risk going blue when we withhold what matters.

When we act on the care we feel between us, being kind strengthens and clarifies our relationships. The simple and authentic touch of a hand, the listening to pain, the quiet holding of a dream, the giving of time and space for honest confusion, the honoring of questions that won't go away—each of these efforts strengthens those involved and makes the Whole that contains them more visible.

At the deepest level, kindness reveals kinship. The tender act of generosity enables us to feel the tug of the Universe. Being kind strengthens the weave of the Universal Fabric, and leaning into the experience and people at hand makes the web of connection palpable. In essence, giving is an aerobic of inner health that allows us to know our place in the vast Universe. And while *being kind* is a gesture we offer, *living kindly* is a way of being we inhabit. Both are invaluable. Our individual health and the health of the Universe depend on the personal practice we develop in both regards: being kind and living kindly.

Living kindly requires a commitment to openness. For under whatever we accomplish or fail to accomplish, staying open is a life-giving act itself. This all points to the spiritual fact that presence—bringing all of who we are without reservation to what is before us—is the eternal wellspring that feeds whatever acts of kindness we can offer. Our relationship to presence determines both how we give and how we receive.

Once we accept that the world is not just one house of sameness, the spiritual aim widens and deepens into seeking as many views, stories, insights, dreams, and histories as we can find. For all views together contribute to a living Whole that no one view can approach. And so, living kindly, in a daily way, involves meeting people where they are.

When we judge and compare, we stop the flow of presence. When we refine our list of requirements in order to love, the exchange of aliveness that comes from giving goes elsewhere, the way water will flow around an obstacle. That quiet teacher, the sun, shows us how to live kindly, as it has no requirements for anything to receive its light.

It helps to think of ourselves as *spiritual emissaries*, committed to speaking as many languages of experience as possible. It doesn't matter how many different names there are for that which is larger than us, that which precedes us, or that which will live on after us. The generosity of our presence and openness—*our commitment to living kindly*—can help us listen for the Unity that lives beyond the various names we pray to. It's the timeless and nameless Source, no matter what it's called, that joins us. Only in kindness can we find our gifts and our nameless kinship.

We are here to love the light out of each other. It's not something

we can plan or build, only ready ourselves for. This is what relationships
that endure can do. When we lend a hand, we open a way for our heart
to touch the heart of everything.

> ∿ *Too often, we cut our connection to the sacred by critiquing
> what matters rather than taking in what matters.*

A Reflective Pause

○ *Describe someone you admire whose deep passion comes from
their connection to life. If still alive, go to them, and ask about
their passion and their understanding of what matters.*

○ *Describe someone who loves the light out of you. How does this
happen and what does it feel like? If you haven't, tell them of the
power and gift of their love.*

○ *What is the one thing your heart needs from the world to open
completely? And what is the one thing your opened heart can give
to the world?*

RELIABLE TRUTHS

▶ ▶ ▶

I know what the cure is: it is to give up, to relinquish, to sur-
render, so that our little hearts may beat in unison with the
great heart of the world.

—HENRY MILLER

AS PEOPLE SPEAK different languages from all over the world while
standing on the same Earth, people speak different truths while
standing on the ground of all truth. As personalized as each journey is,
we all touch the same foundational truth of existence.

Ultimately, no one can tell you what a truth is. We need to discover
what is true and believe it for ourselves. We need to discover for ourselves the touchstone of the common foundational truth that we all
stand on; no matter how differently we come to it. We need to arrive
at some felt, embraceable sense of which truths are worth returning
to. What is the bedrock of truth that we each find reliable? By reliable,
I mean, what you can return to that will hold you up. What is foundational? What won't let you down? These are unnameable truths that can
help us restore what matters when we lose our way.

▶ ▶ ▶

Here are some reliable truths that I return to:

○ *It is rare to be alive.* When I slip and take life for granted, my
return to the astonishing fact that we are here at all grounds me
and I become wholehearted again. None of this—waking to
another day, or taking the dog out to pee and seeing dawn light
the underside of a bank of clouds, or being touched by music
I've never heard—none of it has to be happening. Each thing
we care for, like each twig in each bird's mouth, is a small object
of wonder that we build our nest with. We have to discover
what is possible, again and again, by opening our heart.

○ *There's a common well of being at the center of everything.* There
is something unnameable, mystical, and eternal at the center of
all life that we all share. Great love and suffering bring us to our
knees where we remember to drink from the center of life. This
always makes me strong enough to stand again and make my way.

○ *We are all connected by invisible threads maintained and repaired
when we love.* When I forget that everything is connected,
the world becomes a dark, chaotic machine. Then, I eventually
bump into some invisible but felt way that we are knit together.
Without notice, light comes through a cloud to paint a stranger's
face on the train and the journey we share, though I don't know
her name, is again knowable. And this softens the ride.

○ *Kindness is in our very nature.* The impulse to give and join is
in our spiritual DNA. Kindness reveals the web of connections.
In addition to helping others and to growing our integrity of
relationship, kindness reveals kinship. Kindness reveals our
relationship to everything. Whenever I follow my impulse to be
kind, I begin to experience the Oneness of Things.

○ *There's a sweet ache to being alive that lets us know we are here.*
Below any sadness or sense of exhaustion, I feel the tug and
pull of everything alive that moves through each of us. More
than concepts or theories or principles, it is this sweet ache just

behind my heart that lets me feel my tether to the invisible
depth that roots the world.

○ *Saying yes is how Spirit keeps moving through us into the world.*
  I keep returning to this dynamic teacher: What's in the way
  is the way. Saying yes to what I'm given, though I often resist
  it, always helps me grow. Saying yes always shows me a way
  through. Saying yes, the gift I've carried since birth is given a
  way to show itself.

Returning to any of these animates my sense of what is possible,
renews my sense of relationship with life, and re-inspires my inborn
faith that everyone in the world, regardless of what each believes to be
true, is a light that love gives form to.

When Lost

And when I can't find any of the truths I rely on, when I'm so lost or
confused that I can't find myself in the mirror, I need to rely on the
foundational truth of love. We are never far from the need to complete
each other by bearing witness to each other's journey. To be seen and
heard for who we are is a steadfast truth that is often overlooked and
underestimated. When held and listened to in earnest, we grow.

After all these years, I'm fairly practiced at being myself. And yet, it
was traveling all the way to Maui last year to be interviewed by Oprah
Winfrey that helped me grow. Before we began taping, Oprah took my
hand and said, "This is your time. I don't want you to leave anything
unsaid that's in your heart." I immediately felt deeply received and
accepted. When the cameras began to roll, we entered a depth together
in which we both were gentle, honest, and strong in owning our own
experience at being a spirit in the world.

We filmed for over two hours. When we came to the wonderful
silence at the end of our conversation, we looked at each as we would
at the end of a hike to the top of the island. We had glimpsed eternity.
And to my surprise, I stood a few inches taller, was breathing a few

inches deeper. I left that day inhabiting a few inches of my soul more fully. This fullness hasn't left. This is what being held and listened to, in earnest, can do.

....

∽ *As personalized as each journey is, we all touch the same foundational truth of existence.*

....

Inwardly Reliable

The faithfulness of the magnificent Impressionist painter Claude Monet (1840–1926) to what he felt and saw is instructive. Toward the end of his life, Monet developed double cataracts. He painted right up till the end. He painted his famous *Water Lilies* through the film of his cataracts. He tried to restore his sight and volunteered to have one of the very first cataract surgeries, but it didn't work.

Monet seldom spoke about his work and rarely gave interviews. In his later years, he was so famous throughout the world that people were publishing complex interpretations of his work. This prompted the aging painter to break his silence. He granted a single interview. When the journalist came all the way to Giverny, about seventy-five kilometers northwest of Paris, Monet said, "There is no interpretation. I am simply painting what I see. That's it. I paint what I see." And he ended the interview.

What if Monet developed his amazing vision and gift of painting over a lifetime so that he could retrieve his masterpieces—his *Water Lilies*—by seeing *through* his cataracts and being faithful to painting just what he saw?

The courage and steadfastness of Monet to paint what he saw is an example of what it means to be inwardly reliable. We're constantly asked to stay faithful to what is before us till the gift reveals itself, independent of what we think is clear or what we think is true. Life's inner curriculum is solely dependent on our commitment to never stop feeling, expressing, and conversing with what comes through us.

The Rough Chalice of Now

Earlier, I spoke about the practice of accepting what we're given as a way to become intimate with the nature of the living Universe. I spoke about the need to meet our experience with our own notion of what it means to say yes, as a way of being that strengthens us to grow. I spoke about Beethoven's demand of musicians to play through challenging movements without pause; a call to each of us to stay in relationship to life and adjust as we go, even when out of tune. That we need to work with what we're given, that we need to say yes to life in order to grow, that we need to live at times without pause, adjusting as we go—these, too, are reliable truths we are always returned to.

I work with these conditions as they work with me, almost daily. But opening my heart yet again, this time to the death of my father and the evaporation of my mother's mind, I find myself out of tune, struggling without pause to get back to the surface. I feel the substance of life seeping back into its invisible ground, withdrawing from the borrowers it has lent itself to.

My father is gone and my mother is going and, despite all our difficulties, I love them both. After all these years, their personalities are etched in me: so painful in the carving, but the scars have tarnished into lines that make up my face. So saying yes, here, is swimming into the incomprehensible depth of feeling that losing them opens, neither sorting nor explaining these feelings away.

When I can touch that depth and feel the bottom of my grief— for what we managed in this life and what we failed to bring to each other—it opens yet another grief. I am brought to the inescapable fact that life will leave me, too. In my own way, in my own time, I will arrive here. Their going brings my own death closer. This begins to explain the dark pain under my heart. For I love life so much. I'm not ready for death to come closer. No one is. No one wants this majestic and difficult ride to end. It seems so simple and obvious, but when I let myself feel the end of my own life—look it in the face—I am strangely returned to a reliable truth I've been devoted to for years: to hold nothing back in order to find the fullness of life in the moment at hand.

Strangely, facing my own death only reawakens my devotion to saying yes to life.

No matter how the weather of life twists us about, surviving and thriving always comes back to entering what's before us, to pouring our entire being into the rough chalice of now. As one of its endless borrowers, I bow to life, like so many before me, saying yes one more time, standing tall while pleading with an open heart, "Let me borrow what matters a little while more."

....

     ∿ *We are all connected by invisible threads maintained and repaired when we love.*

....

Blessing Doorways

Since the beginning of time, we have found ways to return to reliable truths to help us endure. In the early period of the Chán school in China (sixth century BC), teachers passed on personal items to students as a sign of Dharma transmission. These items served as symbols of kinship, of unbroken lineage from one generation to the next. The personal items of a teacher were considered sacred reminders of the fundamental nature of things that no one can escape—truth, beauty, suffering, and peace—and the truest values that we can always rely on—honesty, wonder, compassion, and equanimity.

Teachers would give their students robes they had worn for years, or alms bowls they had carried through winter. A teacher might give a student a portrait or a bit of calligraphy, an armrest or a fly whisk. The reliable truth here is that when a student could touch something the teacher had touched, it would serve to reanimate their common connection to all that matters.

We've always done this. Though, without a context for why we carry such items, they're reduced to souvenirs or the bric-a-brac of nostalgia. My life is filled with symbols of transmission. I need them as stones to step on in my journey. There's my grandfather's Talmud that he brought from Russia with its crumbling cover, which I found in the Brooklyn basement of my youth. It helps me return to the endless immigration I'm always a part of, from the ancient to the new. There's my grandmother's mezuzah that I have nailed to the doorway of the study I'm writing this in. When I touch my hand to my lips and then to the mezuzah, I feel her kissing it, and her mother before her kissing it in Katarinaslav, south of Kiev. It helps me remember that there is more to life than what is visible. There's my father's awl, the tool he made holes in wood with, a tool his grandfather made holes in leather with. When I hold it, I feel my father's lifelong commitment to craft. There's my first copy of Pablo Neruda's poems, which my dear friend Robert gave me when we were graduate students and which I wouldn't return, so uplifting and familiar was Neruda's voice. And there's the broken shell I found in the Caribbean that looks like a beak. It reminds me that all poets sing their poems through the break that nature creates in us.

With the aid of these totems passed on by my teachers, I can return to what is reliable and unseen: that what is holy is always with us, no matter what sea we're asked to cross; that blessing doorways can make doors open; that, though skill alone can't give us meaning, a devotion to craft can; that if we dare to stay vulnerable, we'll find a brother or sister somewhere near; and that, painful as each break is, each can open us to our deepest song.

The return to what is reliable begins with a willingness to receive what has meaning and a commitment to pass on what matters. As you put this book down and move through your day, as you leave loved ones and meet strangers, ask yourself, What am I open to receive today, this moment, and what do I carry that is worthwhile enough to pass on? Who might I give this to and when?

⯈　⯈　⯈

We are always at this spiritual fork in the road: to tell ourselves stories to uphold our illusions or to exercise the effort and courage to meet our experience completely by which we can discover our reliable truths. The edge between a reliable truth and an illusion is very thin. So much depends on a constant honesty with ourselves and on the constant love of honest friends.

Returning to what matters gives us access to resilience, which comes from having the strength to lean into whatever life brings us, while opening our vulnerability to absorb it. This is not the kind of strength we can summon or concentrate, but one that we open to the way a flag opens to wind. So we access resilience by showing up and participating fully. The more we can do this, the more available resilience is.

It seems that staying in relationship to what is true is the wellspring of resilience. Staying in relationship to what is true is how we return to what is reliable. For me, what is true lives in the quiet that illuminates the core of every pain, in the depth that is the bottom of every turbulence, in the light that waits to break through every cloud, and in the safety that incubates in the center of every fear. I don't know how to find this bottomless truth or to release it, but I know it's there. If we reach softly into what waits beneath what you and I hold to be true, we will feel a deeper truth that belongs to everyone, and accepting this together, we can be surprised again by everything that lives.

A Reflective Pause

○ *In your journal, describe two, three, or four reliable truths that you've discovered in your life that are foundational, that no one taught you. How did you discover them? If you arrive at something that other people feel is true, what a blessing. Your truth doesn't have to be different for the sake of being different. Rather something you know through your own experience to be foundational.*

○ *In conversation with a friend or loved one, speak of these reliable truths as old friends you haven't seen in a while. Offer a question you would ask of each of them.*

OUTLASTING THE GLARE

▼ ▼ ▼

Up close, the path is seldom what it looks like from afar.

M Y JOURNEY HAS taught me that *the acceptance of what is* is the doorway to our true self and to the one true world. Implied in such acceptance is the constant practice to look at life beyond the glare of the light and the veil of the dark.

Consider how we approach darkness as children. A playful notion is seeded that there's a boogeyman in the closet. Eventually, if we find the courage to open that closet and enter the darkness, it's normal not to see at first. *Accepting what is* is how our eyes grow accustomed to the dark. Because what's there is not really dark, just dark to us. Once still enough, long enough, what seems dark has spaces in it, and we begin to see in those spaces. Carl Jung said, "One does not become enlightened by imagining figures of light, but by making the darkness conscious." So *accepting what is* allows us to enter the one true world. How? By being present enough to outlast the glare of the light and brave enough to part the veil of the dark.

Here's another way to understand this. I'm standing on a hill and looking at a field, struck by how beautiful it is in the sunlight. It seems magical and there's a beautiful glare, which is just as confounding as the darkness we can't see in; except the darkness makes us want to run from it and the glare makes us want to run toward it. Now I say, "Wow, this is idyllic. I wish my life was more like this hill in the sun." So I run up the hill. But always, as we enter reality, the grit of detail presents itself. Now, I'm *in* nature and there's a dead tree trunk and worms burrowing in its stump. And over the hill there's the carcass of a deer beyond a broken fence. The grass and weeds are coming up. It's still beautiful, but now it's stark in its particularity.

Entering life always causes the glare to recede. This holds true for fantasies and illusions and the things we dream of, as well as the things that scare us and hurt us. As we lean into them, the extremeness of their illusion starts to fade and we see things as they are. Now the challenge is to love what's before us all the more, because joy arises from embracing what's before us and being with it until the shimmer of the Universe shows itself through every authentic detail.

Do I feel the shimmer of the particular in every moment? No. Because as a human being, I fall in and out of accepting things as they are. One day, I'm feeling at peace when I drop the groceries and cut my hand picking up the broken mayonnaise jar. I wonder, why me? I feel somewhat cursed to have things break around me. But I pick up the pieces and go back for more, wondering where the peace went. Though the peace goes nowhere.

We struggle with these jarring experiences of being human, unsure whether the broken jar defines our time on Earth or if all the breakage is part of a larger Whole that holds us up. This is our challenge: How to live our small daily lives within the context of all the depth the world comes from? How to grind out the music of who we are, while trying to listen to the larger music of life?

When younger, my first experience of the one true world was startling and amazing. It led me into the high of revelation—the intoxication of new insight. As I've grown older, my experience of insight has become more subtle. I find there's less of a contrast between insight and being, the more grounded I am in life. There was a time about five or six years ago when I wondered, *Am I losing touch with all that is precious? Am I becoming jaded? Am I taking life for granted?* But after living in the depth of things as they are, I can affirm that life keeps revealing itself as more knit in my skin. When I can outlast the glare, what matters presents itself as an ongoing depth that is less outside of me and more a part of me.

With this in mind, I encourage you to look closely at the particulars of your life until you can sense the largesse of being that holds you. I encourage you to accept things as they are until you can feel the gritty mystery of life. When we begin to outlast the glare and the dark inherent in living, the resources of life start to show themselves.

The Glare of Another

Upon approach, the luminous aura of life takes our breath away and, just as often, the living details of reality knock the wind out of us. This is the mystical inhalation and exhalation of experience. It's how the soul breathes. So it's important to resist the urge to settle on one fixed side of life that tells us that things are either all bright and luminous or all dark and tangled. The real question is how to keep inhaling and exhaling, letting all of life move through us.

When we begin to love someone, the aura and glare of another's soul can take our breath away. Yet when we eagerly descend into the piece of Heaven we've discovered in another, the working details of that relationship will often lead us through briars and past a carcass or two among the weeds. This, too, can knock the wind out of us. With our hands on our knees and our hearts in our mouths, we think we've made a bad choice, and this can be true, or that we've been fooled, which can also be true. But more often, if we can stay committed, the deeper truth is that this is how souls grow together on Earth—our deep effort to love makes living together beyond the glare possible.

Yet it's so easy to run from the work of love and to become intoxicated with the glare of another. We can easily run from the glow of one person to the next, yearning for the high of being blinded by something more lighted than us. We can, in fact, become addicted to the sudden brightness of another that takes our breath away. We can stop facing ourselves and become addicted to the glare. We can do this with loves or dreams or careers or with the need for new experience, running from the detailed work of tending the hill we've climbed, because we're intoxicated with the glare of the next hill and all its possibility.

To make the journey even more difficult, there's the dark glare of fear that blinds us to the next small step. If allowed to take over, our fear can mimic death until we hold our breath. Fear and the dark glare it conjures can trigger a spiritual form of arrhythmia in which the heart skips a beat. The danger comes when we believe that holding our breath in fear is all there is. Then the road to everything narrows and we risk the heart stopping.

And while we can't prevent having our breath taken away or having the wind knocked out of us or having our heart skip a beat out of fear, we can outlast these enervations the way divers outlast their brisk entry into the deep.

Accepting what is allows us to enter the one true world, by being present enough to outlast the glare of the light and brave enough to part the veil of the dark.

To Champion Life

Working with all this, I wake with some sadness today and some compassion for how we're tempted by light and dark every day. Right now, after days of rain, the April light is glistening and a large slick crow is preening on a branch whose curl of morning light seems to hold up the world. I notice that birds move to the light, moles to the dark. Snakes do both. And bats navigate the world through their blindness. Much like us.

I have two friends who make their way by their fear of the dark and so they miss much of the light. One is alarmed at every turn. For him, the unknown equals catastrophe. He can hardly be consoled. He feels the Universe is not to be trusted. The other also moves by fear of the dark, but she tries to manage the darkness by ascribing it to people. She uses skepticism as a shield and appears worldly and savvy, almost impenetrable. All her decisions are based on avoiding the worst possible outcome. I've known these two for years. But today, as the April rain clears and the thin ribbon of light on the branch appears to hold up the world, I'm certain that the foundation of their way is terribly incomplete.

I'm not sure what makes me sad today. I only know that I want to champion life in all its complexity and practice the art of finding the light, both inner and outer, while learning from the dark. I believe in making decisions based on what calls me into the open. I believe in going where life takes me while not stepping into holes along the way, if I can help it.

Yet, when still enough, the dark mysteriously lightens. My eyes adjust. And adjusting to the dark is different than resigning to the dark. Adjusting means there is more room to move in a given situation. Resigning means there is less. I don't know why but I trust the Universe. I just accept that it requires my attention and diligence not to hide in the light or the dark.

While I've been thinking my way through this, the crow has gone on, but the branch with its ribbon of light is still holding up the world. Without the darkness of the crow to point it up, I wouldn't have noticed the light on the branch.

Personal Fundamentalism

During periods of constriction and insecurity, we can become so fearful of difference and so in need of preserving our fragile hold on things that we can fall under the spell of our own glare and retreat into a form of *personal fundamentalism*. While religious or political fundamentalism appears as an extreme adherence to a single code or set of views with no exceptions, personal fundamentalism appears as the same extreme adherence but as a desperate effort to uphold our individual experience.

Such personal rigidity manifests as a continual judgment that keeps other forms of life at a distance because our inflexible understanding of the world can't withstand the beautiful and mysterious diversity of life, which won't succumb to any one view. So we deem anything different than us as inferior or not as virtuous, while we secretly scramble like the Wizard of Oz behind our curtain of right and wrong, trying to boom our authority over the world though we fret meekly, afraid we'll be found out. Of course, when rigid and fearful like this, we become prisoners of our own moral scheme.

In the end, judgment and criticism are harsh gatekeepers who push life away. They keep others from climbing our walls while we lean against them, feeling so alone, bemoaning how hard it is to find worthy company.

It's a terribly frightening and lonely way to go through life. In such a state, grace can save us in the form of one gentle and honest friend who might take our hand when no one is looking and say, "Please, give it up. You're no better than the rest of us. It's really all right."

The Dramatic and the Subtle

We live in an age where information, demands, and choices are more plentiful than ever. This rush of possibility gives us the illusion that we can do anything without limit, another form of glare. With all this possibility and the illusion of no limits, we can be seduced into an excitement that stirs a relentless urgency to do it all. In the end, this urgency is oppressive in its allure, the way the sun in its impossible glare intoxicated Icarus to want to touch it. Of course, while we are meant to be lighted, we are not meant to touch the sun. If we try, we will perish. Like Icarus, if we try to do everything without limit, our wings will melt and we'll drown in the sea.

Life is constantly moving between the dramatic and the subtle, between the sun and what it lights. Try as we do to inhabit peak moments only, no one can live like this. In fact, shunning what is subtle is how we miss the miracle that lines everything. As we revel in our desire to be extraordinary, to be the sun, we miss the miracle waiting in the ordinary gift of light.

Beneath the glare of all this possibility and our want to be special, life in its infinite detail is ready to humble us and renew us. After a beautiful day, we settle into a gray one. After an exceptional conversation, we're asked to be patient with that awkward silence, when it seems like there's nothing left to say. After feeling well received, we're challenged to ready ourselves for the disorientation that comes when misunderstood. This is how life moves: from the lift to the sigh and back, from the wide eye to the sleepy one, from the stunning way we see something that was there all along to the repetition of carrying water so many times that we grow tired of spilling it. Once opened, the heart lets in the truth of everything.

Still, facing whatever life brings is like looking into a sudden flash of heat. There's an initial blowback, a wave of distorted clearness we must endure and look through before landing rawly in the situation at hand. While the first courage asks us to look, it's the second courage that allows us to see.

And while outlasting the glare of our stubborn views is never easy, outlasting the glare of what everyone dreams for us is just as essential. We make our way between the dramatic and the subtle, between the horizon of our dreams and the particular shimmer of living them. We look and sometimes see, listen and sometimes hear. We sleep, dream, and bring something back into the world. Our charge is not to isolate and judge the parts we find, but to champion the Physics of the Whole.

We are not bereft when sleeping, we are en route. We are not untethered when dreaming, but mining the core. We are not out of order when naming wonder where we find it, but breaking ground like a flower. Like sunlit threads in a spider's web, we are lumens connecting everything. How does this happen? No one really knows. But our job as ethical beings has always been to outlast what gets in the way and to bring what is inner out.

And so, in the tumble of my days, I work not to be defined by the glare of the light or the veil of the dark but to be in conversation with the particulars that live beneath them, so I might wake in the aliveness that has no history.

As we revel in our desire to be extraordinary, to be the sun, we miss the miracle waiting in the ordinary gift of light.

A Reflective Pause

○ *In your journal, describe a time when someone or some dream looked different from afar and what meeting that person or living that dream looked like up close. How did you understand the difference and what did the journey from the imagined to the real teach you?*

○ *In conversation with a friend or loved one, tell the story of a time when you insisted on your own point of view to the exclusion of other viewpoints. What made you do this and how did your insistence affect those involved? If you could relive the incident, what if anything would you do differently and why?*

THE MAGIC OF PEACE

When the center of the flower
feels its petal opening
and the petal opening
feels the nectar at its center,
the flower is at peace.

I T HELPS TO examine what peace means for each of us. How do we recognize it? How do we receive it? How do we enter it? Once we identify who we are, once we move into relationship, once we quiet our self-centeredness, once we emerge from the pain of becoming, how do we open our hearts to the magic of peace?

After all these years, I'm beginning to see that tranquility is the depth of being that holds what we think and feel, not the still point after we've silenced what we think and feel. Serenity is the depth of being that holds difficulty, not the resting point after we've ended difficulty. And peace is the depth of being that holds suffering and doubt, not the raft we climb on to avoid suffering and doubt. This leads us to joy, which is much deeper and larger than any one feeling. Happiness, fear, anxiety, contentment, doubt, regret, unworthiness, anger, despair—all these and more are the waves that rise and fall in the sea of being. Joy is the ocean that holds all feelings.

This spiritual law reveals the truth that though we can quiet our mind and heart, there is no end to what we think and feel. Though we can solve and lessen the difficulties we face, there is no end to difficulty.

And though we can endure suffering and engage our doubt, there is no end to suffering and doubt. This would be devastating if not for the living truth of Wholeness. For neither is there an end to tranquility, serenity, and peace. It is important to accept these fundamental notions of reality. Otherwise, we can waste our energy trying to bring an end to things that have no end, rather than develop the inner skills to navigate these timeless currents.

I admit I'm still trying to let all my feelings meet and rest in the sea of peace. Our learning never ends. And so, I keep returning to the ever-present riddle that being who we are is the necessary adventure. It unlocks everything, not because our self is so important but because the essential nature that our self carries is the immediate doorway to everything that is life sustaining.

Under all our trouble, it's clear that being who we are not only unfolds our integrity and deepens our relationships, but being true to our own nature allows us to experience the Unity of Things. Regardless of the names we give to that Unity, touching into it cleanses our minds and hearts and we see the world differently. This is the vantage point of peace.

The Majesty and Mess of Feelings

To understand the magic of peace, we need to refresh our understanding of feelings, because only through the majesty and mess of feelings can we approach peace. When seen all the way through, the journey of feeling leads to the tranquility that informs everything. Just as all music begins and ends in silence, all feelings begin and end in peace. For me, the smallest thing covered in light helps me settle to the bottom of whatever I'm feeling. It could be a stone, a blade of grass, the splintered side of the bluebird house. Somehow, the world seems possible again when something very small glows. Somehow, the puzzle that is me seems possible again, if a fallen branch can be surrounded in light. Unexpected light reminds me that what is essential waits at the bottom of whatever I'm struggling with.

∽ *Peace is the depth of being that holds suffering and doubt,*
not the raft we climb on to avoid suffering and doubt.

Like most of us, I've had to learn about the properties and physics of feelings on my own. Because we're sorely mis-educated about the life of feelings and how to respond to them. Early on, we're taught to sort feelings with our mind as a way to neutralize their surprise and power. But the heart is designed to bring us alive by *meeting* our feelings and *relating* to them. The deeper we go, the more feelings appear simultaneously. Over the years, I've learned that the depth of living reveals its meaning when we let the heart merge and integrate our feelings. Letting the heart do its work as an integrating agent lets us experience the energy of life.

In a culture that represses the full range of our humanness, we tend to work at one steady tone of personality, rather than let a steady center hold the human variety, which is necessary if we are to be fully alive. By narrowing what we're allowed to feel, we often shun or exile the array of moods and confusions that come with being human. Then, when the rich depth of being human shows up, it frightens us, as if we're being taken over by some strange alien form. In this way, all the body snatcher and exorcist movies are a projection of how we demonize what we deny.

When we muffle aspects of who we are, when we refuse to stay in relationship with the rich variety of all our human moods, we can't drop into the bottom of things. Instead, we live sideways. Soon, we're overrun by the single mood we resist—doubt, fear, anger, pain, confusion—and for the moment or season, that one mood defines us, or so we think. While it's understandable to be overwhelmed by any moment of acute feeling, we're not that one feeling. At times, doubt and hesitation can grip us so completely that we assume that such fear or worry or unworthiness is who we are.

The image of the many waves and the ocean that holds them is helpful here as well. Again, each mood or feeling, no matter how acute or present, is just one wave in the sea of our being, which at its depth is indistinguishable from the sea of all Spirit. For every individual feeling, if felt and lived through, leads to the depth of all feeling. Yet, at times, we collapse our entire identity into the one difficult mood and lose touch with the ocean of being from which that feeling rises. We all do this and when we do, the days become sharp and jagged.

At times, we become so preoccupied with the one difficult feeling that it becomes our guide or dark master. But the work of loving yourself, which we can always return to, is to stay in conversation with the great living depth from which all these moods and feelings rise. The work of loving yourself, day to day, is to outwait the dark mood, the way you might outwait the turbulence on the water's surface till you can once again see clear to the bottom. And then, to listen to what the depth has to say.

....

∾ *Just as all music begins and ends in silence, all feelings begin and end in peace.*

....

The Edge of Vastness

There's an important difference between peace as a moment of stillness and a state of being. For sure, we need to experience both. Yet, while the calming of agitation is a welcome moment of stillness, peace as a state of being is the edge of vastness that contains all of our psychological habits. As joy holds all our feelings, peace holds all our psychologies. Like human fish, we fin our way through eddies and pools, through turbulent tides, looking for expansive stretches of calm. No one knows exactly how to do this, but we each must try.

For me, leaning into my feelings at the edge of vastness means surrendering my anxious need for order, which never really quiets the unpredictable rise and rush of feelings. Seeing my feelings through means withstanding the disorientation of receiving the emotional surf we live in without knowing what those feelings mean or where they are leading me.

As I mentioned earlier, the older I get, the more I feel in any given moment. This means experiencing more than one feeling at a time. Even when one feeling is pronounced, others are nearby. This is the unifying experience of depth. We're asked to lean into this merging, not resist it. I can feel happy and sad at once. I can feel clear and confused at the same time. I can feel pain and beauty at the same time. Because the current of experience, which never stops, wears the opening of the heart wider and deeper, so it can receive more of life at once. While this is challenging, it's a good thing. It brings us closer to the flow of aliveness.

Regardless of its intensity or subtlety, every feeling is a doorway to the generative core of all feeling. Understandably, we resist difficult emotions, like sadness or despair, even though seeing them through will open us to the depth of all being. It's as if a thousand separate corridors of mood lead to the same depth chamber. There's no way into that core without following one of the corridors to its center. This core depth is the vast center of all being, from which singular feelings arise and take their form.

It's becoming clear that emotional maturity evolves, often against our will, as we're drawn to feel our singular feelings through their very bottom to where we begin to feel the inseparable totality of all feeling. Facing our experience this deeply not only brings us closer to the edge of vastness from which peace arises, but informs a living soul with a lasting sense of being that softens the acuteness of each feeling experienced at the surface. What this means is that while we can't avoid the burn of experience that comes with pain, grief, sadness or worry, if felt to our core, that burn can in time be transmuted into the warmth of light. This dissipation of fire into light is the appearance of peace.

Every individual feeling, if felt and lived through, leads to the depth of all feeling.

Faceless Masters

We never know when we'll come upon models of how to be. I was in the Shedd Aquarium in Chicago when I stumbled into an exhibit of jellyfish from around the world. The room was softly lit and the transparent creatures floating through the tanks seemed iridescent, all aglow. I watched them pulse and move in slow motion, their entire being in unison.

Watching them, I slowed in the half-light myself. I noticed others around me had softened. I focused on the movement of one delicate master, opening and closing its umbrella-shaped bell, streaming its trailing tentacles. It was the crystal jelly, found off the west coast of North America. Its ease of being stunned me.

I want my movement through life to be as complete and seamless. I want to be as transparent. I want my opening and closing to move me forward into life in one continuous devotion, the way inhaling and exhaling, and perceiving and expressing move us so completely when we slow ourselves enough to receive them.

There are two promising traits that jellyfish offer. First, their larvae can stay dormant for decades, drifting until the right condition for birth appears. They are in no hurry. I find this affirming, as we can stay dormant for years, just waiting for the right condition of birth to appear. I often forget this. Birth, especially along the way, begs for our patience. And secondly, some jellyfish, like this crystal jelly, are blessed to emit their own light. This is the by-product of being true to our own nature. While emitting light in a jellyfish is called *bioluminescence*, emitting light in a person is called *the Spirit's glow*.

This mirrors my learning: that authentic living begins when we face and see our way through what we're given. Then the light of the soul emits from within us to meet the light in the world. In those hard-earned moments, we glow in all directions.

I stood for a long time before the crystal jelly and, after a time, I began quite naturally to breathe in unison with its slow opening and closing. After a while, I could feel my soul opening and closing. Later, I wondered if I was softly emitting my own light.

I've been thinking about the jellyfish for days, seeing the faceless masters drifting in their clear world, trying not to lose their wordless wisdom. I've been trying to remember that peace is the depth of being that holds my suffering and doubt, trying to see my feelings all the way through to the edge of vastness they come from. I keep opening myself so I can drop into the calmness I was born with.

This morning there is a glow edging up through the tall, bare trees that decorate our world. And birds are singing in counterpoint as they anticipate what we call morning. And I wonder if the age we wake in is a clear tank, and if we're small, transparent creatures opening and closing our way through the deep. I wonder if being aware of this makes us glow, and if that moment of glow coursing through me is the magic of peace.

A Reflective Pause

○ *In your journal, describe your felt experience of peace, however briefly it might appear. When does this feeling rise in you? When does it seem farthest away? What people, settings, or conditions bring the feeling of peace closer to you?*

○ *In conversation with a friend or loved one, tell the story of a moment in which you have felt more than one feeling at the same time. If you were to give this combined feeling a new and personal name, what would it be?*

○ *In conversation with a friend or loved one, discuss how your understanding of peace has shifted over the years.*

TAKING TURNS AT THE EDGE
OF THE WORLD

▼ ▼ ▼

The Tōjinbō Cliffs in Japan

THE TŌJINBŌ CLIFFS are a series of basalt stone outcroppings in Fukui Prefecture, north of Kyoto, on the western coast of Japan. These stone croppings are unusual. They seem to rise out of nowhere, gigantic columns of rock eroded into jagged hexagons and pentagons by the long waves of the sea. Known as columnar jointing, this geological phenomenon can only be seen in a few places around the world, such as Geumagangsan in Korea, Norway's western coast, and at Tōjinbō, where the cliffs face the Sea of Japan.

The Tōjinbō Cliffs are a well-known site for suicide. Perhaps because of their sharp drop into an immensity that seems as comforting as it is sudden. Perhaps because, for the long moment at the edge, everything seems easier if we could just surrender to that vastness. And this is true. The soul knows under all its pain that it's the immensity we need, the Oneness that can hold us till we are whole again. But in our pain we can make the wrong jump. This is the aching twist of the want *out*: out of pain, out of sadness, out of the press of life that won't let go. When hurting, this has always been the allure of death (death of self, death of pain, death of regret): the want to surrender into a vastness that will give us peace, that will end our pain and preoccupation with self. Yet, in our pain, it's hard to believe that what will relieve us, what will save us, is a jump more fully *into* life.

No one knows what led the first lone soul to jump at Tōjinbō. Legend says that Tōjinbō was a dissolute Buddhist monk who fell in love with a beautiful princess, Aya. They say that, disliked by everyone, Tōjinbō was tricked by another admirer of Princess Aya and pushed to his death. Others tell a softer story of how Aya kissed him once, then married another. And driven crazy by the one kiss, he was unable to be held by anything but the vastness which stilled his heart as he fell to the rocks. Ever since, Tōjinbō's fallen spirit has cried inconsolably and his cries have stirred the strongest winds and rain. Decades later, an itinerant priest felt such empathy for the dissolute monk that he held a memorial for Tōjinbō. Such compassion soothed the forlorn ghost and the storms ceased for years. Yet every time someone jumps to their death, Tōjinbō joins their fallen spirit and howls like a monkish wolf and the cries of the fallen stir the winds and rain again. And every time someone stops to feel the cries of the fallen, to remember their pain, the storms cease and the sea goes calm.

Today Tōjinbō is separated into three parts: the cliffs themselves; a red bridge under which the bodies wash up; and an island that the red bridge leads to, which is said to be the resting place of the fallen. It's believed that the broken spirits float at night around the bottom of the cliffs. When the moon is full or new, completely lit or completely dark, their grief and the grief of their loved ones can be heard in the crash of the waves up the sheer walls.

So how do we hear the fallen? How do we calm the sea by feeling their pain? How are we not drowned by them? I only know that when I stop long enough to feel my own pain, and long enough for that to subside, then I can feel the pain of those I know. And beyond, the pain of those I'll never know. Then I drift in the immensity and there I can feel the windedness of soul that makes good-hearted people think they can't go on. Then I want to say to them, "Hold on . . . the puncture of this pain, that seems more than anyone could bear, this pain will pass . . . Hold on . . ."

Recently I learned from an article in *Time* magazine that someone stands watch at Tōjinbō today. He is:

> Yukio Shige, a retired detective from nearby Fukui City, and he patrols the cliffs two or three times a day. He senses the ones who've come to jump. They can barely look to the sky. They play cat and mouse with the edge. He often walks up slowly, smiles, and says, "Hello." He might ask how they came there and at what inn they are staying. Sometimes after a light touch to their shoulder, they will burst into tears, and Shige will begin to console them. "You've had a hard time up until now," he says, "haven't you?" After he talks them off the cliffs, Shige takes them to his small office, where two gas heaters keep a kettle boiling, ready to make them tea.

Now it seems clear that the itinerant priest who first heard Tōjinbō and Yukio Shige are related. They stand the same watch, the watch of compassion. Now I feel certain that we are all related, that each time we're pressed, we have a choice about which way to jump: into death or into life. Each time we feel we can't go on, the lineage of the fallen pulls at our mind and each time we feel compelled to talk the fallen back into life, the lineage of those who stand watch lifts our heart.

The truth is the cliffs are everywhere, as is the immensity. Perhaps the cliffs are there to bring us to the immensity, where we need each other to remember the bare value of living. And every day, we take turns: teetering at the edge of the world and caring for each other's souls; feeling tired enough to jump and talking each other back from the ledge. This is the simplest and most enduring form of friendship and community. This is the work of cliff-love that will go on forever.

When close to the edge, I feel the pull of the fallen and the lift of those who stand watch. But today, something makes me want to move to the cliffs and apprentice with Shige till I can hear Tōjinbō and all his descendants. Maybe in time I could learn that small touch of shoulder, that soft step away, and how to warm the soul with a cup of tea.

A Reflective Pause

○ *In conversation with a friend or loved one, describe a time when you gave more than you thought you had to give; how that felt and how doing so changed you.*

THE ONE TRUE WORLD

There is only one truth.
When we see clearly, the great teachings are the same.
What can ever be lost? What can be attained?
If we attain something, it was there from the beginning of time.
If we lose something, it is hiding somewhere near us.

—RYŌKAN

I ALWAYS FEEL tender and well rooted as I near the end of a book. I always feel that there's so much more to explore together and, at the same time, what else is there to say? But here we are: taking turns at the edge of the world, trying to become just the person we were born to be, overwhelmed by what life demands of us, though renewed by the most delicate thing. It could be the reflection of a gull on top of a mast. Or the water lapping in the harbor. Or the eyes of a child following clouds. Or the light off the alley window making the broken glass look like a diamond. But that's the secret: the broken glass *is* a diamond and the diamond carries within it the history of all broken glass. And every broken heart carries the history of all broken hearts as it shines through its break. I think that's the purpose of the break: to let the gem of light we carry way inside be known in the world.

All I can say is that the light inside the break of our heart and the light on the bits of broken glass are the same light. And when the light in our heart touches the light in the world, we find our original home.

In those moments, all we know gives way to a deeper knowing we can't put words to. In those tender moments, we wake in the One True World.

What do I mean by the One True World? Throughout the history of souls, there's an opening we all fall through or are lifted into in which we know with absolute certainty that we're fully alive. In that opening, we join the stream of aliveness that has come before us and that will go on after us. We can call this unending, unnameable stream of life that touches all generations, the One True World. And we're not the first to stumble into such deep and wordless knowing.

One old soul who speaks of the One True World is Ryōkan, the quiet Buddhist monk cited above. Born three hundred years ago to live most of his life alone, he was sensitive enough to cry on the handwritten pages that elders left long before he was here. And he was given to stop and play with children along the road. He was deep and light and known as a broad-hearted, generous fool.

But it takes a broad-hearted, generous fool to surface the wisdom of the Universe. Let's look at his quote:

There is only one truth. When we see clearly, the great teachings are the same. When broken of our stubbornness, we come to know this in our bones. As all trees root in the same earth, as all fish swim in the same water, as all birds fly in the same sky, all the different teachings are the same. When needing to feel special, we fight the underlying Oneness wherever it appears. But when drawn to feel life more than understand it, the One True World is comforting.

What can ever be lost? What can be attained? Despite all our struggles, the substance of all that matters never leaves us. In our pain and fear, it is we who doubt the presence of light because for the moment we can't see. In our numbness, it is we who doubt the value of the heart because for the moment we can't feel. In our weariness, it is we who think that music has left the Earth because for the moment we can't seem to hear.

If we attain something, it was there from the beginning of time. The One True World never goes away and so the first work of faith is to honor its depth as coming through us and not solely from us. Whatever we achieve is a rejoining of the part that lives in the world to the depth that holds up the world. This does not minimize our great efforts, but opens us to the great resource they come from. As the bottom of a lake is felt in the hand that works the oar, the One True World is felt through the work of caring hands.

If we lose something, it is hiding somewhere near us. Dropping what matters doesn't mean it has vanished but that we misplaced it. While being human involves constant loss, what matters is never lost, just somewhere out of view. And so, the second work of faith is to keep looking for what matters.

That all this comes from a quiet monk who stopped to play with children shows that sincerity is the greatest form of intelligence, the most reliable oar we can drop into the water of our lives.

....

↶ *Every broken heart carries the history of all broken hearts as it shines through its break.*

....

Below All Names

I must confess that I tripped into the One True World during the most pressing part of my cancer journey. It was years ago. Things were getting more and more difficult. When close to death, there was a moment in which I forgot my name. Almost dying was like falling from a height into a body of water. And the sting of going below stunned me into an extraordinary clarity that slowed down everything. As I sank below the living, my name and identity—where I lived, what I did, all the outer roles and circumstances I was struggling with—seemed to float like clothes on the surface above me.

Thankfully, I was returned to life and asked to put my name back on. But I was forever changed for being so deeply naked. Ever since, I've lived below the roles and names others keep trying to give me. For nearly dying made me realize that life and death are knit together and we are stretched between them, needing both surface and depth. We need to clothe ourselves in the circumstances we move through, the relationships we work at, the histories we create, and the names we go by in order to survive the world. And we need to go below these outer garments in order to find meaning and to inhabit life fully.

After all this time, I am more thoroughly me, but I live closer to the Source and accept my name and identity as the necessary cup that holds my share of all that is unnameable and uncontainable. Who we are is the necessary self that carries the Spirit we are born with through the world.

Since the beginning of time, the call of sages and poets has always been to help us understand and navigate the tension between the inner life and the outer life. Like the earliest Hindu rishis, Vedic poets who praised the unseeable hymns of the Universe, each of us has a poet in our soul who is eager to show us how to go below the surface of things. Not to escape the surface world, but to refresh our being so we can resurface in the world, the way whales launch themselves into the breach, saturated and glistening with the deep.

We have no choice but to live in this rhythm: unthreading the tangle of the daily world and diving into the eternal mystery that informs it. And when the waters of life rise in me, appear in me as tears, it's not always because I'm sad. When this feeling of depth makes me dial your number so we can meet, this is the proper use of names—so we can find each other! Yet, once together, the love moving between us makes us drop our names like ancient robes. This is the gift of friendship. Then, suddenly, despite our histories, we're adrift in that moment when everything touches everything else.

The Essentializing Journey

Still, we are never exempt from the friction of living in the world and how it essentializes us, day by day. There is no preventing this, only helping each other survive the abrasion of the process. With each hardship and loss, friendships matter more and not just with people, but with nature and time and with life itself. This last decade has made me more vulnerable and stronger at the same time.

I think I've been reduced to what is elemental, less able to pretend or look away. I still get tripped up by fear and worry and at times forget where I've been and who I am. But this is all part of the endless practice. I remain a student of things as they are and this has led me to the astonishing guidance that all things are true. I simply have to keep my heart open long enough to keep discovering how.

When I can keep my heart open, it's as if there's an invisible string that connects me to you and everything else. And when you move, it tugs on me. That tug not only confirms that we're connected but I feel an ache wherever you go. That pull of the barely seeable threads that connect us and the ache that binds us is the slack and tension of compassion as all of life moves together. On the inside, I'm coming to know joy as an expansive sense of being, and out in the world, when I don't hide, I find that singing is dreaming outloud.

And so, I ask you to remember—and if we meet, to remind me—that when all seems broken and we can't bear to feel one more thing, our heart is always deeper and stronger than we think; ready to hold us and soften us the way a great sea shapes a stubborn shore. Humbly, when we feel we have nothing left to give, this is just when the gift that only we contain is about to show itself. For though we're battered about by the difficulties of life, the heart is only made more potent, condensed by our trials into something like a diamond.

In ancient India, it was believed that diamonds were created when bolts of lightning struck rocks. They were crystallizations of power sent by the gods. As such, diamonds were placed in the eyes of statues honoring the gods. In the traditions of Buddhism and Hinduism, the diamond quality of spirit, crystallized as a moment of gem-like clarity, is known as *vajra*, a Sanskrit word meaning both thunderbolt and diamond.

Through the difficult and essentializing journey of being human, the lightning of being becomes the diamond of the heart, a unified center point of presence where our depth of feeling and clarity of mind are briefly one and the same. While no one can live in such a condensed depth state permanently, our brief experience of such heartfelt clarity can inform the rest of our lives. So as you meet what is yours to meet, trust the clarifying process that your spirit is being strengthened by. One drop of truth seen through the diamond heart can soothe a thousand wounds.

Each Trial and Blessing

As I grow older, my wonder widens and softens. As I become more humble, I keep finding that we're all of the same awakening tribe; forgetting and remembering our way, dropping and picking up the one truth that there is nowhere else to go but here, no one else to do the caring but us, no one else to care for but each other. With each trial and blessing, I keep discovering how to let the heart do its job, to let it protect us—not the other way around.

And now, if pressed to speak of God from this place of wonder, I'd have to say that God *is* the One True World, the all-embracing ocean that is home to every fish. If pressed to speak of God from inside all I've suffered, I'd have to say that God is the Unnameable Unity that continually brings us as alive as possible, the way the sun makes everything grow. If pressed to comment on the human journey, I'd have to say that the soul is the common center of Universal Spirit that seeds each human being, which is why when in the depths of our soul, we feel a kinship with all living things.

No matter how we want to spare ourselves the roughness of the ride, we can't bypass the human journey. It's the cocoon that releases our Spirit. When we can accept the inescapable gift of being here, it becomes clear that the real value of listening is that it leads us outside of ourselves and eventually back into who we are, only more enlivened, complete, and awake.

After all the conversations, all the lessons, all the setbacks and unexpected blessings that seem to come from nowhere, I wish for you and me the continued chance to learn from our heart, so we can be awake enough to do small things with love. And the strength of heart to turn the sorrow that endures forever into the peace that abides in each moment. My vow remains the same as those before me: to stay a committed, animated, obedient learner, always asking, Of what use and bridge can I be?

....

∾ Though we're battered about by the difficulties of life, the heart is only made more potent, condensed by our trials into something like a diamond.

....

Another Day

When parting after a long journey, it helps to gift each other something by which to remember what we have seen together. I offer you a few more shiny things from the deep.

▸   ▸   ▸

Is there anything worth knowing that the heart doesn't already know? If a seed contains the entire tree, doesn't the heart contain every gift? Doesn't the ounce of spirit we are given contain the river of what-is? Isn't this what we feel streaming by when we close our eyes and hush our mind? Hasn't the work always been to water the heart so it might sprout what it knows?

▸   ▸   ▸

Kindness and suffering are wordless teachers, ready to bend and soften us until we accept that we are here; that, try as we will, we can't build our way out of existence or dream our way out of being human. Once opened in this way, we come to know in a felt way that we are already in the One True World and the only thing to do is to love being here.

▸   ▸   ▸

In the way that the sun encourages all things to grow without choosing some as more worthy of light than others, there are always those luminous beings in each generation who love with great attention and with no preference. They can be seen as spiritual enhancers and models for what we are all capable of. For we are all luminous beings who can give without limit. In those moments of unrestricted flow of inner to outer, we are the person we were born to be. In facing the age-old storms of fear and violence, we are sorely in need, as generations before us, of precise and warm beings who shine and give. We need a million little suns, of which you are one.

❧   ❧   ❧

When I fall down, I try to remember that we can never eliminate obstacles. Like rocks in streams, it's their presence that makes the river sing. And so, I ask myself: Where can I stop and bow, even briefly, so the song of everything larger can come through me? When feeling like a snail tired of its shell, I try to close my mind and drink from life.

❧   ❧   ❧

And one more story, always one more story. I was in the market recently, when I closed my eyes until the cup without thought at the base of all I know began to collect the tenderness of those who've gone before us and I heard the cries of the world. I looked at everyone walking by and it was clear. It's tenderness that forces us to be kind till our only reason for being is to soften the pain hardening in others. I looked about and knew that what matters is carried in those who can't close, no matter how we try to shut ourselves down or run away. And just when I was ready to give up and turn to stone, the blind doves of acceptance fluttered in my face. It was then an old friend came upon me in the market staring at the fish. Without a word she knew, it was just another day, each of us this close to everything.

GRATITUDES

This book is dedicated to my grandmother, Maijessca Nepo, who I knew as Grandma Minnie, and her son, my father, Morris Nepo. In their own way, each modeled the endless practice. Grandma made her immigrant way through the mud of the twentieth century and the poverty of the Great Depression, meeting everything with a large and open heart. She showed me the ordinary nobility of making a feast of whatever she had. My father came from her as a child filled with wonder and creativity. He showed me what comes from immersing yourself in the details until they form a new and vibrant whole. They are the lineage of heart and perseverance that I come from.

Deep gratitude to Brooke Warner for her integrity and a grace beyond her years. And to my agent Jennifer Rudolph Walsh and the WME team for their magic, care, and excellence. And to my editor, Leslie Meredith, for lending her eye and deep knowledge to help me surface what I'm trying to say.

Gratitude to my dear friends for the endless practice of how we bear witness to each other with honesty and care. Especially Eileen, Bob, George, Don, Paul, Skip, TC, David, Karen, Paula, Ellen, Eleanor, Linda, Michelle, Rich, Sally, and Joel. And to Oprah Winfrey, who breaks a trail and shares the way.

And more than I can say to Paul Bowler, who held me in the dark. And to Robert Mason, who holds the mystery like a washcloth to my worried head. And to my wife, Susan, for always putting living things first and for showing me what it means to love.

NOTES

Epigraphs and poems without attribution are by the author.

To My Reader

xvi *I believe and give my heart to:* This passage is from my essay "The Wisdom of an Open Heart," which appeared in *The Oprah Winfrey Show: Reflections on an American Legacy*, edited by Deborah Davis. New York: Abrams Books, 2011, p. 122.

The Daily Migration

5 *We have been stopped:* From "The Synthesist: Shine a Little Light," Alan Burdick, in *OnEarth*. New York: NRDC, Spring 2011, p. 24.

5 *Environmentalist Alan Burdick:* The author of *Out of Eden*. He wrote the article from which I learned about zooplankton, "The Synthesist: Shine a Little Light," Alan Burdick, in *OnEarth*. New York: NRDC, Spring 2011, p. 24.

Six Practices

8 *There comes a moment:* Jaime Buckley, from his novel *Prelude to a Hero*. He is a publisher of comic books, and the author of graphic novels and the online comic *Wanted Hero*. Please see http://wantedhero.com and http://jaimebuckley.com.

16 *Old Age: Journey into Simplicity:* Helen M. Luke. Great Barrington, MA: Lindisfarne Books, 2010, from the first chapter, "The Odyssey," pp. 1–24.

The Necessary Rain

25   *my brother:* Howard Nepo is a gifted visual artist, photographer, and life-long teacher.

27   *outwait the clouds:* I explore this notion further in the chapter "Outwaiting the Clouds" in my book *Seven Thousand Ways to Listen*. New York: Free Press, 2012, p. 150.

The Sanctity of Experience

28   *Every [person's] condition:* Ralph Waldo Emerson. This important quote is worth returning to. I first explored it in *The Book of Awakening*. Berkeley, CA: Conari Press, 2000, March 3, p. 75. I have updated the quote regarding gender.

33   *Things That Hearten and Dishearten:* This passage first appeared in my article "How to Return to Your Center," published online for Oprah.com, February 12, 2013.

35   *"We may mis-understand":* Vine Deloria Jr., Standing Rock Sioux, 1991, from *Words of Power: Voices from Indian America*, edited by Norbert S. Hill, Jr. (Oneida). Golden, CO: Fulcrum Publishing, 1994, p. 31.

36   *"If you were given the truth":* Umberto Eco, from *The Sun*. Chapel Hill, NC, Issue 389, May 2008, p. 48.

What's in the Way Is the Way

37   *There's a thread you follow:* From *The Way It Is: New & Selected Poems*, William Stafford. St. Paul, MN: Graywolf Press, 1998, p. 42.

Our Inch of Light

43   *If there occurs an emergency at night:* Robert Temple, *The Genius of China: 3,000 Years of Science, Discovery, and Invention*. New York: Simon & Schuster, 1986, p. 98.

Losing Yourself

50   *The more uncertain I have felt about myself:* Carl Jung, from *The Sun*. Chapel Hill, NC, Issue 439, July 2012, p. 17. Originally from *Memories, Dreams, Reflections*, Carl Jung, edited by Aniela Jaffe. New York: Random House, 1961.

50   *Bob starts talking:* This paragraph is from my poem "Losing Yourself" in *The Way Under the Way*, a book of poems in progress.

51   *"For the raindrop":* Ghalib, from *Nine Gates: Entering the Mind of Poetry*, Jane Hirshfield. New York: HarperCollins, 1997, p. 5.

Meeting Difficulty

67 *Returning to Center:* This section first appeared in my article "How to Return to Your Center," published online for Oprah.com, February 12, 2013.

Just This Person

72 *"The Friendship of Tung-Shan and Yün-Yen":* This story about Tung-Shan (807–869) and Yün-Yen (d. 850) comes from a note in *The Enlightened Heart*, edited by Stephen Mitchell. New York: Harper & Row, 1989, pp. 163–64, and the lines Tung-Shan wrote are from Stephen Mitchell's translation on p. 37. For another version of the story and more of Tung-Shan's journey, please see *The Record of Tung-Shan*, translated by Liangjie Dong and William F. Powell. Honolulu: University of Hawaii Press, 1986, chapter 9, pp. 27–28. "Tung-Shan was an active participant in what was perhaps the most creative and influential phase in the development of Chán Buddhism in China. He is regarded as the founder of the Ts'aotung lineage, one of the Five Houses of Chán, and it was his approach to Buddhism that attracted the great thirteenth-century Japanese monk Dōgen during his stay in China. Dōgen carried Tung-Shan's lineage back to Japan where it became known as Soto Zen, which remains one of the major Zen sects today." From *The Record of Tung-Shan*, back cover.

A DREAM WE'RE CLOSE TO LIVING

77 *If we hold what has suffered:* From "Where the HeartBeast Sings," in my collected essays, *Unlearning Back to God: Essays on Inwardness, 1985–2005*. London/New York: Khaniqahi Nimatullahi Publications, 2006, p. 100.

Hearing the Cries of the World

81 This chapter first appeared in *Parabola*, Issue 150, March–April 2013.

81 *"Perhaps the most important reason for 'lamenting' ":* Black Elk was a Native American sage of the Oglala Sioux. This quote is from *The Sacred Pipe: Black Elk's Account of the Seven Rites of the Oglala Sioux*, recorded and edited by Joseph Epes Brown. Norman, OK: University of Oklahoma Press, 1953, p. 46.

81 *A saint [is one] who:* From *The Earth Is the Lord's: The Inner World of the Jew in Eastern Europe*, Abraham Joshua Heschel. Woodstock, VT: Jewish Lights Publishing, 2001, p. 20.

83 *"Held back, unvoiced":* Ghalib, translated by Jane Hirshfield, in *The Enlightened Heart*, edited by Stephen Mitchell. New York: Harper & Row, 1989, p. 105.

84   *That we go numb . . . to revive us:* This passage first appeared in my article "How to Return to Your Center," published online for Oprah.com, February 12, 2013.

85   *the grisly spectacle of gladiators . . . Roman crowd:* The barbaric gladiator combats were extensively showcased in the Roman Coliseum, peaking in popularity between the first century BC and the second century AD. The Coliseum was built just east of the Roman Forum. Construction started in 72 AD under Emperor Vespasian and was completed in 80 AD under Emperor Titus. Seating fifty thousand spectators, the amphitheater was also used for public spectacles such as mock sea battles, animal hunts, and executions.

Always Beginning

90   *Emerson's letter to Whitman:* For the entire letter, see http://www.class roomelectric.org/volume1/belasco/whitman-emerson.htm.

90   *Whitman tells us:* Walt Whitman, from *Specimen Days*, Philadelphia, PA: David McKay, 1892, #238. "Boston Commons—More of Emerson": "Up and down this breadth by Beacon street, between these same old elms, I walk'd for two hours, of a bright sharp February mid-day twenty-one years ago, with Emerson, then in his prime, keen, physically and morally magnetic, arm'd at every point, and when he chose, wielding the emotional just as well as the intellectual. During those two hours he was the talker and I the listener. It was an argument-statement, reconnoitering, review, attack, and pressing home (like an army corps in order, artillery, cavalry, infantry), of all that could be said against that part (and a main part) in the construction of my poems, 'Children of Adam.' More precious than gold to me that dissertation—it afforded me, ever after, this strange and paradoxical lesson; each point of E.'s statement was unanswerable, no judge's charge ever more complete or convincing, I could never hear the points better put—and then I felt down in my soul the clear and unmistakable conviction to disobey all, and pursue my own way. 'What have you to say then to such things?' said E., pausing in conclusion. 'Only that while I can't answer them at all, I feel more settled than ever to adhere to my own theory, and exemplify it,' was my candid response. Whereupon we went and had a good dinner at the American House. And thenceforward I never waver'd or was touch'd with qualms."

90   *"Children of Adam" poems:* "Originally entitled 'Enfans d'Adam' in the 1860 edition of *Leaves of Grass*, this cluster of poems celebrating (homo) sexuality was called 'Children of Adam' in 1867 and thereafter. The poems, openly 'singing the phallus' and the 'mystic deliria,' were too bold for their time and often got Whitman into trouble. His relationship with Emerson cooled after he refused Emerson's advice in 1860 to drop the sex

poems; in 1865 he lost his job in the Interior Department in Washington for writing 'indecent' poems; and he had to withdraw the 1881 edition of *Leaves* from publication in Boston when the Society for the Suppression of Vice found it immoral." —James E. Miller Jr., from *Walt Whitman: An Encyclopedia*, edited by J. R. LeMaster and Donald D. Kummings. New York: Garland Publishing, 1998, http://whitmanarchive.org/criticism /current/encyclopedia/entry_11.html.

The Goldweigher's Field

101 *"in one apartment"*: From *The Innocents Abroad*, Mark Twain. New York: Signet Classics, 1966 (originally published in 1869).

The Last Quarter

105 *I've reached the age of self-knowledge:* Wisława Szymborska (1923–2012) was a precise and deeply ironic Polish poet who won the Nobel Prize in Literature in 1996.

112 *Henri Bergson:* Bergson (1859–1941) was a profound and poetic French philosopher who explored and affirmed immediate experience and intuition as more significant than rationalism and science in understanding reality. His major works include *Time and Free Will* (1889), *Matter and Memory* (1896), and *Creative Evolution* (1907). He won the Nobel Prize in Literature in 1927.

What Do We Do With What We Feel?

113 *So, through me, freedom and the sea:* From "Poet's Obligation," in *Selected Poems of Pablo Neruda*, edited by Nathaniel Tarn. New York: Vintage Classics, 2012, p. 428.

114 *The riverbed and its banks:* I first began to explore this image in "What We Bring Along" in *The Book of Awakening*. Boston: Conari Press, 2000, August 7, p. 259.

119 *the philosopher's stone:* A legendary alchemical substance said to be capable of turning base metals, such as iron or lead, into gold or silver. It was also believed to be an elixir of life, a remedy for rejuvenation and achieving immortality. For many centuries, it was the most sought-after goal in Western alchemy.

Mention of the philosopher's stone can be found as far back 300 AD in *Cheirokmeta* by Zosimos of Panopolis. See *A History of Science in Society: From Philosophy to Utility* by Andrew Ede and Lesley B. Cormack. Toronto: University of Toronto Press, p. 66.

According to legend, the thirteenth-century scientist and philosopher

Albertus Magnus discovered the philosopher's stone and gave it to his pupil, Thomas Aquinas, shortly before his death, circa 1280. See *A Survey of the Occult,* Julian Franklyn and Frederick E. Budd. Electric Book Company, 2001, pp. 28–30.

In Buddhism and Hinduism, *Cintamani* is a wish-fulfilling jewel, equivalent to the philosopher's stone. See *Symbols of Sacred Science,* René Guénon. Hillsdale, NY: Sophia Perennis, 2004, p. 277.

Our Ring of Fear

125 *Morihei Ueshiba (1883–1969):* Ueshiba founded the martial art of aikido as the culmination of three spiritual experiences that awakened him.

In 1925, after Ueshiba defeated a naval officer's attacks while unarmed himself and without hurting the officer, Ueshiba walked into his garden and had a spiritual awakening. He later wrote: "I felt the universe suddenly quake, and a golden spirit sprang up from the ground, veiled my body, and changed my body into a golden one. At the same time my body became light. I was able to understand the whispering of the birds, and was clearly aware of the mind of God, the creator of the universe. At that moment I was enlightened (and realized): the source of *Budo* [Japanese for the Spirit of the Warrior] is God's love—the spirit of loving protection for all beings . . . Budo is not the felling of an opponent by force; nor is it a tool to lead the world to destruction with arms. True Budo is to accept the spirit of the universe, keep the peace of the world, correctly produce, protect and cultivate all beings in nature." (See *Aikido* by Kisshomaru Ueshiba. Tokyo: Hozansha Publications, 1985.)

In 1940, Ueshiba was performing *misogi,* a Japanese ascetic practice involving exhaustive activities such as extended periods without sleep, breath training, and standing under waterfalls. Later, he wrote: "Around 2 a.m., I suddenly forgot all the martial techniques I had ever learned. The techniques of my teachers appeared completely new. Now they were vehicles for the cultivation of life, knowledge, and virtue, not devices to throw people with." (See *The Art of Peace* by Morihei Ueshiba, translated by John Stevens. Boston: Shambhala Publications, 1992, pp. 5–10.)

In 1942 during the worst fighting of World War II, Ueshiba had a vision of *the Great Spirit of Peace* and later wrote: "The Way of the Warrior has been misunderstood. It is not a means to kill and destroy others. Those who seek to compete and better one another are making a terrible mistake. To smash, injure, or destroy is the worst thing a human being can do. The real Way of a Warrior is to prevent such slaughter—it is the Art of Peace, the power of love." (See *The Art of Peace* by Morihei Ueshiba, translated by John Stevens. Boston: Shambhala Publications, 1992, pp. 5–10.)

125 *"the Way of unifying [with] life energy"*: From *The Principles of Aikido* by Mitsugi Saotome. Boston: Shambhala Publications, 1989, p. 222.

125 *"the Way of harmonious spirit"*: From *Aikido and the Dynamic Sphere* by Adele Westbrook and Oscar Ratti. Tokyo: Charles E. Tuttle Company, 1970, pp. 16–96.

129 *Wanting to reform the world:* Ramana Maharshi, found in *Tao Te Ching, Lao Tzu,* translated by Stephen Mitchell. New York: Harper & Row, 1988, note to chapter 29, p. 96. Ramana Maharshi (1879–1951) is regarded by many as the greatest Hindu saint of the twentieth century.

The Troubles of Living

130 *It begins in mystery:* Diane Ackerman, from *The Sun.* Chapel Hill, NC, Issue 387, March 2008, p. 48.

131 *poetry and peace-building:* The invitation to be with these students around this wonderful topic was the inspiration of the visionary peace builder John Paul Lederach. Please see John Paul's books, *The Moral Imagination* and *The Journey Toward Reconciliation.*

132 *Matsukura Ranran:* Please see my dream of meeting Matsukura in the reflection "The Radiant Flow" in my forthcoming book *Things That Join the Sea and the Sky,* p. 89.

135 *Our schizophrenic patient:* Joseph Campbell, from *The Sun.* Chapel Hill, NC, Issue 427, July 2011, p. 48.

135 *"Things fall apart . . . of passionate intensity":* From "The Second Coming," in *The Collected Poems of W. B. Yeats,* edited by Richard J. Finneran. New York: Scribner, 1996.

138 *"The [dove] that remain[s] at home":* Rainer Maria Rilke, from *The Enlightened Heart,* edited by Stephen Mitchell. New York: Harper & Row, 1989, p. 145.

The Sweet Ache of Being Alive

139 *The Sweet Ache of Being Alive:* This chapter weaves together themes of inquiry from many books, themes I keep returning to.

139 *When the sweet ache of being alive:* This is my poem "The Moment of Poetry," from a manuscript in progress, *The Way Under the Way.*

139 *We are each born with a gift and an emptiness:* This passage first appeared as part of the article "The One Conversation," published online for *Super Soul Sunday*/OWN TV, January 19, 2012.

140 *the tuning fork of my soul:* From "A Steadfast Teacher" in my book *Seven Thousand Ways to Listen.* New York: Free Press, 2012, p. 196.

142 *an autobiography of his mind:* Albert Einstein, from *Autobiographical Notes,*

translated and edited by Paul Arthur Schilpp. Chicago: Open Court Publishing Company, 1979. Open Court published an astonishing series during the mid-twentieth century, inviting leading thinkers to write an autobiography of their mind. This book is part of that series, as well as *Meetings* by Martin Buber.

143 *When everything you've put off is here:* The epigraph to the chapter "The Gift of Surprise" in my book *The Exquisite Risk.* New York: Harmony Books, 2005, p. 114.

The Flute of Interior Time

146 *The Flute of Interior Time:* The title of this chapter is the title of the poem on p. 150, which is from my book *Surviving Has Made Me Crazy.* Fort Lee, NJ: CavanKerry Press, 2007, p. 13.

The Hard Human Spring

153 *The Hard Human Spring:* I'm indebted to my friends at Sounds True for transcribing three live sessions I offered for my online course, *A Pilgrimage of the Heart.* In these sessions, I was able to surface and express the themes I've been puzzling through in a unified way that would have been hard to reconstruct. Having the verbatim notes from these talks proved invaluable in creating these three chapters, "The Sweet Ache of Being Alive," "The Flute of Interior Time," and "The Hard Human Spring."

154 *to hold nothing back:* My first exploration of this key theme appears in my book *The Exquisite Risk.* New York: Harmony Books, 2005, p. 54. I also created a two-CD audio program devoted to this theme, *Holding Nothing Back* (Sounds True, 2012).

157 *"I am alone":* Rainer Maria Rilke, from *Selected Poems of Rainer Maria Rilke,* translated by Robert Bly. New York: Harper & Row, 1981, p. 25.

158 *We're each born with a gift . . . the whole world will eat of its nectar:* This paragraph is a prose version of my poem "The Hard Human Spring," from a manuscript in progress, *Returning to Where I've Never Been.*

THE MARK OF OUR HANDS

163 *Freedom is presence, not absence:* From *Centering in Pottery, Poetry, and the Person* by M. C. Richards. Hanover, NH: Wesleyan University Press, 1989.

Beyond the Old Protections

175 *You can avoid reality:* Quoted in *The Week,* Volume 12, Issue 597, December 21, 2012, p. 15.

Staying in Relationship

180 *there is one word for being and doing, iwa:* I am indebted to the linguist Dr. Olasope Oyelaran for his deep knowledge of the Yoruba culture and language. He was the director of the College of Arts and Sciences in the School of International Studies at Western Michigan University. Born in Nigeria and educated in the United States, Dr. Oyelaran has been instrumental in higher education in Nigeria for many years.

If Just for a Moment

184 *Like Paul Cézanne:* One day in late October 1906, Cézanne was caught in a storm while working in the field. Only after working for two hours in a downpour did he decide to go home. On the way he collapsed. He was taken home by a passing driver. His old housekeeper rubbed his arms and legs until he regained consciousness. He died of pneumonia a few days later on October 22, 1906, at the age of sixty-seven (from *Cézanne* by Ambroise Vollard. England: Courier Dover Publications, 1984, pp. 113–14). After his death, fifty-six of his paintings were exhibited in Paris in a large retrospective in September 1907. The Cézanne retrospective at the Salon d'Automne (Autumn Salon) greatly influenced the avant-garde in Paris. He was quickly considered one of the most influential artists of the nineteenth century, a forerunner of Cubism. In 1903, the first Salon d'Automne was organized by Georges Rouault, André Derain, Henri Matisse, Angèle Delasalle, and Albert Marquet as a reaction to the conservative policies of the official Paris Salon. The exhibition immediately became the showcase of innovations in twentieth-century painting and sculpture. In his 1945 essay entitled *Cezanne's Doubt*, the French philosopher Merleau-Ponty, a pioneer of phenomenology, discussed how Cézanne gave up classic artistic elements such as pictorial arrangements, single-view perspectives, and outlines that enclosed color in an attempt to get a "lived perspective" by capturing all the complexities that an eye observes. A new, comprehensive biography, *Cezanne: A Life,* by Alex Danchev, was published in 2012.

184 *"The moon bobs in the Great River's flow":* Tu Fu, from "Night Thoughts Aboard a Boat" (circa 767 AD), translated by James J. Y. Liu and Irving Y. Lo (1975), one of thirty-five known translations. Tu Fu (712–770) is one of the great sage-poets of China. Often paired with his contemporary Li Po (701–762), they appear in a lineage of other contemporary pairs, well known and unknown in their lifetime, such as Wordsworth and Coleridge, and Emerson and Thoreau. Like Coleridge and Thoreau, Tu Fu was unknown and more introverted than the more vivacious, renowned Li Po. Together, Tu Fu and Li Po are often considered China's

Shakespeare. I have always been drawn to Tu Fu's palpable humanness from first reading him when in my twenties. During my cancer journey, in my thirties, Tu Fu appeared to me in dream as a guide. Please see my poem "Tu Fu's Reappearance" in *Suite for the Living,* CA: Breed for the Journey International, 2004, p. 51.

The Most Difficult Two Inches on Earth

190 Passages in this chapter first appeared as part of the article "Listening Is a Form of Faith," published as a guest column online for *The Washington Post,* October 9, 2012.

191 *"The Swan":* From *Selected Poems of Rainer Maria Rilke,* translated by Robert Bly. New York: Harper & Row, 1981.

192 *"Faith is the state":* From *Dynamics of Faith,* Paul Tillich. New York: Harper and Brothers, 1957, p. 4.

192 *"One may lose faith in four ways":* From "Muhammad b. Fadl Balkhi: The Ostracized Master" by Arnold Combrinck, in *Sufi, A Journal of Sufism.* London: Khaniqahi Nimatullahi Publications, Issue 66, Summer 2005, pp. 47–48.

194 *What Do We Do When We're Broken?:* This section first appeared as an article published online for Oprah.com, November 15, 2013.

195 *not getting what we want:* I explore this more fully in *Seven Thousand Ways to Listen.* New York: Free Press, 2012, p. 220.

196 *I've come to believe:* A different version of this paragraph appears as the poem "Below Our Strangeness," in my manuscript in progress *Returning to Where I've Never Been.*

All Things Are True

205 *As something is breaking . . . the face of God:* These three paragraphs merge prose versions of two poems of mine: "Somewhere" from a manuscript in progress called *Journey with No End* and "Nothing Is Separate" from another manuscript in progress called *Returning to Where I've Never Been.*

Beyond Seeking

212 *"Oceans":* Juan Ramón Jiménez, in *News of the Universe: Poems of Twofold Consciousness,* edited and translated by Robert Bly. San Francisco: Sierra Club Books, 1980.

Born of the Moment

217 *Joshu asked Nansen:* From "Everyday Life is the Path," in "The Gateless Gate," in *Zen Flesh, Zen Bones*, compiled by Paul Reps and Nyogen Senzaki. Boston: Shambhala Publications, 1994, p. 193.

217 *Every [person] has the right:* From the Geneva philosopher, writer, and composer Jean-Jacques Rousseau (1712–1778), from *The Sun.* Chapel Hill, NC, Issue 337, January 2004, p. 48.

219 *the batter checks:* Haiku by Cor van den Heuvel, from *Baseball Haiku*, edited by Cor van den Heuvel and Nanae Tamura. New York: Norton, 2007, p. 18. This is a well-researched and comprehensive anthology of all the known haikus about baseball from Japanese and American poets with an excellent history of the haiku form and how baseball migrated to Japan in 1872.

221 *Rikyū:* Please see my story "The Tea Master and the Warrior" in *As Far As the Heart Can See*, which unfolds the friendship of Rikyū and Taikō. In sixteenth-century Japan, Rikyū was one of the great tea masters whose long friendship with the warrior prince Taikō Hideyoshi was legendary. After many years, a jealous treachery arose toward Rikyū and when a distance grew between Taikō and Rikyū, the enemies of the tea master spread rumors that Rikyū was going to poison Taikō with a cup of tea. Hearing this rumor, Taikō coldly discounted their long friendship and without any further inquiry condemned Rikyū to die by his own hand. Surrounded by his students, Rikyū offered them all a final cup of tea and ended the tea ceremony by breaking the sacred cup to keep it from being misused by others. He then whispered, "Welcome O sword of eternity . . . Through Buddha thou has cleft the way," and fell on his dagger. To learn more about the tea ceremony and the reverent way of life behind it, see the classic *The Book of Tea* by Kakuzo Okakura. It is also of interest that *taiko* means drum in Japanese. In feudal Japan, a *taiko* was often used to motivate troops and call out orders. Entering a battle, the *taiko yaku* (drummer) was responsible for setting the pace of the march.

223 *To be poured into:* Chuang Tzu, from *Chuang Tzu: Mystic, Moralist and Social Reformer*, translated by Herbert A. Giles. London: Quaritch, 1889, chapter 2.

Little by Little

226 *As sticks were rubbed prehistorically:* From "Within a Greater Will," in my collected essays, *Unlearning Back to God: Essays on Inwardness, 1985–2005.* London/New York: Khaniqahi Nimatullahi Publications, 2006, p. 140.

227 *[Our] understanding emerges:* From "Riding the Waves of Chaos: An In-

terview with Tibetan Buddhist Jennifer Fox" in *Sufi*. London: Khaniqahi Nimatullahi Publications, Issue 82, Winter 2012, p. 41.

232 *A tiny, tender wave of love:* Maharishi Mahesh (1918–2008), from *The Traveler's Journal,* edited by Robin Lim and Sam Shapiro. Bali: Half Angel Press, 2007, p. 51.

Without Pause

234 *took the image he had fashioned:* From *The Poetical Works of Oscar Wilde*. New York: Thomas Crowell Co., 1913, p. 297.

235 *Prosecutor Charles Gill; Oscar Wilde; Justice Wills; Oscar Wilde:* Transcript of Oscar Wilde's trial, published online by University of Missouri–Kansas City Law School.

236 *When first I was put into prison:* From the *Complete Letters of Oscar Wilde*, edited by Merlin Holland and Rupert Hart-Davis. New York: Henry Holt, 2000, p. 739.

236 *upon his release:* On his release from prison, Wilde entrusted the letter to his dear friend, Robert Baldwin "Robbie" Ross (1869–1918), a Canadian journalist and art critic who also served as Wilde's literary executor. *De Profundis* was published posthumously in 1905.

THE EXCHANGE THAT BRINGS US ALIVE

241 *On this ever-revolving wheel of being:* From "The Shvetashvatara Upanishad," I, 4–6, in *The Upanishads*, translated by Eknath Easwaran. Tomales, CA: Nilgiri Press, 1987, pp. 217–18.

243 *There is always a practice before the practice . . . that saves us:* A poem version of this passage appears in my book of poems in progress *The Way Under the Way.*

What More Could I Ask For?

247 *The Book of One Thousand and One Nights (The Arabian Nights):* Known in English as *The Arabian Nights, One Thousand and One Nights* is a collection of folktales from west and south Asia, gathered and added to over centuries by many storytellers, authors, and translators. All the stories are housed within the frame of an overarching story of a Persian king Shahryar, whose new bride is unfaithful. He's so heartbroken that he has her executed. In his woundedness and grief, he fearfully concludes that all women are unfaithful. Shahryar begins to marry only virgins, having each executed the next morning, before she has a chance to dishonor him. Eventually the vizier, whose duty it is to provide the king with virgins, can't find any more. To his great dismay, his daughter, Scheherazade, of-

fers herself as the next bride. Once the king hears of this, her father reluctantly agrees. On the night of their marriage, Scheherazade begins to tell the king a tale, but doesn't end it. The king, needing to know how the story ends, postpones her execution to find out what happens. The next night, Scheherazade ends the first story and begins a new one, and the king, eager to hear how that story ends, postpones her execution again. This goes on for 1001 nights, by which time Shahryar has fallen in love with Scheherazade and, made wiser by the tales, he no longer wants to kill her or anyone.

The framing story of Shahryar and Scheherazade is the storehouse for the 1001 folktales Scheherazade tells which have been gathered over time. *The Arabian Nights* as we know it traces back to an Arabic translation of a Persian book, *Hazār Aāān*, meaning "The Thousand Stories." Having stories told within stories is a framing device known as an embedded narrative. An earlier embedded narrative is *The Panchatantra*, an ancient interrelated collection of Indian fables that convey the many lives of Buddha in animal forms. This original Sanskrit work dates back to the third century BC. Notes for this and Aladdin's lamp are drawn from *Wikipedia*.

The Courage Not to Waste Our Gifts

250 *No one can construct the bridge:* From *Untimely Meditations* by Friedrich Nietzsche, edited by Daniel Breazeale, translated by R. J. Hollingdale. Cambridge: Cambridge University Press, 1997.

251 *the psychologist James Hillman . . . believed:* Tim McKee, in "Conversations with a Remarkable Man: Honoring the Late James Hillman," a combined interview over ten years (1990, 1997, 2000) by Sy Safransky, Scott London, and Genie Zeiger, from *The Sun*. Chapel Hill, NC, Issue 439, July 2012, p. 5.

253 *the great epic poem* Khamsa: This epic poem was written in tribute to the Persian master poet, Nizami Ganjavi (1141–1217), and became a masterpiece as an illuminated text created in 1597 by thirty-one artisans under the auspices of the great Mughal emperor Akbar (1542–1605).

255 *a story and a song:* From *Tell These Secrets: Tales of Generosity from Around the World*, an amazing collection of seventy-four stories gathered from twenty-three traditions and edited by Ian Simmons and Margo McLoughlin. Many of these stories are available as a teaching resource at http://www.LearningtoGive.org/resources/folktales.

Reliable Truths

259 *I know what the cure is:* Henry Miller, from *The Sun*. Chapel Hill, NC, Issue 454, October 2013, p. 48.

264 *a portrait . . . a fly whisk:* These details are from *The Roaring Stream*, edited by Nelson Foster and Jack Shoemaker. New York: Ecco Press, 1996, p. 268.

Outlasting the Glare

267 *"One does not become enlightened":* From Carl Jung's autobiography, *Memories, Dreams, Reflections*. New York: Vintage Books, 1965.

The Magic of Peace

275 *After all these years . . . to everything that is life sustaining:* This passage first appeared as part of the article "The One Conversation," published online for *Super Soul Sunday*/OWN TV, January 19, 2012.

Taking Turn at the Edge of the World

282 *The Tōjinbō Cliffs:* Image from http://en.wikipedia.org/wiki/File:Japan _Tojinbo02n4592.jpg.

284 *Yukio Shige . . . to make them tea:* This paragraph is from "Postcard: Tōjinbō Cliffs," Coco Masters. *Time*, Monday, June 22, 2009.

The One True World

286 *There is only one truth:* Ryōkan, in *The Enlightened Heart*, edited by Stephen Mitchell. New York: Harper & Row, 1989, p. 97. Ryōkan Taigu (1758–1831) was a quiet Buddhist monk who lived much of his life as a hermit. Ryōkan is remembered for his poetry and calligraphy and for his love of Dōgen (1200–1253), the Kyoto-born teacher who founded the Sōtō school of Zen in Japan. Ryōkan was born in the village of Izumozaki in Echigo Province. He renounced the world at an early age to train at the nearby Sōtō Zen temple Kōshōji, refusing to meet with or accept charity from his family. He was originally ordained as Ryōkan Taigu. *Ryō* means good, *kan* means broad, and *Taigu* means great fool. Ryōkan, the tender-hearted poet-monk, was known as a "broad-hearted generous fool."

PERMISSIONS

ABOUT THE AUTHOR

MARK NEPO moved and inspired readers and seekers all over the world with his #1 *New York Times* bestseller *The Book of Awakening*. Beloved as a poet, teacher, and storyteller, Mark has been called "one of the finest spiritual guides of our time," "a consummate storyteller," and "an eloquent spiritual teacher." His work is widely accessible and used by many, and his books have been translated into more than twenty languages. A bestselling author, he has published fifteen books and recorded nine audio projects. Recent work includes *Inside the Miracle* (forthcoming from Sounds True, 2015); his latest book of poems, *Reduced to Joy* (Viva Editions, 2013), cited by *Spirituality & Practice* as one of the Best Spiritual Books of 2013; as well as a six-CD box set of teaching conversations based on the poems in *Reduced to Joy* (Sounds True, 2014); and *Seven Thousand Ways to Listen* (Atria), which won the 2012 Books for a Better Life Award. Mark has appeared several times with Oprah Winfrey on her *Super Soul Sunday* program on OWN TV. He has also been interviewed by Robin Roberts on *Good Morning America*. *The Exquisite Risk* was cited by *Spirituality & Practice* as one of the Best Spiritual Books of 2005, calling it "one of the best books we've ever read on what it takes to live an authentic life." Mark devotes his writing and teaching to the journey of inner transformation and the life of relationship. He continues to offer readings, lectures, and retreats. Please visit Mark at http://www.MarkNepo.com, http://threeintentions.com, and info@wmespeakers.com.